Charles Fleet

Glimpses of Our Ancestors in Sussex

With sketches of Sussex characters, remarkable incidents

Charles Fleet

Glimpses of Our Ancestors in Sussex
With sketches of Sussex characters, remarkable incidents

ISBN/EAN: 9783337097431

Printed in Europe, USA, Canada, Australia, Japan

Cover: Foto ©ninafisch / pixelio.de

More available books at **www.hansebooks.com**

GLIMPSES

OF

Our Ancestors in Sussex;

WITH

SKETCHES

OF

SUSSEX CHARACTERS, REMARKABLE INCIDENTS, &c.

BY

CHARLES FLEET,

Author of "Tales and Sketches," "The City Merchant," &c.

"I have some rights of memory in this 'County,'
Which now to claim my vantage doth invite me."—*Shakspeare.*

BRIGHTON:
W. J. SMITH, 41, 42, AND 43, NORTH STREET.

1878.

FLEET AND BISHOP,
PRINTERS,
"HERALD" OFFICE, BRIGHTON.

TO THE READER.

The contents of this Volume appeared in the columns of the BRIGHTON HERALD in the years 1875-6-7, under the title of "GLIMPSES OF OUR ANCESTORS," and the Author of them is induced to re-publish them in their present form by the frequent applications which have been made for the numbers of the Journal containing them. With the hope that they may help to fill up a gap or two in the history of Men and Manners in his native County, and with full acknowledgment of the large debt he owes, in respect to the matter of several Papers, to the contributors to the Collections of the Sussex Archæological Society—especially to his old and esteemed friends, the late Mark Antony Lower and William Durrant Cooper—he commits his work to the indulgent consideration of the Public.

CONTENTS.

1.—THE SUSSEX DIARISTS	1
2.—THE SUSSEX IRONMASTERS	64
3.—THE SUSSEX SMUGGLERS	73
4.—THE SOUTH-DOWN SHEPHERD	87
5.—THE SUSSEX SHEEP-SHEARER	98
6.—SUSSEX CHARACTERS :—	
THE SUSSEX COTTAGE-WIFE.	105
THE OLD SUSSEX RADICAL	112
THE OLD SUSSEX TORY	119
THE SUSSEX COUNTRY DOCTOR	127
SELF-EDUCATED SUSSEX MEN	135
THE LAST OF THE SUSSEX M.C.'S	150
THE LAST OF HIS KIND	156
7.—THE SUSSEX REGICIDES	164
8.—SUSSEX TRAGEDIES AND ROMANCES	188
9.—SUSSEX POETS	224
10.—SOCIAL CHANGES IN SUSSEX :—	
SERVANTS AND THEIR WAGES	271
SUSSEX ROADS	287
MUSIC IN SUSSEX	293

Glimpses of our Ancestors, &c.

THE SUSSEX DIARISTS.

GREAT changes,—material, political, social,—are easily seen. They stand out on the surface. Every body can discern the difference between a railway and a highway; between Fielding's Squire Western and the modern country gentleman. But there are other changes, scarcely less important, which are not so easily to be noted: for instance, between the men who carry on the general trade of country-places in the present day and those who carried it on, say 100 years ago. That such a class as this has participated in the changes which have been going on all over the country, who will deny? But who is to note the change? Who to describe it? Who to draw the portrait of "the general trader" at one end of the century and compare it with the lineal successor of the same individual at the other? How rarely do we get a correct delineation of such classes as these, or, indeed, of any classes in country places. A Fielding will draw the Squire and Parson, the fast young man and poacher and barber of his day, and a Thackeray will do something in the same way in his; but they select different classes and points of view. The one takes the country—the other, the town. We still miss the point of comparison. In fact, the country is passing more and more out of the range of vision of writers of fiction; these writers live in towns, and naturally describe what they see most of: that is, town manners. So, perhaps, 100 years hence, our descendants will wonder what kind of creature was the agricultural labourer, or even the farmer, or small country tradesman of these days. And, unless any of this class happen to have kept a Diary, and this Diary shall happen to have been preserved, the feeling of wonder will go unsatisfied !

But "sufficient for the day is the evil thereof." Let us make use of some of the material which other ages have provided for us and endeavour to present, as much as possible in their own language, some of the moral and social features and characteristics of our forefathers to their successors of the present day, beginning with The Sussex Diarists.

The range of the Sussex Diaries is from 1655 to 1750, Previous to the earlier date, clerkly accomplishments were rare except in the higher spheres of life, and it is not in that sphere that Diaries are to be found. The Duchess of Newcastle (who lived in the reign of the two Charles's) is an exception to the rule ; but she was not a Sussex woman, nor were the Pastons (who kept Diaries during the Wars of the Roses) a Sussex family. Would that they had been ! Sussex had its men of letters in Andrew de la Borde, the original "Merry Andrew," and the author of that "merry conceit," the "Wise Men of Gotham," as also in Nicholas Culpepper, the author of the Herbal. But neither of these men was a Diarist. They were, perhaps, too occupied with other, and, as they thought, higher matters. Men who keep Diaries would seem, according to our Sussex experience, to be "home-staying youths"—men with a certain amount of leisure, and whose minds are more active than their bodies ; not engaged in great affairs,—for these engross the mind and lead it from smaller details, such as make up Diaries, to the contemplation of greater results,—but men in the middle ranks of life, to whom ordinary passing events, such as occur in all civilized communities, possess an interest, and are not as yet so insignificant as to be utterly unworthy to be recorded. We are afraid that such is the case now ; that Diarists are an extinct class. They have been superseded by the newspaper. Of what use, it may now be asked, for individuals to chronicle events which it is the business of the journalist to send forth to the world with all the authority of official and verbatim reports ? The notes of a Pepys or an Evelyn would now only be partial and incorrect copies of the *Times* or the *Telegraph*. No ;

the golden days of the English Diarists are gone; they extend from the period of the Reformation, when the middle ranks began to read and write, up to the introduction of the newspaper.

All our Sussex diaries fall within that period, and they fill up a most important gap in social history. We are afraid the newspaper itself will not supply to coming ages that insight into domestic life and manners—that peep at personal peculiarities—at the little failings and the foibles of men—their peccadilloes and prejudices—which we get in the diaries of the Rev. Giles Moore, Rector of Horstead Keynes; Thomas Turner, general shopkeeper, of East Hothly; Anthony Stapley, Squire of Hickstead Place; Walter Gale, schoolmaster, of Mayfield; Leonard Gale, ironmaster, of Worth; Thomas Marchant, yeoman, of "Little Park," Hurst; Counsellor Timothy Burrell, of Cuckfield; and Dr. Burton, of Oxford.

The names and avocations of the above list of Sussex Diarists bear out our statement that it is the middle classes that have been the largest contributors to this species of literature, and not so much the noble or rich or learned, who might be supposed to have most leisure for such occupation,—not so much these as the ordinarily educated and intelligent man, interested in his own and his neighbours' affairs, and with business habits to which the keeping of a daily record might be a help as well as a diversion.

It is to be regretted that no female diary has been discovered, or published, in Sussex, which might give us a glimpse of the ladies' side of the question! In a description of the hall or refectory of an old English mansion it is said that an aperture was left in the "bower" of the lady in the upper story, through which she could hear the wise, and, doubtless, sometimes the foolish things said by her lord when he was feasting with his friends below. Now, a diary is just such a peephole as this, through which the actions of one generation are revealed to another; and, to be complete, the lady should tell her story as well as the lord. But, unfortunately, no lady thought of doing this in Sussex—at least, if kept, her record has not been found, and so we must be content to take the evidence from the only party who puts in an appearance, and that is the male.

The first witness whom we will call into Court is the Rev. Giles Moore, Rector of Horstead Keynes, whose diary extends from 1655 to 1679. He is methodical, frank, concise, and good-tempered; in fact, has most of the good qualities of a good diarist, and though we could have wished he had told us a little about things more interesting than the price he paid for his extinguishers, his bellows, his grate, the shoeing of his horses, &c., &c., yet, as it was in order to chronicle these items that he kept the Diary, we must take the boon as he gives it, and get as much instruction and information out of it as we can.

The Rev. Giles Moore was, we are afraid, open to the charge of "time-serving." He was one of those gentry called, in the Commonwealth times, " Compounders ; " and it was with his own conscience as well as with the Protector, Oliver Cromwell, that he compounded. He was, in point of fact, a Royalist and an Episcopalian. According to his own statement, he was serving in the ranks of the Royalists (in what capacity he does not say— perhaps as Chaplain) when he was taken prisoner by Essex's army. How long he remained so, we do not know ; but in 1655 he was presented to the Rectory of Horstead Keynes (then vacant by the death of Mr. James Pell) by Mr. William Michelborne, of Broad- hurst and Stanmer, whom he calls his patron, and being admitted by " the Commissioners for the approbation of Publique Preachers sitting at Whitehall " (a body of men, partly ministers, partly laymen, appointed by Cromwell and his Council for the proper filling-up of benefices in England and Wales), he "removed fully and wholly from Lindfield to Horstead Canes " *(sic.)*, where he immediately commenced his Diary (from February, 1655), and continued it up to within a few days of his death in 1679. It occupies 60 pages of the first volume of the Sussex Archæological Collections ; and the greater part of the entries relate to the price of things bought and sold, the amount of tithe taken for lands, crops, &c., and the personal expenses of the Rev. Giles Moore.

But ever and anon a fact crops up which helps to diversify

the otherwise dry and matter-of-fact character of the Diary. Thus, how business was carried on in Sussex more than 200 years ago may be guessed from the fact that the Rector bought his "coverletts," blankets, bolsters, &c., of William Clowson,* "upholsterer itinerant, living over against the Crosse at Chichester, but *who comes about the country with his packs on horseback.*" This, in fact, was the way in which business was chiefly carried on in Sussex in the 17th century. The roads were too heavy for vehicles, and "packmen" who rode on horseback were the chief carriers of "dry goods." Still, some of his heavier furniture Mr. Moore procured from London, notably, "a bed, with purple rug, curtaines, &c., which cost mee altogether £20 16s. 7d."

If this was dear, house labour was cheap. To his manservant, Mr. Moore paid £5 a-year; and to his maid-servant, Rose Colman, £3. What would be said to such salaries at the present time, even if doubled to allow for the depreciation of gold?

If Mrs. Moore had kept a diary (would that she had!) she would doubtless have told us what her weekly household expenses were. Mr. Moore does not do so; but one entry shows that the labour of carrying on "the house" was a divided one—that the wife had her department distinct from the husband's. *Ex. gr.:* "I bought of my wyfe a fat hog to spend in my family, for the which I payed the summe of 30s.; the two flitches of bacon, when dryed, weighed 64lb. I gave her to buy a qr. of lambe 3s. 6d."

Thus buying and selling went on between husband and wife—a novelty to us.

The religious practice of that day—the very acmé of Puritanism—was very strict and severe. Mr. Moore has several entries of the number of communicants at his Church, and in three Communions they numbered on an average above 180 persons. To

---

* Was this William Clowson an ancestor of that William Clowes who went from Chichester 100 years later and established the world-famed printing business of Clowes and Son? Names got very much altered—cropped or augmented—in past ages.

this Mr. R. W. Blencowe (who edits the Diary for the Sussex Archæological Society) attaches a note to the effect that in the three last years (preceding 1848) the average number of communicants at Horsted Keynes at eight sacraments had been 148 persons: that is, considerably less than the number who attended *three* Communions in Mr. Moore's time. But we must bear in mind that the reign of Cromwell and the Puritans was an exceptional period for the practice of religion. And with many, doubtless, religion and morality went hand in hand. But not with all. The license of the following reign showed that, with the majority, both religion and morality were but skin deep, and even in those stern times, when play-houses were shut up and the maypole was pulled down, there did not lack occasional proofs of the weakness of the flesh—even, alas! in the household of the Rev. Giles Moore. Here is one, under the date of November 8, 1659:—

"Thos. Dumbrell came to mee as servant to dwell with mee, with whom I agreed to give after the rate of £5 a yeare. On the 22nd Dec. I payed him up to that time £1 8s.; that same night I found him sleeping with my mayd Mary, and I packed them off. Jan. 2nd I marryed Thos. Dumbrell and Mary his wyfe gratis, and I gave him on his wedding 8 stone of beefe 16s. 8d. a hind qr. of mutton 3s. 4d. and a lambe 7s. 6d., besydes butter, wheate, and fewell."

The Rev. Giles Moore must have been of a more forgiving temper than many of his Reverend brethren in those stern days, or Thomas Dumbrell and "my mayd Mary" would have come off less easily than this!

The above domestic event occurred during the Protectorate. But let not the enemies of Puritanism triumph over that! In 1676, after the King had got "his own again," and the true Church had been reinstated in all its rights, something very much like a parallel event occurs in the household of the Rev. Giles Moore:—

"13th October I marryed Henry Place and Mary Holden, my two servants, and spent at theyr wedding 20s.; I gave the fiddlers 1s. I also gave them a large cake, all theyr fewell, and the use of my house and stables for 2 dayes, with a quart of white wine, being in all not less than 40s. or one yeares wages. On the 6th of February following shee was delivered of a daughter, so that the —— (and here the Rev. diarist uses a very strong expression) went but 15 weekes and five dayes after her marriage."

We are afraid that, so far as the morals of Horstead Keynes were concerned, there was not much to choose between King and Protector !

It will be noticed that there were fiddlers at the wedding of Henry Place and Mary Holden ; and on various other occasions the Rev. Giles Moore makes an entry to the same effect : " I payd the fiddlers 6d.," or 1s. This shows that the fiddlers were a fixed institution in country parishes 250 years ago, and so they continued until our own times, " a case of viols " being kept for their use in most villages. These are the only references to music by the Rector of Horstead Keynes, except a not over flattering entry anent the national instrument of Scotland : " To a begging Welchman and a bagpipe player, 6d. each."

As may be concluded from these entries, the Rev. Giles Moore was very careful in the setting-down of his out-goings ; and the national taxes and poor rates begin about this time to figure rather largely and frequentl yin the Diary. At first the requisitions made by Oliver upon the country for the support of his army, navy, and government generally must have seemed very exorbitant. But it could not be denied that the Protector gave *quid pro quo*, and that the interests and the glory of England were protected by him and the country well-governed. Still, the people rejoiced when Charles the Second was restored in 1660 ; and the Rector of Horstead Keynes, who, as we have seen, fought or prayed—perhaps both—for the Royal cause in his youth, was foremost amongst the rejoicers. As, during the Commonwealth, he had occasionally aired his Latin by giving expression to his loyal feelings in that safe language, so now he poured forth his rejoicings at the restoration of Monarchy in the same classic and orthodox form. But the Rev. Giles Moore soon found that, whether under King or Protector, he had to " pay the piper," and, under the former, to a more lively tune than the latter. Assessments both for King's taxes and for poor-rates became both heavier and more frequent. In April, 1665, the Rector records as follows:—

"A taxe was made for the reliefe of the poor of the parish, at 9d. in the £, I being then raysed from £16 to £30 per an. I payed for the parsonage and glebe £1 2s. 6d. This single time I payd 12s. 6d. extraordinary, through Fields malignity, with Cripps concurrence; the next poore booke, however, I got it downe againe. In Decr. I payed another taxe for the poore at 3d. in the £."

"There are," adds Mr. Blencowe, "two assessments for King's taxes recorded in this year (1665); the share paid by the Rector amounted to £2 12s. 6d." Three years later,—in 1668,—the King's taxes paid by the Rector amounted to £7 6s., or just treble, exclusive of hearth-money and poll-tax; and he began, shrewdly remarks Mr. Blencowe, to show symptoms of what, in after ages, Lord Castlereagh called, an "ignorant impatience of taxation." He was, in fact, paying for his loyalty, and getting very little return for his money; for the foreign wars of Charles (against the Dutch) were disastrous; and the internal government was anything but satisfactory. The poll-tax and hearth-tax referred to in the above entry pressed most unfairly upon the working and middle classes, who paid in respect to the first as much as the wealthy, whilst the latter laid open the habitations of all to the tax-gatherer. That the hearth-tax was not a light one we can gather from the following entry:—

"To Mr. Moore, of East Grinstead, collector, for 8 fire hearths due for one whole yeare expiring at Michaelmas, together with one yeare more for the brewhouse chimney, I payed 18s."

Pepys, who was keeping his diary at the same time as the Sussex Rector, was better informed as to the extravagant expenditure of the Court at this time. "It was," he says, writing in 1666, "computed that the Parliament had given the King for this war only, besides prizes, and besides the £200,000 which he was to spend of his own revenue to guard the sea, above £5,000,000 and odd £100,000, which is a most prodigious sum. It is strange how everybody do now a days reflect upon Oliver, and commend him; what brave things he did, and made all the neighbouring princes to fear him; while here, a prince come in with all the love and prayers and good liking of his people, who have given greater signs of loyalty and willingness to serve him with their estates than was ever done by any people, hath lost all so soon, that it is a miracle what way a man could devise to lose so much in so short a time."

Friend Pepys took care to write in cypher, or this reference to the "brave things that Oliver did" might have cost him dearly!

Poor-rates also continued to increase in Horstead Keynes. In 1730 they had reached 2s. 9d. in the £, and in 1831 they amounted to £2 a-head in a population of 782 persons. Even in 1848 they averaged 6s. 4d. in the £. Horstead Keynes, indeed, was, from some cause or other—perhaps its remoteness from any large town, lying as it does in the very centre of the Weald of Sussex,—one of the poorest and most neglected, though most picturesque villages in the South of England. It was here that the Sussex peasantry met when they broke out into something like rebellion against their lords and masters, and made the reporter of the *Brighton Herald* (professionally present at their meeting) a few hours' prisoner in order that he might put into shape the rough draft of their petition to Parliament for a redress of grievances. On a subsequent occasion the Riot Act was read (by Mr. Mabbott, if we recollect rightly) and the agricultural labourers of East Sussex were put down with a strong hand.

But enough of taxation. Let us turn to more agreeable matters. What will Rectors' wives of the present day say to this indication of the tastes of Mistress Giles Moore?—" Tobacco for my wyfe, 3d." It was, really, a little too bad of the Rector to put down this. Why couldn't he let his "wyfe" have her threepenny worth of tobacco without telling all succeeding generations of it? Oh, that Mrs. Moore had only thought of setting down all the Rector's little indulgences!

"For a lb. of sugar, to preserve quinces, 1s." shows the high price of colonial produce at that day (Oliver had only recently annexed Jamaica to the English Crown). There are numerous other proofs of it, whilst, on the other hand, home produce was very cheap. Thus, in 1662, "I pay'd for 3 pecks of barley malt 2s. 7d.; for 11lbs. of beef, 2s. 2d."

Wine was also cheap. Claret and "sack,"—that is, dry sherry (sherry *sec*) were chiefly drunk; the former was 1s. per bottle, and the latter little more. Here is one entry: "1st April, 1662. I had 5 bottles of claret, and as many of sack from London, for which I payed, and for the bringing them down, at 2d. the bottle, in all 12s. For a pint of old sack 6d., 2 quarts of muscadine 3s. 2 ounces of tobacco 1s. For a sugar loafe weighing 4 pounds 1s."

Mr. Giles Moore was evidently a temperate man for the times; and this entry in February, 1668, on the principle of the exception proving the rule, shows it :—

"This evening, between nine and ten o'clock, when I had began prayers with my family, I was so overpowered with the effects of some perry which I had taken, not knowing how strong that liquor was, that I was obliged to break off abruptly. O God! lay not this sin to my charge!"

The original entry, we may add, like the Rev. Diarist's political effusions of an earlier date, is in Latin.

Close to this entry we have two "signs of the times," *videlicet:* "I was with Mistress Chaloner and bargained with her at £12 per an. for board and schooling for Mat." "I gave Mr Salisbury, a begging Minister, 4d."

The Mistress Chaloner to whom Mat. (an adopted daughter of the Diarist), was sent for a year's schooling and board at £12 a year (!), was, doubtless, a member of the great Chaloner family, whose Sussex seat in the 17th century was at Kennard's, Lindfield, and whose head, now in exile,—"Ye Major Chaloner of Kennard's,"—had been an active adherent of the Commonwealth, and was punished by the confiscation of his estates. His family, doubtless, shared in this reverse of fortune, and this "Mistress Chaloner" had to keep a school in London, to which "Mat." was sent, on terms which would make the heads of modern Seminaries cast up their eyes in wonder. The "begging Minister" was, doubtless, as Mr. Blencowe surmises, one of those unfortunate Ministers of the Church of England who, admitted, like Mr. Giles Moore, to benefices during the Commonwealth, refused,—unlike him,—to conform to the new doctrines introduced after the Restoration, and so "went out"—one "black Monday"—to poverty and often destitution, to the number of 2,000. Non-conformists do not forget this little fact even at the present day.

Two circumstances point significantly to the alteration in diet which has taken place since the days of the second Charles. The first is, the frequent reference in this and other Diaries to fresh-water fish, now so insignificant a matter in domestic economy; the other is, the total absence of any mention of the potato. It was, as Mr. Blencowe remarks in a note, introduced into England —probably by Raleigh—in the reign of James I., for, in an account of the household expenses of his Queen, there is an entry of their purchase at 2s. per lb. But the cultivation of it was slow, "and," says Mr. Blencowe, "before the year 1684, when they were first planted in the open fields in Lancashire, they were raised only in the gardens of the rich." And then Mr. Blencowe gives the following interesting account (on the authority of his friend, Col. Davies), of the introduction of potatoes into Sussex :—

"'William Warnett, of Horstead Keynes, yeoman, who is turned of 90, but in full possession of his faculties, says that before the year 1765, when he was seven years old, potatoes had never been heard of in this neighbourhood; that in that year the late Lord Sheffield, who had recently purchased the Sheffield estate, brought some, as it was reported, from Ireland, and that his father received a few from his lordship's gardener. He adds, that no one knew how to plant them, but that they got a man who worked on the road, and who came from some distant County, to plant them, which he continued to do regularly on old Lady Day for many years, and it was very long before they began to plant them in the fields. They used in those times to leave their potatoes in the ground all the winter, covering the ground with brakes, and taking them up as they wanted them for use. Before potatoes came into use, pease pudding was usually part of the dinner. So strong was the prejudice against them, that, at the elections which took place at Lewes about this period, it shared with Popery the indignation of the people, and 'No Popery, no potatoes!' was the popular cry.'"

In France the cultivation of the potato by the poor was still more tardy than in England; and, doubtless, our readers will call to mind the graphic account which is given, in MM. Erckmann-Chatrian's " History of a Peasant," of the excitement produced at Phalsbourg when the first crop of potatoes ever raised in Alsace made its appearance in the garden of the blacksmith, Maitre Jacques, — the ridicule which attended the planting of the peelings, which had been brought from Germany —the curiosity excited by the first appearance of the green sprouts above the ground, and the triumph with which the wonderful roots were dug up and the gusto with which they were eaten. It marked an era in the life of the French peasant.

The introduction of the potato and other vegetables and fruits, and their greater use by all classes, contributed not a little, doubtless, to check the prevalence of that "dire disorder," the scurvy, from which the Rector of Horstead Keynes himself suffered and for which his brother in the Isle of Wight constantly sent him " scurvy water and scurvy grass."

Another mode of curing (?) this and all other diseases was by " letting blood." Such entries as this constantly occur in the Diary :—" I was bled as usual at hæmorroyadal times the quantity of 10 oz., for which I paid Mr. Parker 3d." On which entry, Mr. Blencowe remarks, " The custom of being blooded at the Spring and Fall of the year prevailed till within a few years. The labourers generally attended the village surgeon on a Sunday morning, that their week's work might not be interrupted; the charge for bleeding them being 6d. each."

It is only in our days that this most pernicious practice has been completely exploded, though Le Sage had made it the object of his satire, directed against Dr. Sangrado, in *Gil Blas*, 150 years before.

Newspapers had no existence in the Rev. Giles Moore's days; but the "Gazettes" and "Letters" out of which they sprang had made their appearance during the preceding civil war, and they were not to be rooted out by the Licenser of the Press, Sir Roger L'Estrange. Our Sussex Diarist had evidently acquired a taste for them. *Ex. gr.*:—" To John Morley, for gazettes read from Lady Day till Midsr., at 1d. per each gazette, 1s. 3d. I payed him for 1 qr. newes bookes, 2s. 6d.; and I promised him a paier of old breeches for his letters." A mode of barter not very complimentary to literature. But, doubtless, John Morley was only the carrier, not the inventor of the news! Another entry of a payment to the same person has a curious *addendum*:—" I payed John Morley for a letter 2d., for carrying news books 2s. 6d., and 6d. more gratis to stop his mouth." Doubtless there had been some scandal at Horstead Keynes which the Rector did not wish to spread!

One entry would puzzle modern readers, did not Mr. Blencowe kindly append an explanation to it. It is this:—" 26th Dec. I gave the howling boys 6d." This was *not* the waits! " On New Year's Eve," writes Mr. Blencowe, " it was, and it still continues to be the custom, to wassail the orchards. At Horstead Keynes and elsewhere, the ceremony retains the name of 'Apple Howling.' A troop of boys visit the different orchards, and encircling the apple trees, they repeat the following words:—

> ' Stand fast root, bear well top,
> Pray the God send us a good howling crop.
> Every twig, apples big;
> Every bough, apples enou;
> Hats full, caps full,
> Full quarters sacks full.'

They then shout in chorus, one of the boys accompanying them upon the cow's horn. During this ceremony they rap the trees with their sticks. This custom is alluded to in Herrick's 'Hesperides,' p. 311 :

> 'Wassail the trees that they may beare
> You, many a plum, and many a peare :
> For more or less fruits they will bring,
> As you do give them wassailing.'

This practice is not confined to Sussex; it prevails in Devon and in Herefordshire."

Evidence of the manners of the day crops up here and there in the Diary. *Ex. gr.:* "To Mrs. Stapley, I lost 1s. at *cards.*" "I bought for my wyfe a new horse pillion, for which I gave 8s." "I payed Wm. Bachelor, at the Tiger Inn, at Lindfield, for a dinner for 12 persons, £1 4s. ; for beer, bread, and tobacco, 7s. 7d. ; 3 bottles of sack, 5s. ; horse meate, 8d."

The Tiger Inn still stands at Lindfield, and a curious old building it is !

The fashion of tradesmen to put up signs over their doors was in full vogue in Mr. Moore's days. He made not infrequent journeys to London, always riding on horseback, as was the practice in those days, when, indeed, in Sussex there were no roads for vehicles ; and he duly sets down his purchases. Here is one entry as a sample of numerous others :—" For 6 yards of black cloth to make a cloake, bought of Mr. Theophilus Smith, at the White Lion, Pauls Church Yard, I payd £4 16s., and for 7 yards of calaminko to make a cassock £1 4s. 6d., and 1 qr. of a yard of velvet 6s. ; I bought of Mr. James Allen, at the Hat and Harrow, a new hat, costing mee £1 ; I bought for my wyfe a lute string hood, costing 6s."

And so this amusing and instructive Diary goes on from its beginning, in 1655, to its termination, in August, 1679, when it closes in the following suggestive entry :—

"3rd of August, I payed to Capt. Fishenden for a cephalic playster, and to Mr. Marshall, of Lewis, for a julep, and for something to make mee sleep, 2s, 6d."

The narcotic must have had the required effect, for the next extract, from the Parish Register, is as follows:—

"Mr. Giles Moore, Minister of this parish, was buryed the 3rd of October, 1679."

So the Rector of Horstead Keynes slept the long sleep to which there is only one awakening. But his Diary survives, and in it he and his doings will live for many a day, to amuse and interest Sussex people.

The Stapleys, of Hickstead Place, in the parish of Twineham, may be said to have been a family of Diarists. Their memoranda, in account books and journals, extend from 1607 to 1743—a period of 136 years! The example was set by John Stapley, who, in addition to being the Squire of Hickstead Place, was a Trainband Captain. His career was in the latter years of the reign of "Good Queen Bess" and the earlier ones of James the First; but his memoranda, or what remains of them, are limited to one item, namely, "that for all my landes within the whole parish I am to impaile of the churchyard of Twineham 174½ feet. The churchyard is in compass 28 rods and 2 feet."

This refers to a custom still, according to the late Rev. E. Turner, observed in some places, of the fences of the churchyard being kept up by the landowners according to the number of acres they possessed in the parish. But, for the most part, we take it, the custom is obsolete, and the burthen is borne by the whole of the parishioners.

At this early period,—1607-10,—the prices of all home-productions were very low, as compared with those which they now fetch. Of course, the value of money has depreciated; a sovereign, a shilling, and a penny 250 years ago were worth double or treble their present value. But, even allowing for this, an ox which weighed "600lbs. the foure quarters," would be very cheap at £9 10s., and 2s. 3d. the stone of 8lbs. for mutton would be very acceptable to consumers of butcher's meat. Lambs, too, at 6s. 8d. each (the weight is not specified) would not be dear. And these were the prices of 1610 for meat, whilst those for wheat and eggs may be learnt from the following stanzas of an old ballad ;—

> "Ill tell what, old fellowe,
> Before the friars went hence,
> A bushell of the best wheate
> Was sold for fourteen pence.
> And forty egges a penny
> That were both good and newe,
> And this, I say, myself have seene,
> And yet I am no Jewe."

Forty eggs for a penny! Will not that make our modern housewives' mouths water?

In 1662 wheat was 30s. per quarter; peas, 24s. per ditto; lime, 12s. per load—so that even in the half century which followed 1610 prices had risen. And they have not ceased to do so from that time to this.

The Diary of the Rev. Giles Moore bore testimony to the low rate of educational charges in the Charles's day, and the Stapley Diaries confirm it. But we should note that we have now reached the Stapley Diarists Proper. These were the two sons of the before-mentioned John Stapley, the Trainband Captain, and successively the owners of Hickstead Place, namely, Richard Stapley up to 1724 and Anthony up to 1738. These two Stapleys systematically recorded their expenses and the chief events of their lives from 1657, which is contemporaneous with Giles Moore's Diary, and when Oliver Cromwell was England's ruler, until 1738, when George the Second was King; and Richard Stapley, the son of Anthony, adds a closing memorandum in 1743. What a momentous period in the history of this country! What vast changes—social, religious, political, and, above all, scientific and economical,—took place in the interval of the commencement and the closing of these Stapley Diaries! and yet, in the retirement of this little Sussex homestead, the current of life seems to have flowed on with a quietude that no civil or political convulsion could disturb. There were Restorations and Revolutions—Plots, sham and real—civil and foreign wars—victories and defeats—the rise and fall of Ministers, the death and banishment of Kings; great discoveries in science, by a Newton, a Hervey, and a Boyle; great changes in the industrial world, such as the introduction of coal and the substitution of the iron of Wales for the iron of Sussex. But, of all these changes, we get little or no indications in the Stapley Diaries. A Sussex village like that of Twineham must have been, in those days of impassable roads, almost as remote from the great movements of life at the centres of civilization as the islands of the South Seas are now; and those who lived in them seemed to concern themselves as little about such movements. They paid taxes, of course—and these kept on increasing!—and we presume that they occasionally gave a vote at County elections. But, if so, no note is made of such voting. As Mr. Blencowe remarks, a battle like that of Naseby might have been fought in another County and the news of it never have reached such a village as Twineham!

But there *were* events and incidents even in the Stapley world. There were children born into the world, and they had to be taught to read, write, and reckon. How cheaply, we may infer from the entry (May, 1731) that "Anthonie Stapley went to school to Thomas Painter by the week; to learn to write and read, and cast accounts, *at 6d. per week.*" Previous to this the same Anthony (a son of Anthony Stapley, we presume) had been to a Brighton boarding school, and we have this entry: "Paid Grover and Browne, of Brighton, £7 6s. 10d." Doubtless for the year: for at the same period, we are told, "Sarah Stapley went to William Best's to board at 3s. 6d. per week. She is to go to Miss Leach's school at 6d. per week; and Jane, and John, and Samuel went to Dame Bellchamber's the same day,—the boys at 2d. and Jane at 4d. per week." Again (May 20th, 1735) "Carried my son John to Mr. Browne, of Lindfield, to be boarded by him at 3s. per week. And on the 23rd he is to go to school to John Wood, to learn to read and write, at 6d. per week."

Verily, the education rate was not a heavy one at Hickstead Place!

The practice of sending children to board with one person, and to another to get their schooling, seems to have been a common one; and, certainly, the bodily food was better paid for than the intellectual! *Ex. gr.* " Paid Thomas Burtenshaw his half-year's salary, for teaching the girls and boys, £1 10s." As much is now often paid for a single lesson on the pianoforte!

Domestic servants were a different class of persons in the 17th century from what they are now. They came, indeed, from the same ranks of life—those of the agricultural labourer. But their pretensions were much humbler, and their affections seem to have been much more constant. Instances were not rare of both male and female servants devoting their whole lives to their masters and mistresses, and periods of 10, 20, and even 30 years of service in the same family were common; and that, too, at wages which would now be laughed at. Here are some entries by Mr. Anthony Stapley—who kept three men and three maid-servants—of the wages he paid them:—

"1730. Mary White began her year May 1st, and is to have £1 5s. if she stay until May, 1731. Hannah Morley came, and is to have £2 if she stays until Lady Day next. Paid Edwd. Harland and George Virgoe ½ year's wages each, £3 5s. James Hazelgrove came to live with me at £6 5s. per annum.

"1740. Sarah Chandler came to live with me, and she is to have £2 10s. if she stays until Lady Day, 1741. But as she left my service in about 8 weeks I gave her 1s. only. Sarah Martin left me, and William Sully. Also Mary White, who went back to Bolney; and Thomas Fairhall, whose loss of time was a week, and he allowed me a shilling for it. Richard Sayers took his place, and is to have £2 15s. if he stays twelve months. He stayed with me but a very short time. Paid Thos. Avery his wages in full, though he was sick part of the time.

"1741. John Steer went away from my house Dec. 16th. He was with me about a year, and I had just given him a coat, waistcoat, breaches, and hat, and 3 shirts, which cost me £5 1s.

"1742. Sarah Juppe came to live with me March 25th, and is to have £2 10s. if she stays with me to Lady Day, 1743. But this she did not do. For she left me Nov. 7th, and came to me on the 16th of the same month."

Mr. Turner suggests a reason for this quitting service one day and returning to it two or three days later. It was to avoid making a servant chargeable to the parish by an uninterrupted twelve months' hiring. One of the blessings of the old Poor Law!

Like most country gentlemen, the Stapleys were sportsmen, and there are numerous entries concerning dogs, guns, foxes, and even hawks, showing that falconry was not yet an obsolete sport. Thus, in 1642, "Bought a hawk for £2, and in 1643 bought another at the same price." These must have been well-trained birds, to fetch such high prices.

There is nothing about music in the Stapley diaries—no mention of concerts or pianofortes or even fiddles; but Mr. Richard Stapley had an ear for one species of music. *Ex. gr.:*— "Paid to William Ashford, for two beagles, *which make my cry complete*, £4 15s."

This expression calls to mind the beautiful lines uttered by Theseus in *A Midsummer Night's Dream*:—

> My hounds are bred out of the Spartan kind,
> So flew'd, so sanded; and their heads are hung
> With ears that sweep away the morning dew;
> Crook-knee'd and dew-lapp'd like Thessalian bulls;
> Slow in pursuit, but match'd in mouth like bells,
> Each under each. A cry more tuneable
> Was never holla'd to, nor cheer'd with horn,
> In Crete, in Sparta, nor in Thessaly:
> Judge, when you hear.

On the 5th of October, 1739, Mr. Stapley records a sad misfortune to his canine establishment:—"I had a mad dog in my kennel, and was obliged to kill all my hounds. Six of them were all hanging at the same time."

Mr. Anthony Stapley had the feelings of "a gentleman and a Christian" for his dumb servants. Here is an example:—

"1735, Octr. 9th. James Matthew had my old white horse away, which I gave him to keep as long as he should live, and when dead to bury him in his skin, and not to flaw him or abuse him in any way."

By a later entry it appears that this old horse died May 21st, 1736, and was buried in the sawpit in the Laines Wood. His age when he died was supposed to be 35 years.

In all articles of home-produce the rise of prices has been immense since the Stapley's days; and horse-flesh has "gone up" with the rest. In May, 1737, Mr. A. Stapley records that "Chowne bought me a mare, which cost me £10 10s, and I gave him 1s for bringing her." Again, in 1739, "Bought a black mare for John Stapley to ride; she cost £5, with bridle and saddle in." 1740: "Bought a mare of John Daulton, for which I gave him £5."

Sometimes, however, a higher figure was reached, as in 1741, when he "bought a mare of John Lindfield, of Dean House, for which I paid him £15."

They were great meat-eaters at Hickstead Place; but they did not go to the butcher for it. "The calves, sheep, and lambs," writes Anthony Stapley, "which I have killed in my house this year (1642) are 4 calves, 20 sheep, and 45 lambs." The practice of neighbours exchanging meat with each other was, it is evident, common: Thus, in 1645, "Had of Georg Luxford, of Hurst, 21 nailes of beef, which I have since repaid him." And in 1654, "Goodman Butcher owes me 15 nailes of beef and 2 lbs., and he has been paid all the beef I owed him."

It was very convenient, doubtless, when it was necessary to kill a sheep in order to get a leg or shoulder of mutton, to exchange in this way with a neighbour.

Brewing, of course, was carried on at Hickstead Place, for home consumption, and, doubtless, very good ale was brewed. There are numerous entries of the purchase of malt. The average consumption at Hickstead was, says Mr. Turner, until 1746, about eight bushels a month. In speaking of malt the Stapley accounts generally describe it as *barley* malt. This (remarks Mr. Turner) doubtless is done to distinguish it from malt made of other grain. In the early part of the reign of Edwd. II. great quantities of wheat were made into malt, and this, towards the close of his reign, he found it necessary to prohibit. But this practice was subsequently resumed, for in the "Chronicles of London" we find the following receipt: "For brewing 60 barrels of good Songel Beer, 10 quarters of Barley Malt, 2 do. of Wheat do., 2 do. of Oats do., and 40lbs. of Hoppys." And this appears to have gone on until the year 1630, when wheat was again prohibited from being made into malt by royal proclamation, and it was further ordered that "no grain, meet for bread to feed men, be wasted and consumed in stuff called starch," which was profusely used for stiffening the ruffles, and cuffs, and other linen attire which an ostentatious and inconvenient fashion had been the means of introducing into the habits both of the gentlemen and ladies of the times of Charles the First and Second.

Hops, though grown at Twineham, were also bought by the Stapleys in large quantities.

Whilst upon this subject of liquor, we may note that claret was the principal wine drunk by the Stapleys, and doubtless other families of the period, with a certain quantity of sherry, under the name of sack. Thus (1646), "I had from Cleer, of London, one runlet of sacke, and 3 runlets of claret." "For sack, when strangers were here, 12s 6d." "Had a dozen of white wine and one gallon of sack, which cost me £1 17s 4d."

We have referred to the absence of politics in these Diaries, and to the utter ignoring of the rise and fall of Kings and Governments. Only in the payment of taxes, which all Governments, Kingly or Republican, levy, can we detect any signs of the great events going on in England, and this is shown in the curious admixture of "King" and "Parliament" in the following entries :—

"1644. To the King, £1 4s 2d. To William Dumbrell for tax, £1 15s 2d. To the Parliament, £1. To Goodman Erle for a six months' tax, £2 7s 6d.

"1645. To the Parliament, £1 7s 6d.

"1646. Taxes for the Parliament, April 8th. To Arthur Luxford for four months' tax, 10s. To William Dumbrell for eight months' tax, £1 0s 4d. To do. for twelve months' tax, £1 10s 6d.

"1649. To William Dumbrell for a tax, 13s 5d. To Thomas Averie for a do., 14s 6d. To Thomas Marchant, of Hurst, for a tax for the Parliament £3. To Arthur Luxford for the use of the King and Parliament, 14s. To William Dumbrell for an eight months' tax, £2 10s 6d. For the King's Provision, 14s 8d."

The contribution to King and Parliament is pretty equal, and perhaps the feelings of the Stapleys,—who counted Roundheads and Cavaliers among their successors, and one of whom was a friend of Cromwell, and figured as a Regicide,—were pretty equally balanced. All that they cared for at Twineham was to be let alone!

As we go through the entries of the Squires of Hickstead Place, as to their eatings and drinkings, buyings and sellings, we cannot help wishing that they had given us a glimpse of themselves, and of their "interior"—the ways and fashions of the house and of its inmates, male and female. But we look in vain for anything of the sort. It was a Diary for the use of Richard and Anthony Stapley, and not for the information of those who might come after them. If it had not been for entries of fees paid to Mr. Nightingale,—"for his journey half-a-guinea, and 2s for things which he brought with him"—we should scarcely have known that Richard Stapley had a wife, until her death, from a cause which is thus quaintly but forcibly described :—" Struck with the dead palsy from head to foot, in a moment of time."

For pictures of the mode of life of such families as that of the Stapleys—the Squires or gentry of the 17th and 18th centuries—we must go to other sources. The Rev. E. Turner, who edited these Stapley Diaries for the Archæological Society, and who had other sources of information as to the manners of Sussex people in their day, drew the following lively picture of the style in which our forefathers lived 200 years ago :—

"They dined at one or two o'clock, and many now do the same; the only difference between them and us being, that what they called dinner we call luncheon. They sat down to a substantial meal at half-past seven or eight o'clock, and so do we; and this they called supper, but we call dinner. And as soon as supper was over the squire sat down at the shovel-board table, with his canine pets about him ; and his tenants and retainers being called in, they smoked their pipes and quaffed they grogs—unless any of the party preferred instead potent home-brewed October ale—discussing all the while the business as well as the passing events of the day. And this continued—varied, perhaps, with now and then a hunting song, in the chorus of which all heartily joined, or with a game played with cards—until it was time to prepare for bed, which, in well-regulated families, was seldom later than ten o'clock ; while in another part of the hall, if it was spacious enough to admit of it, or if not in some adjoining apartment opening into the hall, sat the lady of the house, with her family and any female friends that might be staying with her, busily engaged in spinning. Pianofortes, now to be found in every tradesman's and farmer's house, were unknown even in the houses of many of the gentry in those days. The drone of the spinning-wheel was the music they most delighted in ; and singing, or, as one of my church choir used to call it when he was in a grandiloquent humour, 'the tuneful music of the vocal voice,' was all the melody that arrested the ear within the substantial walls of the Place House ; and profitable music it was, for all the linen of the house, body, bed, and table, was, for the most part, thus supplied ; the maid servants, as well as the mistress of the house, her daughters and her friends, employing all their not otherwise occupied time in the same way. Tea was a repast not then much appreciated, even if it was known ; the article itself—from a decoction of which the meal took its name—being far too costly during the period under consideration to be much used in a common way, even in the houses of the better class ; though it appears to have been occasionally indulged in at Hickstead ; the price given for the article thus consumed being charged, according to the accounts, at 25s. and 30s. per pound. The family breakfasts at this date were upon the substantial Elizabethan scale. They consisted for the most part of hot meats, with a liberal supply of well-matured nut-brown malt liquor. A hot beef steak, with no scant measure of two years' old ale, was no unusual thing for the lords and ladies of Queen Elizabeth's Court at breakfast to indulge in ; and her most gracious Majesty did the same. And at Hickstead this meal was taken at a somewhat unusually early hour, so that by eight o'clock the squire was ready either for business or pleasure. If, during the hunting season—

> ' A southerly wind and a cloudy sky
> Proclaimed a hunting morn,'

the hounds were unkenelled, and every servant that could be spared from his customary duties in and about the house, each with a hunting pole in his hand, attended his master to the cover, and the welkin soon rang with the music of their tuneable voices ; for game was far too plentiful in the Hickstead woods and hedgerows in those days to be long in being found. Or if the day was better adapted to shooting, the old Sussex spaniels, for which Hickstead was then famous, were brought out, and the squire spent his morning in trying either the covers for pheasants or the stubbles for partridges ; and by twelve o'clock he was able to return home with a well-filled bag."

For a contemporary picture of Sussex manners in the 18th century, though not of a very flattering character, we are indebted to Dr. Burton, the learned Greek Lecturer of Oxford, who, in 1751, was bold enough to "go down, through muddy, fertile, pastoral Sussex," to Shermanbury, to see his mother, who had married the Rector of that place, Dr. John Bear. Here he had an opportunity of seeing a little of the people who constituted the society of Sussex 137 years ago,—the squires and yeomen of the County,—and he draws the following not over-flattering sketch of them :—

"You should observe that the farmers of the better sort are considered here as squires. These men, however, boast of honourable lineage, and, like oaks among shrubs, look down upon the rural vulgar. You would be surprised at the uncouth dignity of these men, and their palpably ludicrous pride ; nor will you be less surprised at the humility of their boon-companions *(compotantium)*, and the triumphs of their domineering spirit among the plaudits of the pothouse or kitchen ; the awkward prodigality and sordid luxury of their feasts ; the inelegant roughness and dull hilarity of their conversation ; their intercourse with servants and animals so assiduous, with clergymen or gentlemen so rare ; being illiterate, they shun the lettered ; being sots, the sober *(sobrios bibaculi)*. Their whole attention is given to get their cattle and everything else fat, their own intellect not excepted. Is this enough about the squires? Don't ask anything further about their women. They who understand Latin will feel that these remarks do not apply to them ; they who do not, I need not dread their abuse."

This is certainly not very complimentary to the Sussex gentry of 1751.

To the ladies he is a little more polite, but it is at the expense of their lords and masters :—

"You would probably admire the women if you saw them, as modest in countenance and fond of elegance in their dress, but, at the same time, fond of labour, and experienced in household matters ; both by nature and education better bred and more intellectual generally than the men."

In social position, as in worldly possessions, Thomas Marchant, of Little Park, Hurst, who follows next in order of the Sussex Diarists, was a degree below the Stapleys, of Hickstead Place. They were Squires, and one (Richard) was a Justice of the Peace. Thomas Marchant was a Yeoman. Yet they touched closely upon each other, and mixed with and were probably related to the same families : the Campions, Courthopes, Dodsons, Scutts, Harts, Turners, Whitpaines, Lindfields, Stones, &c. For Thomas Marchant belonged to that higher order of English Yeomen who farmed their own land, and the house he resided in at Hurst was one of some pretensions. It had originally belonged to Sir William Juxon, of whom it was bought by Mrs Annie Swaine, of Hurstpierpoint, and was purchased of her son and heir by the father of Thomas Marchant. Little Park is now the property of Col. Smith Hannington, who acquired it from the Executors of the last male representative of the Marchants of Hurst. Thomas Marchant, our Diarist, was the second of his family who held Little Park, and he began his Diary in September, 1714; a few years before that of the Stapleys was brought to a close.

There is a certain family resemblance between the Stapley and the Marchant Diaries. Both illustrate the character of the times—one of great material prosperity, but, in country places, at all events, of little intellectual activity, and of peaceful pursuits. The sword had, in very truth, been turned into the ploughshare. The campaigns of Marlborough were brought to a close, and the next 50 years were passed, with only rare exceptions, in profound peace, and in a state of material prosperity which has perhaps never been exceeded in England. But it was of a gross kind. This is reflected in the Diary of Thomas Marchant, of Hurst; in that of Thomas Turner, of East Hoathly; and others of the same period. They are redolent of eating and drinking and of the dealings connected therewith. People married, begat and christened children, eat and drank "hugely," amused themselves in a coarse kind of way, bought and sold, died, and were buried. And all this went on in an uniform way as if there were nothing more in life, and as if life would always go on in the same way. The education of the lower classes was utterly neglected, and their morals did not improve. But they were fed well—to a large extent in the houses of their employers, who were not much superior to them in manners or in education. It was the period, perhaps, when the relations of the farmer and the labourer were closest to each other. The time was yet to come when they were to separate: the former struggling to maintain their position and eventually rising in the scale; the latter sinking more and more into poverty and pauperism, until poor-rates threatened to swallow up rents, and then a reactionary movement set in towards independence, which, assisted by new forces, is going on in our own day.

But these changes were far off in Thomas Marchant's days. The Civil Wars were well nigh forgotten; the great wars in Flanders, where our soldiers fought so well and swore so terribly, were over. Sir Robert Walpole was entering on his long lease of political power, and finding out the price at which men were to be bought; peace being the great object of his policy, and a gross national prosperity the reward of it.

Thomas Marchant, of Little Park, Hurst, was, we may be sure, one of those who accepted this policy, and his life was a capital illustration of it. He had received a practical kind of education—could read, write, and keep accounts, and was, in all probability, rather superior in these respects to his neighbours; for he was frequently selected as executor to their wills, and as Overseer, &c.; and was eventually chosen by the owner of Petworth, the "proud" Duke of Somerset, to be his Steward, and for some time filled that post, living then near Petworth. But, at the time he began this Diary, he was at Little Park, farming his own land there, and doing a great deal as the breeder of freshwater fish, for which, it is clear, there was a much greater demand in those days than there is now. In every way, indeed, he was a good man of business—ever ready to turn a penny and make a bargain. The first day's entry, September 29, 1714, is not a bad sample of the character of the whole Diary. Here it is :—

"John Shelley went away. Set 4 pigs to fatting yesterday. Lent James Reed 4 oxen. Paid John Gun 1 guinea. Went by Henfield to Steyning fair : and received 31s. 6d. of John Goffe, as part paiment of 3 guineas which I had lent him. Bought five runts of Thomas Jones for £16. Drank with Thomas Vinal of Cowfold at J. Beard's. Met with J. Gold of Brighthelmstone at Bramber as we were coming home ; and concluded that he should have a load of my wheat at £7 10s.—which is to be delivered on friday se'nnight next at the Rock. We did not agree for any Barley ; because some one had told him, that my Barley was all of it mowburnt. Ned Grey kept holiday. The day was dry ; we took in the evening 22 pigeons."

And so the Diary of Thomas Marchant runs on, filled with details which are purely personal, and, for the most part, relating to business matters, and pounds, shillings, and pence—scarcely a reference to national affairs, which now occupy so much of men's thoughts—of the great contests of parties or collisions of Empires —hardly a thought beyond the parish in which Mr. Marchant lived, or its immediate neighbourhood. Brighthelmstone, indeed, figures more than once in the Diary, and Lewes pretty frequently, Mr. Marchant going to the Sessions on parochial business, disputed settlements being a fertile source of litigation between neighbouring parishes, which rejoiced in their triumphs over each other as though it were a gain to the community that some unfortunate labourer, who had strayed from his parish, was transferred from Hurst to Cuckfield, or *vice versa*, as the case might be.

"Went to the Sessions at Lewes, where we had a trial with the parish of Cuckfield about the settlement of Thomas Mitchell: *and we cast them.*"

With what exultation did Thomas Marchant make that entry, not forgetting the inevitable sequel: "Dined at the Crown,"—the parish paying for the dinner to celebrate the victory over Cuckfield *in re* Thomas Mitchell, pauper!

Obsolete customs, coins, and terms crop up here and there. *Ex. gr.:* "Sold John Smith a steer at £6 certain; and, if he prove worth it, I am to have a *noble* more."

How long is it since nobles disappeared from our current coin?

Thomas Marchant was not an intemperate man; but all men in those days, in all ranks of life, drank freely, and at times deeply, and our Sussex Diarist does not blink the matter. At Danny, on one occasion, he, his wife, and others "staid late and drank too much." On another occasion, at Mr. Whitpaine's, "staid late there and *drank enough.*" Again, at John Smith's, "stay'd late and drank too much." Nor was he very particular with whom he drank. A mountebank came to the town (Hurst), and Mr. Marchant records, " Mr. Scutt and I drank tea with the tumbler. Of his tricks (he modestly writes) I am no judge; but he appears to me to play well on the fiddle."

Perhaps the trick of playing the fiddle was to Thomas Marchant (as, indeed, it was at a later date to Dr. Johnson) the most wonderful of all tricks! The arrival of a mountebank was evidently an event at Hurst. In subsequent entries we are informed, "A mountebank man here the 2nd time. * * * I drank with him yesterday at the Swan." And, later on, "The mountebank in the town. A smock race in our field." Probably in honour of the mountebank! The visits of mountebanks are rare enough now; but the visits of another sort of gentry have died out quite. "Mr. Russell, the non-juror, came there (to Mr. Dodson's, the Rector of Hurst) in the evening." Non-jurors were those clergymen of the Church of England who refused to take the oaths of allegiance to the new dynasty and denied the orthodoxy of the Bishops who recognised William and Mary as their Sovereigns.

Bleedings and shavings of the head are frequently recorded, and cyder is still brewed. Side by side with these old fashions, now extinct, are symptoms of new ones, which still flourish. Thus, in 1717, "Willy went to see a cricket match,"—an early record of that now national game. In Whitsuntide of the same year "the new singers began to sing in the Church," and Mr. Blencowe adds, in a note, that the then Bishop of Chichester granted a faculty at this time for a singing gallery at the west end of Hurst Church, where, doubtless, the "new singers" were located. "Carried flax" is a reference to a growth now seldom seen in Sussex. The Sussex iron mills were in full work; prize-fighting was in vogue; "Will and Jack went to Lewes to see a prize-fight between Harris and another." Horses and carts were "mired" in Sussex roads, and people died of the small-pox in a way which would gladden the hearts of modern anti-vaccinators! "Crying lost goods in Church" is a custom "more honoured in the breach than the observance." But there are some signs of civilization : "Mr. Lun, the dancing-master, began teaching at Kester's." Tea begins to be drunk with greater frequency, and the following entry—" Paid Norman 6d. for the reading of a book yesterday, and recd. a case to carry pen and ink and sand"—indicates that letters were not quite neglected. Indeed, this Diary itself is a proof of this. But, at the same time, it proves the slight extent to which literature had penetrated to the middle classes at the beginning of the 18th century. In the Diary of Thomas Turner, mercer, of East Hothly, we shall find great advance in this respect. He was a reader of books, and had a taste for their contents. To Thomas Marchant, as to the Stapleys, they appear to have been totally closed. The only books they were acquainted with, judging from their own records, were account books. Yes, one book is named by Thomas Marchant : it is a book entitled "Lex Testamentaria" (the law of Wills), which he received from Mr. Norman, and he couples the fact with another : "paid 20s.

for a ribbon and slouch for Molly Balcombe!" We wonder if Mrs. Marchant was privy to this purchase!

In fact, the whole time and attention of the country gentry and farmers of that time were absorbed in *res angusta domi*, but which to them were a source of pleasure as well as of profit. It was a prosperous period; but the leisure which prosperity produces had not yet begun to give that refinement and taste for luxuries which were to follow. The men eat, drank, fished, shot, hunted, bought and sold, raised stock, sowed and reaped, married and begot children; and these, with a little parish business, or a County election now and then, and an occasional bout of drinking, made up life,—at least, there are signs of little more in the Stapley and Marchant Diaries. The political allusions, as to the Coronation Day of George I. (October 18, 1714), his death, and the accession of George II. (1727); the report about the Duke of Ormond, the great supporter of the Chevalier St. George, commonly called the Pretender, "going off at Shoreham," with Sir Harry Goring, Mr. Middleton, and one or two more, are of the most meagre kind. There is a little more detail than usual about the contested election for Sussex which followed on the accession of George I., and in which the Whigs gained the victory "by a vast majority," but, as Mr. Marchant (who had Tory, if not Jacobite proclivities) insinuates, "by all manner of indirect practices." But these are "few and far between," and show the faint interest taken in politics in those days, compared with present times. In one respect they seem to have had the advantage over us: there was, to all appearance, a more free mixture of classes—less separation between the degrees of social rank which made up the rural community. Mr. Thomas Marchant, although only a yeoman, farming his own land, dines and sups at Danny with the Campions and the Courthopes, and goes to Mr. Dodson's at the Rectory, and mixes with the Whitpaines, the Scutts, and other members of the landed gentry living at or near Hurst, on terms of perfect equality. One of the last entries tells us how "three of Sir George Parker's daughter's supt and spent the evening here." In fact, there is no evidence of social differences or jealousies in the Marchant Diary, and we are afraid that such would not be the case if one of the same rank were to keep a Diary in the year of our Lord one thousand eight hundred and seventy-eight !

The first and foremost of our Sussex Diarists, in Diaristic ability, though, in order of time, he came last, is, without question, Thomas Turner, general dealer, of East Hothly. He is our Sussex Pepys, and possesses many of the qualities of that Prince of Diarists. He is intelligent, frank, open-speaking, rather fond of recording his own failings, disposed to be social, a good man of business, but yet with a decided bent towards literature. In all these points, Samuel Pepys, Secretary of the Admiralty, and Thomas Turner, grocer, draper, haberdasher, hatter, clothier, druggist, ironmonger, stationer, glover, undertaker,—for Thomas Turner was all of these, *cum multis aliis*,—resemble each other, and if one enjoys a world-wide fame and the other only a local reputation, it is owing, perhaps, to the Fate that placed them in such different spheres.

Still, in his own sphere, Thomas Turner is a man to be esteemed, and he has performed a work,—namely, that of describing the life of a Sussex rural tradesman 100 years ago,—for which he ought to be held in high regard by all students of social history in England.

He was not a native of Sussex. He was born in 1728 at Groombridge, in Kent; but he claimed descent from an old Sussex family—the Turners of Tablehurst, at East Grinstead—and he must have settled in Sussex pretty early in life, for he begins his diary in 1754, at which time he was only 26 years of age. Where he was educated we are not told; but he had evidently received an education above the average, and though, as was the failing of the times, his orthography was by no means perfect, he expresses himself with ease and force, and has a considerable command of language. In this, indeed, and in other respects, he is far above the Stapleys and Marchants, or even the Rev.

Giles Moore. Take, as a sample, the sentence with which he opens his Diary on Sunday, Feb. 8, 1754:—

"As I by experience find how much more conducive it is to my health, as well as pleasantness and serenity to my mind, to live in a low, moderate rate of diet, and as I know I shall never be able to comply therewith in so strickt a manner as I should chuse, by the unstable and over-easyness of my temper, I think it therefore fit to draw up Rules of proper Regimen, which I do in the manner and form following, which I hope I shall always have the strictest regard to follow, as I think they are not inconsistent with either religion or morality."

As is the wont of young men beginning life,—young women, too, perhaps,—Thomas Turner forms a number of good resolutions, which—but the sequel will show how he kept them. He determines to rise early, to breakfast between seven and eight, and to dine between the hours of twelve and one; eating sparingly of meat, but plenty of garden-stuff; his supper to consist of weak broth, water-gruel, or milk pottage, varied occasionally with a fruit pie.

"If," he says, "I am at home, or in company abroad, I will never drink more than four glasses of strong beer; one to drink the King's health, the second to the Royal Family, the third to all friends, and the fourth to the pleasure of the company. If there is either wine or punch, never upon any terms or perswasion to drink more than eight glasses, each glass to hold no more than half a quarter of a pint."

He concludes with the resolution, "allways to go to bed at or before ten o'clock."

Mr. Turner was at this time a married man. Men married early 100 years ago, in all ranks of life; for competition was not so fierce as it is now, and men were less ambitious in their aims and women less expensive in their dress and houses. His wife, too, shared in his literary tastes, for an early entry tells us that on one occasion "my wife read to me that moving scene of the funeral of Miss Clarissa Harlow" (in Richardson's novel), and thereupon he makes the edifying remark :—

"Oh, may the Supreme Being give me grace to lead my life in such a manner as my exit may in some measure be like that divine creature's."

And let it not be supposed that the East Hothly grocer's readings was limited to novels. In the course of five or six weeks, say the editors of his Diary (Messrs. R. W. Blencowe and M. A. Lower), "we find him recording his perusal of Gray's *Poems*, Stewart *On the Supreme Being,* the *Whole Duty of Man, Paradise Lost and Regained, Othello,* the *Universal Magazine,* Thomson's *Seasons,* Young's *Night Thoughts,* Tournefort's *Voyage to the Levant,* and *Peregrine Pickle.*"

A very good six weeks' reading for a man engaged all the day in trade! Another day we find him reading part of Boyle's Lectures; then he turns from science to politics, and reads "several numbers of the *Freeholder,*" which, he adds, "I think, is a proper book for any person at this critical juncture of affairs "— it was in April, 1756,—and from politics to poetry; for on the same day he read "Homer's Odysseyss" (*sic*), and thus records his opinion of it :—

"I think the character which Menelaus gives Telemachus of Ulisses, when he is a speeking of his warlike virtues, in the 4th Book, is very good. Read the 13th Book, after supper; I think the soliloquy which Ulysses makes when he finds the Phœnicians have in his sleep left him on his native shore of Ithaca, with all his treasure, contains a very good lesson of morality."

At the same time he copies out in full the passages he admired from Pope's translation.

As some explanation, however, of this unusual taste for literature in a Sussex tradesman of that day, it should be noted that Mr. Turner began his career at East Hothly as a schoolmaster. It was not a long nor apparently a successful career, for in May, 1756, he resigned his school and scholars to Mr. Francis Ellis, and entered on the more lucrative vocation of a general shopkeeper. But he did not give up his reading. To the last we find him deep in such solid works as "Burnett's History of the Reformation," and Beveredge's "Thoughts," varied by Shakspeare's plays and John Wilkes's "North Briton."

It would have been well for Thomas Turner if he had been constant to his books, and had not indulged in another habit more in keeping with the times; and that was of excessive drinking. The reader will not forget the good resolution with which he started, "never upon any terms or persuasion to drink more than eight glasses (of wine or punch), each glass to hold no more than half a quarter of a pint."

Quite enough, one might have thought, for a moderate man. But Thomas Turner was, it is evident, not proof against temptation, and his lapses from sobriety commence early and recur only too frequently. Here is the first set down :—" I went to the audit and came home drunk. But I think never to exceed the bounds of moderation more."

Alas ! for the frailty of human nature. Close upon the above is the following :—" Sunday, 28th, went down to Jones, where we drank one bowl of punch and two muggs of bumboo ; and I came home again in liquour. Oh ! with what horrors does it fill my heart, to think I should be guilty of doing so, and on a Sunday, too ! Let me once more endeavour never, no never, to be guilty of the same again."

Can any reader tell us what "bumboo" is ? But perhaps it is as well they should not know !

It is amusing, but scarcely edifying, to find our Diarist perfectly awake to the enormity of his offence, and yet still offending. "In the evening"—so runs one of his entries—" I read part of the fourth volume of the *Tatler;* the oftener I read it the better I like it. I think I never found the vice of drinking so well exploded in my life, as in one of the numbers."

So of his attendance, or rather non-attendance, at church. He plainly saw the right road, and he followed the wrong one.

Yet never was a man—who kept a Diary—less disposed to screen his weaknesses, or more ready to lay the lash upon his own back! In the making of good resolutions, too, he was decidedly strong. We have had some specimens. Here is another:—
"June 20th. This is my birthday, in which I enter the 29th year of my age; and may I, as I grow in years, so continue to increase in goodness; for, as my exit must every day draw nearer, so may I every day become more enamoured with the prospect of the happiness of another world, and more entirely dead to the follies and vanities of this transitory world."

The next entry, June 21, is a curious comment on this:—

"June 21st. Attended the funeral of Master Goldsmith at Waldron; this was the merriest funeral that ever I saw, for I can safely say there was no crying."

There is, indeed, throughout Mr. Turner's Diary, a comical contradiction of precept and action. The writer is a sage and moralist in theory; in practice he is—but we will leave him to name himself:—

"Aug. 22nd. I sett off for Piltdown, where I saw Charles Diggens and James Fowle run twenty rod for one guinea each. I got never a bet, but very drunk."

"Tuesday, 23rd. Came home in the forenoon, not quite sober; at home all day, and I know I behaved more like an ass than any human being—doubtless not like one who calls himself a Christian. Oh! how unworthy am I of that name!"

The reader, perhaps, has had enough of these lapses from sobriety and self-criminations. Let us turn to another page in Mr. Turner's Diary, in which, with a frankness very unusual in our Sussex diarists, he introduces us into his family interior and imparts to us his domestic troubles. He had taken to himself a wife soon after his arrival at East Hothly, and we presume that she was a native of that place, for he refers to his mother-in-law, Mrs. Slater, as a "very Xantippe," with a "great volubility of tongue," "especially if I am the subject." This lady was one of the stirrers-up of dissension between Mr. and Mrs. Turner. Another cause of conjugal irritation was Mrs. T.'s inclination to visit her friends at Lewes, on occasions when her absence from home [was inconvenient to Mr. T. "I have," he writes on one occasion, "several journeys to go next week, which I must postpone, on account of her absence. But, alas! what can be said of a woman's temper and thought? Business and family advantage must submit to their pride and pleasure. But tho' I mention this of women, it may perhaps be as justly applyed to men; but most people are blind to their own follies."

The way in which these journeys were made by Mr. Turner's better-half would astonish ladies of the present day. In the first place, a horse had to be borrowed, and then both man and woman had to mount it: the latter riding on a pillion behind her lord. And sometimes Master Dobbin was indisposed to bear the double load, and behaved accordingly:—

"My wife having hired a horse of John Watford, about four o'clock we set out on our journey to Hartfield, and as we were riding along near to Hastingford, no more than a foot's pace, the horse stood still, and continued kicking-up until we was both off, in a very dirty hole (but, thanks be to God, we received no hurt). My wife was obliged to go in to Hastingford House, to clean herself. My wife and I spent the even at my father Slater's. We dined off some ratios [rashers] of pork and green sallard."

Mr. Turner often particularises the dishes off which he dined, and certainly they were not epicures in those days. This is a Sunday's meal:—"Sept. 18th. My whole family at church—myself, wife, maid, and the two boys. We dined off a piece of boiled beef and carrots, and currant suet pudding."

It will be observed that the whole household—boys, maids, and all—dined together,—a custom long disused.

Up to this point—that is, some three or four years after marriage—the domestic happiness of the Turners had not been much disturbed, except by Mrs. Slater's tongue and her daughter's frequent illness. But now we come to a very tragic entry :—

"This day how are my most sanguine hopes of happiness frustrated !—I mean the happiness between myself and wife, which hath now continued for some time ; but, oh ! this day it has become the contra ! I think I have tryed all experiments to make our life's happy, but they have all failed. The opposition seems to be naturally in our tempers—not arising from spitefulness ; but an opposition that seems indicated by our very make and constitution."

John Milton himself could have set down no stronger reason for that right of divorce for which he pleaded so eloquently, and, in his days, ineffectually ! And from this time there is a continual recurrence of these doleful entries. "Oh !" Mr. Turner breaks out on Nov. 3, "how transient is all mundane bliss ! I who, on Sunday last, was all calm and serenity in my breast, am now nought but storm and tempest. Well might the wise man say, ' It were better to dwell in a corner of the house-top, than with a contentious woman in a wide house.' "

He had, however, his intervals of calm, and seems to have enjoyed them. Thus, " 1751, Jan. 9, Mr. Elless (his successor in the school), Marchant, myself, and wife sat down to whist about seven o'clock, and played all night ; very pleasant, and, I think I may say, innocent mirth, there being no oaths nor imprecations sounding from side to side, as is too often the case at cards."

And, again, Feb. 2, in the same year, "We supped at Mr. Fuller's, and spent the evening with a great deal of mirth, till between one and two. Tho. Fuller brought my wife home upon his back. I cannot say I came home sober, though I was far from being bad company. I think we spent the evening with a great deal of pleasure."

Cards all night, and merriment till between one and two in the morning, do not say much for the habits of the day ! to say nothing of carrying home ladies pick-a-back ! But this is nothing to what took place on the succeeding 22nd and 25th of February :—

"About 4 p.m. I walked down to Whyly. We played at bragg the first part of the even. After ten we went to supper, on four boiled chicken, four boiled ducks, minced veal, cold roast goose, chicken pasty, and ham. Our company, Mr. and Mrs. Porter, Mr. and Mrs. Coates, Mrs. Atkins, Mrs. Hicks, Mr. Piper and wife, Joseph Fuller and wife, Tho. Fuller and wife, Dame Durrant, myself and wife, and Mr. French's family. After supper our behaviour was far from that of serious, harmless mirth ; it was downright obstreperious, mixed with a great deal of folly and stupidity. Our diversion was dancing or jumping about, without a violin or any musick, singing of foolish healths, and drinking all the time as fast as it could be well poured down ; and the parson of the parish was one among the mixed multitude. If conscience dictates right from wrong, as doubtless it sometimes does, mine is one that I may say is soon offended ; for, I must say, I am always very uneasy at such behaviour, thinking it not like the behaviour of the primitive Christians, which I imagine was most in conformity to our Saviour's gospel. Nor would I be thought to be either a cynick or a stoick, but let social improving discourse pass round the company. About three o'clock, finding myself to have as much liquor as would do me good, I slipt away unobserved, leaving my wife to make my excuse. Though I was very far from sober, I came home, thank God, very safe and well, without even tumbling ; and Mr. French's servant brought my wife home, at ten minutes past five" (probably, add the Editors of the Diary, on his back).

This is pretty well in the way of "fooling ;" but what follows beats it :—

"Thursday, Feb. 25th. This morning, about six o'clock, just as my wife was got to bed, we was awaked by Mrs. Porter, who pretended she wanted some cream of tarter ; but as soon as my wife got out of bed, she vowed she should come down. She found Mr. Porter, Mr. Fuller, and his wife, with a lighted candle, and part of a bottle of port wine and a glass. The next thing was to have me down stairs, which being apprized of, I fastened my door. Up stairs they came, and threatened to break it open ; so I ordered the boys to open it, when they poured into my room ; and, as modesty forbid me to get out of bed, so I refrained ; but their immodesty permitted them to draw me out of bed, as the common phrase is, topsy-turvy ; but, however, at the intercession of Mr. Porter, they permitted me to put on my ——, and, instead of my upper cloaths, they gave me time to put on my wife's petticoats; and in this manner they made me dance, without shoes and stockings, until they had emptied the bottle of wine, and also a bottle of my beer. . . . About three o'clock in the afternoon, they found their way to their respective homes, beginning to be a little serious, and, in my opinion, ashamed of their stupid enterprise and drunken preambulation. Now, let anyone call in reason to his assistance, and seriously reflect on what I have before recited, and they will join with me in thinking that the precepts delivered from the pulpit on Sunday, tho' delivered with the greatest ardour, must lose a great deal of their efficacy by such examples."

Most unquestionably there are few in these days who will not give a hearty approval to these sentiments of Mr. Thomas Turner. Perhaps it was in a vein of satire that, immediately after chronicling the above nocturnal orgies, our Diarist adds:—"Sunday, March 3. We had as good a sermon as I ever heard Mr. Porter preach—it being against swearing."

Drinking would have been a topic more to the point.

We have before remarked on the greater freedom of intercourse between different classes in country places in former days. And here, in the above entries, is another instance: not very edifying certainly, but forcible.

Nor was this an exceptional meeting. Another is entered on the following March 7th, at which the same party,—with the addition of a Mr. Calverley and Mrs. Atkins,—met to sup at Mr. Joseph Fuller's, "drinking," says our diarist, "like horses, as the vulgar phrase is, and singing till many of us were very drunk, and then we went to dancing and pulling of wigs, caps, and hats; and thus we continued in this frantic manner, behaving more like mad people than they that profess the name of Christians."

Three days after this they sup at Mr. Porter's, with a repetition of the same excesses, except that (perhaps in deference to the recent exhortations from the Rev. gentleman's pulpit) "there was no swearing and no ill words, by reason of which Mr. Porter," he says, "calls it innocent mirth, but I in opinion differ much there from."

The next day Mr. Thomas Turner was "at home—very piteous," and certainly deserving no pity. For, yet once more, on the following Friday, the orgies were renewed at his own house, and then, he adds, "all revelling for this season is over; and may I never more be discomposed with so much drink, or by the noise of an obstreperious multitude, but that I may calm my troubled mind, and sooth my disturbed conscience."

A more striking illustration of the grossness of the manners of the age will scarcely be found,—even in the pages of Fielding or Smollett. That the clergyman of the parish, and a man of learning, as Mr. Porter evidently was, should have joined in such scenes shows to what a low point "the cloth" had sunk, and that the Trullibers and Thwackams and Squareums of fiction were not mere "inventions of the enemy."

Thomas Turner did not take the same trouble as Samuel Pepys did to conceal what he wrote. He had not the same reasons for doing so, for he was not the servant of a jealous Government nor did he live in a scandalous Court, which might not have been too well pleased to have its doings handed down to posterity. He wrote his Diary in a fair legible hand, in some 116 "stout memorandum books," and the manuscript went down to his son and his grandson, by the latter of whom it has been given to the world. But in Turner's own life-time he must have kept it very close. His first wife, his "dear Peggy," we are certain, never saw it, or it would scarcely have survived to the present day! He must have written it "on the sly," and it must have taken up a good deal of his time. Yet he had a large business to attend to. What were his motives, then, for keeping so voluminous a Diary? Why did he chronicle with such minuteness his own doings and those of his neighbours—not always of the most creditable kind? Why did he so often enter such good resolutions, and alas! why did he so frequently have to chronicle that he had broken them? There can be little doubt that Thomas Turner had a "tender conscience"—that he really *did* grieve when he drank too much, gambled away his money, and played the fool; and probably he had some idea that in recording his delinquencies he made some reparation for them and strengthened himself for better things. He was also, it is plain, of an open, social, communicative temper—in this resembling his great prototype, Pepys. He did not live in a great city or see much of life; but he got as much as he could out of the little rural community in which he did live. He was a lively actor in it, and he was an acute observer. He was a good business man, too, in the habit of keeping accounts, and, from making entries of his business dealings, there was but a step to making entries of his personal affairs—his pleasures and his troubles—his discretions and his follies. It was a diversion from his more sedate occupations. There was, too, doubtless, a little smattering of vanity in it. He was the hero of the drama—at once the victor and the sufferer. If he sinned, it was some consolation that he also inflicted the punishment; if he suffered (and as he had a Xantippe for his mother-in-law there is no doubt he did!) there was some solace in giving expression to it. If he failed, he could condole with himself. If he succeeded, did he not prolong the pleasure of success by setting it down in his Diary? And then there was, as we have said, a little vanity mixed up with it. It is not every man that can keep a Diary—of any kind; and Thomas Turner's was not an ordinary Diary. He had some literary taste and ability, and must have felt, as he made his entries, that he was doing what no other man in his parish—perhaps in the County—could do. He was, perhaps, prolonging the memory of his name to other ages—conferring on himself a species of immortality! We have reason to be thankful that he did it. The result is, that we have a picture of rural manners in the last century which is worth a whole library of learned essays or sermons or fashionable novels, and that we can see here how Englishmen of the middle classes actually passed their lives in those small communities, composed of clergyman, Squire, a few farmers and shopkeepers, and a large gathering of labourers and of labourers' wives, sons, and daughters, which made up the greater part of England 100 years ago—how they worked and played—eat, drank, rode, and smoked, swore and prayed—quarrelled and amused themselves. Such a picture as this does

Thomas Turner, general dealer, of East Hothly, give; and, whatever his motives may have been for doing so, we are thankful that he kept a Diary.

Now, to leave our speculations and resume our quotations.

The spirits of Thomas Turner rose and fell with business, according as it was dull or brisk. In July, 1757, he chronicles " a most prodigious melancholy time, and very little to do," adding, in a moralising vein, " I think that luxury increases so fast in this part of the nation, that people have little or no money to spare to buy what is really necessary. The too frequent use of spirituous liquors, and the exorbitant practice of tea-drinking, has corrupted the morals of people of almost every rank."

The conjunction of spirituous liquors and "the exorbitant practice of tea-drinking" as corrupting the morals of the people will be a novelty in the eyes of tee-totallers of the 19th century! Mr. Turner makes this conjunction more than once, and, although he was a seller of tea, evidently did not look upon it with favourable eyes.

On the previous Sunday a brief had been read in East Hothly Church "to repair the groins and fortifications of the town of Brighthelmstone, against the incroachments of the sea on that coast, which, if not timely prevented, will in all probability eat in and destroy the town, several houses having in a few years been swallowed up by the sea." Times are changed with Brighton as well as with tea!

If it be any consolation to know that there were wet summers in former days, it may be found in the following entry in July, 1757: " This is the 29th day on which we have had rain successively." And yet some people think that the sun always shone in the olden summers.

Manners and morals go, as a rule, together. When the former are gross,—and Thomas Turner's diary is full of evidence that they were such in the middle ranks of society 100 years ago, —we may be pretty sure that the latter were not very pure. The matter-of-course tone in which Mr. Turner sets down certain family facts which, in the present day, supposing them to occur, would be kept out of sight as much as possible, indicates that they were comparatively ordinary occurrences. Thus he records, on May 26th, 1764, that "My brother Moses came to acquaint me of the death of Philip Turner, natural son of my half-sister, Elizabeth Turner (the boy we had the care of, as also his maintenance, according to the will of my father); he died this morn about five o'clock, of a scarlet fever, aged fifteen years."

And again, immediately after this, "In the morn I went over to Framfield, and, after taking an account of the gloves, hatbands, favours, &c., I set out for the funeral of Alice Stevens, otherwise Smith, natural daughter of Ben Stevens, at whose house she died."

Upon these facts, occurring in families of good repute, the Editors remark, "Natural children, one hundred years ago, were considered the most natural things in the world." The example was set by the higher classes. "Mistresses" were an established part of the household of a great man 100 years ago, and when they had lost their early bloom, the ladies were, according to Macaulay, handed over to the domestic chaplains as wives. That the conjunction was not so very unequal we may conclude from some of the entries in this Diary in respect to the clergy—amongst them the following:—" Mr. ———, the curate of Laughton, came to the shop in the forenoon, and he having bought some things of me (and I could wish he had paid for them), dined with me, and also staid in the afternoon till he got in liquor, and being so complaisant as to keep him company, I was quite drunk. How do I detest myself for being so foolish!"

The great nobleman in the neighbourhood of East Hothly was the Duke of Newcastle, the first and last of the House of Pelham who bore the title, and whose seat, Halland House, was situated at Laughton, and was the scene of great festivities—in other words, of much dissipation, upon which Mr. Thomas Turner does not omit to pass some severe and just strictures, though, considering from whom they came, it is a little like the pot calling the kettle black! "Oh, how glad," he exclaims on one occasion, " am I that the hurry and confusion is over at Halland, for it quite puts me out of that regular way of life which I am so fond of, and not only so, but occasions me, by too great hurry of spirits, many times to commit such actions as is not agreeable to reason and religion ! "

Cock-fighting was at this period one of the "national" sports. *Ex. gr.* :—" Was fought, this day, at Jones's, a main of cocks between the gentlemen of Hothly and Pevensey."

The grossness of manners that showed itself, in private life, in inordinate drinking and "romping," and the carrying home of each other's wives on their backs, was, as might be expected, not without its public phase. Mr. Turner occasionally attended Vestry meetings, and he does not speak of them in the most flattering terms. Thus, "after dinner I went down to Jones, to the Vestry. We had several warm arguments at our Vestry to-day, and several vollies of execrable oaths oftentime redounded from almost all parts of the room. A most rude and shocking thing at publick meetings."

In the midst, however, of the hard drinking and swearing and coarse immorality of the day, indications occur in Mr. Turner's diary of the deeper current that was setting in. Literature entered largely into the delights of our East Hothly trader, and science put in an occasional appearance, though as yet she was a wonder and a mystery. "There being at Jones's a person with an electrical machine, my niece and I went to see it ; and tho' I have seen it several years agoe, I think there is something in it agreeable and instructing, but at the same time very surprising. As to my own part, I am quite at a loss to form any idea of the phœinomina."

Though Mr. Turner was not quite at home in scientific terms, this entry is creditable to him, and is a great advance on Mr. Marchant's admiration of the tricks of the "tumbler" at Hurst.

Mr. Turner also had his opinions in politics, and was not afraid to read the *North Briton,* nor to express his approval of its contents :—"July 13, 1763. In the even read several political papers called the *North Briton,* which are wrote by John Wilks, Esq., Member for Ailesbury, Bucks, for the writing of which he has been committed to the Tower, and procured his release by a writ of *Harbus Corpus.* I really think they breathe forth such a spirit of liberty, that it is an extreme good paper."

Well done, country trader of a hundred years ago! There is many a country trader in the present day who would hesitate to speak out so boldly as this! It may be doubted, indeed, whether the position of the country shopkeeper has not degenerated in the last hundred years, both in respect to the amount of trade done and the character of the men who carry it on. It is clear that Mr. Thomas Turner, general dealer, of East Hothly, was a man of some importance and standing. He and his wife associated, as we have seen, on equal terms with the clergyman and the clergyman's wife, and he was "hail fellow, well met" with the gentry and farmers. He carried on a very extensive trade, and it is recorded of his son and successor that he "turned over" £50,000, and, in one or two years, as much as £70,000 a year: the profits upon which, we may be sure, were much larger than they would be at the present day. "It is," say the Editors of this Diary, "certainly a fact that several County families in Sussex can, if they are so disposed, trace their pedigree up to the mercers of bye-gone times." We do not for a moment suppose that they are so disposed! Country mercers are not the men they were: a large part of their custom has been diverted to towns, now so numerous and accessible, and we question if the County families of the future will be much recruited from their ranks.

The indignation with which our East Hothly general-dealer looked upon any intrusion on his ground is shown by the following note, in which he refers to the first appearance in the parish of a licensed hawker :—

"July 6. This day came to Jones's a man with a cartload of milinery, mercery, linen-drapery, silver, &c., to keep a sale for two days, which must undoubtedly be some hurt to trade ; for the novelty of the thing (and novelty is surely the predominant passion of the English nation, and of Sussex in particular) will catch the ignorant multitude, and perhaps not them only, but people of sense, who are not judges of goods and trade, as indeed very few are ; but, however, as it is it must pass."

Novelty, the passion of Sussex in 1763! What would Thomas Turner say now?

We have said that the beginning and the middle of the last century was a time of prosperity, though gross in manners and low in morals. The state of crime shows it :—" Monday, Aug. 11, 1754. This day the Assizes at Lewes, and only one prisoner." Thirty-two years later, after the American war, there was a different tale to tell. "I preached," writes the Rev. Mr. Poole, "before the Judge in the College Chapel at East Grinstead, the Church being in ruins. A very full Assize and heavy calendar; twenty-six prisoners; nine condemned, and six for execution." Possibly for what would now be treated as light offences; for the penal code was Draconic, and Jack Ketch flourished under it!

Before we take up the thread of Mr. Turner's domestic history, we will note one or two points of interest to the archæologist. In 1756 he attended a sale at Lewes, and the mode of auction was, that the last bidder whilst a candle burned was the buyer. The candle was lighted before four o'clock and burnt till eight; four hours being occupied in the disposal of property worth £420! Pepys notices the same custom :— "Sept. 3, 1662. After dinner we went and sold the Weymouth, Success, and Fellowship Hulkes, where it was pleasant to see how backward men are at first to bid; and yet, when the candle is going out, how they bawl and dispute afterwards who bid the most first. And here I observed one man cunninger than the rest, that was sure to bid the last man, and to carry it; and inquiring the reason, he told me, that just as the flame goes out, the smoke descends, which is a thing I never observed before, and by that he did know the instant when to bid last."

Few of our readers, we take it, have ever heard of "pandles." It was "the good old Sussex word (so says Mr. Lower) for shrimps," which latter word is comparatively modern. Mr. Turner writes: "In the morn Fielder brought our herrings, but could get no *pandles*."

The fear of over-population had not yet come upon the

nation. In fact, Mr Thomas Turner evidently thought that there was room for a large increase :—

"Nov. 14. This day was married, at our church, Mr Simonds Blackman and Mary his wife (*alias* Mary Margenson). She being under age, some months agoe they went into Flanders, and was married at a place called Ypres ; but, as this marriage was not in all respects agreeable to the laws of England, in regard to their issue enjoying the gentleman's estate, they was married this day by a licence, which styled her Mary Margison, otherwise Blackman. In my own private oppinion, I think, instead of making laws to restrain marriage, it would be more to the advantage of the nation to give encouragement to it ; for by that means a great deal of debauchery would, in all probability, be prevented, and a greater increase of people might be the consequence, which, I presume, would be real benefit to the nation ; and I think it is the first command of the Parent and Governor of the universe, 'Increase and multiply,' and the observation of St. Paul is, that 'marriage is honourable in all men.'"

But then at this particular moment the mind of our Diarist was again directed towards matrimony. He had lost his "dear Peggy," and is as melancholy under the affliction of her death as he was in her life-time under the infliction of her temper. There can be but little doubt that he did value her highly, though his grief is probably a little exaggerated when he says, "with the incomparable Mr. Young" ("Night Thoughts"), "Let them who ever lost an angel, pity me !" Perhaps there was a twinge of remorse for past entries to the prejudice of "dear Peggy" in the outbursts that now meet us, or perhaps (and we think this is the fact), in the absence of Mrs. Turner, his old temptation proved too strong for him. There are signs of it :—" I lodged at Joshua Durrant's, and my brother and Mr. Tomlin lodged at my house "—a funny arrangement, this, but with the same consequences to both parties, for "not one of us went to bed sober, which folly of mine makes me very uneasy. Oh, that I cannot be a person of more resolution." And immediately upon this we have the following :—

"July 27. Very bad all the even. Oh, my heavy and troubled mind ! Oh, my imprudence pays me with trouble !"

"July 28th. I am intollerable bad : my conscience tears me in pieces."

"Aug. 5. Almost distracted with trouble : how do I hourly find the loss I have sustained in the death of my dear wife ! What can equal the value of a virtuous wife? I hardly know which way to turn, or what way of life to pursue. I am left as a beacon on a rock, or an ensign on a hill."

In his "grief and melancholy" Mr. Turner takes to "sawing of wood" in his leisure hours,—trade being dull, and time hanging heavily on his hands. It was, he says "a melancholy time in trade" throughout the County, and he has "no friend —no, not one—with whom I can spend an hour to condole and sympathise with me in my affliction." In this frame of mind he goes and dines with "my father Slater," and came home—" I cannot say thoroughly sober—I think it almost impossible to be otherwise [than drunk?] with the quantity of liquor I drank." "But," he proceeds, " however much in liquor I was, my reason was not so far lost but I could see a sufficient difference at my arrival at my own house between the present time and that of my wife's life, highly to the advantage of the latter. Everything then was serene and in order ; now, one or both servants out, and everything noise and confusion. Oh ! it will not do. No, no ! it never will do."

Clearly, Mr. Turner was thinking about the wisdom of taking unto himself another wife ! " If," he says, a little further on, " if ever I do marry again, I am sure of this, that I will never have a more virtuous and prudent wife than I have been already possessed of ; may it be the will of Providence for me to have as good an one ; I ask no better."

We may set it down for a certainty that when a widower begins to asseverate to himself or to his friends that he will never get so good a wife as she whom he has just lost, and "asks no better," he is very far on the road to a second marriage ! .

Another consequence of " single blessedness " now breaks upon his mind. " For want of the company of the more softer sex, and through my over much confinement, I know I am become extreme awkard, and a certain roughness and boisterousness of disposition has seized on my mind, so that, for want of those advantages which flow from society, and a free intercourse with the world, and a too great delight in reading, has brought my mind to that great degree of moroseness that is neither agreeable to myself, nor can my company be so to others."

A more considerate man, to his friends, never breathed than Thomas Turner! If he marry again, it will clearly be for the advantage of East Hothly society! But then how repair the loss of his "dear Peggy?" How find a counterpart to that incomparable one? "I know not," thus he bursts forth, in his despair, "the comfort of an agreeable friend and virtuous fair; no, I have not spent an agreeable hour in the company of a woman since I lost my wife, for really there seems very few whose education and way of thinking is agreeable and suitable with my own."

We have our doubts whether we ought to make this exposure to the world of the weak side of a widower! But then why did Mr. Thomas Turner keep a diary? However, we are drawing to a close. Who can doubt to what all this woe and lamentation tends? Still, despite these scientific "approaches" to the inevitable result, it comes upon us in the end rather suddenly. Perhaps our Diarist intended to be "sensational":—
"Sunday, Dec. 9. After dinner Jenner and I walked to Lewes, in order to see a girl I have long since had thoughts of paying my addresses to, and he for company. I was not so happy, shall I say, as to see her, or was I unfortunate in having only my walk for my pains, which, perhaps, was as well?"

Who can answer this question? Still, the quærist's temper was not improved by the failure of this first step, for his "cuz, Thos. Ovenden" coming to see him, and staying to sup with him, he thus tells us what he thinks of Mr. Thos. Ovenden:—"I think I never see a more stupid young fellow in my life than my couz. Thos. Ovenden: his discourse is one continued flow of oathes, almost without any intermission."

Poor Thos. Ovenden! He came across his "cuz." in an unlucky moment. A little later, and his "flow of oathes" might

E

not have been thrown away upon unappreciative ears. For, a day or two later, our widower made another attempt, and this time all went smoothly :—

"March 28. In the afternoon rode over to Chiddingly, to pay my charmer, or intended wife, or sweetheart, or whatever other name may be more proper, a visit at her father's, where I drank tea, in company with their family and Miss Ann Thatcher. I supped there on some rasures of bacon. It being an excessive wet and windy night, I had the opportunity, sure I should say the pleasure, or perhaps some might say the unspeakable happiness, to sit up with Molly Hicks, or my charmer, all night. I came home at forty minutes past five in the morning—I must not say fatigued ; no, no, that could not be; it could only be a little sleepy for want of rest. Well, to be sure, she is a most clever girl ; but, however, to be serious in the affair, I certainly esteem the girl, and think she appears worthy of my esteem."

We suppose it was the fashion, 100 years ago, for wooers to stay up all night with their fair ones ! It had its dangers, and also its inconveniences, as appeareth by the following:—" Saturday, April 7. In the even very dull and sleepy ; this courting does not well agree with my constitution, and perhaps it may be only taking pains to create more pain."

Really this last expression is highly dramatic—not unworthy of a man who had read and appreciated Shakspeare !

This, however, was only a passing cloud, to give a deeper azure to the coming sky :—

"Sunday, April 15. After dinner I set out for Malling, to pay Molly Hicks, my intended wife, a visit, with whom I intended to go to church, but there was no afternoon service. I spent the afternoon with a great deal of pleasure, it being very fine, pleasant weather, and my companion very agreeable. Now, perhaps, there may be many reports abroad in the world of my present intentions, some likely condemning my choice, others approving it ; but, as the world cannot judge the secret intentions of my mind, and I may therefore be censured, I will take the trouble to relate what really and truly are my intentions, and the only motive from which they spring (which may be some satisfaction to those who may happen to peruse my memoirs).

First, I think marriage is a state agreeable to nature, reason, and religion; I think it the duty of every Christian to serve God and perform his religious services in the most calm, serene, and composed manner, which, if it can be performed more so in the married state than a single one, it must then be an indispensable duty. . . . As to my choice, I have only this to say:—the girle, I believe, as far as I can discover, is a very industrious, sober woman, and seemingly endued with prudence and good nature, with a serious and sedate turn of mind. She comes of reputable parents, and may perhaps, one time or other, have some fortune. As to her person, I know it's plain (so is my own), but she is cleanly in her person and dress, which I will say is something, more than at first sight it may appear to be, towards happiness. She is, I think, a well-made woman. As to her education, I own it is not liberal; but she has good sense, and a desire to improve her mind, and has always behaved to me with the strictest honour and good manners—her behaviour being far from the affected formality of the prude, on the one hand; and on the other, of that foolish fondness too often found in the more light part of the sex. For myself, I have nothing else in view but to live in a more sober and regular manner, to perform my duty to God and man in a more suitable and religious manner, and, with the grace of the Supreme Being, to live happy in a sincere union with the partner of my bosom."

This, we admit, is rather long and prosy. But we owe it to Thomas Turner to give it *verbatim et literatim*. It is his justification to the world—to all who read his Diary, and it is obvious that he intended it should be read. He was not afraid to exhibit his follies and weaknesses—his resolutions and his failures—to the world. He had an inkling that there was something in the Diary that " the world would not willingly let die," and he was quite right. It is a very valuable picture of the times, and a very amusing one of an individual man. There are not many such genuine ones in the whole range of literature. We get from this Diary a more lively conception of life and manners and morals in the middle of the 18th century than from any book of history or divinity that was ever writ. We cannot part from Thomas Turner without acknowledging his rare merits—his frankness, simplicity, honesty, and desire to do what is right and proper, albeit he sometimes fails. This he does, indeed, to the very last, for, in the last entry but one, taking " a ride to pay my intended wife a visit," after a " serious walk " he takes his leave at the very proper hour of ten o'clock, but, " after parting with her, I went to take my horse, and, happening into company—[alack, that company was to Thomas Turner, as to Jack Falstaff, the ruin of him !]—I staid till ten minutes past 12 and came home about four o'clock."

Let us hope that this was the last lapse, and that "his dear Molly" kept him in better order than his "dear Peggy," and never required to be taken home on Mr. Tho. Fuller's back! He was married to her by his old friend and boon companion, Mr. Porter, on the 19th June, 1765, and now, he writes, "thank God, I begin once more to be a little settled, and am happy in my choice. I have, it's true, not married a learned lady, nor is she a gay one; but I trust she is good-natured, and one that will use her utmost endeavour to make me happy. As to her fortune, I shall one day have something considerable, and there seems to be rather a flowing stream. Well, here let us drop the subject, and begin a new one."

And so we part with Thomas Turner. Here he dropped his Diary, and did not commence a new one; at least, none has been preserved. Perhaps Molly found it out, and put a stop to such waste of time, or she may have burnt it, finding some impertinent reference to herself, or used it as waste paper, or——but there, let us rejoice that we have got so much as we have. The Diary, the Editors of it tell us, was originally in at least 116 stout memorandum books, and these, with the exception of a few, have been preserved. They may be ranked amongst the literary treasures of Sussex, of which, as we have already said, Thomas Turner is the Pepys—the first of the Sussex Diarists.

Walter Gale, schoolmaster at Mayfield, was a contemporary of Thomas Turner, general dealer at East Hothly. Both "flourished" in the middle of the last century; both belonged to the middle class of life; and the educational gifts of each were of much the same extent. The chief difference in their career was, that Thomas Turner began as a schoolmaster and ended as a trader; whereas Walter Gale, beginning as an Officer of Excise, ended as a schoolmaster. How he came to fail in the former capacity admits of very little doubt; he shared in the general failing of the age: an inordinate love of drink. He had been discharged from his office, and he was not so enamoured of the instruction of youth but that he was desirous to be replaced in it, and, in an application to a friend with that view, he states that "the many vicissitudes of fortune which I have experienced since my being discharged from the office [of Exciseman] would constitute a pretty good history."

Perhaps a pretty bad history would have been nearer the mark. There can be little doubt that, though Walter Gale was a clever man and could turn his hand, as his diary shows he did, to a good many things, he was not at all fitted, by his habits or inclinations, for the office of a schoolmaster. But that office stood at a very low ebb in the middle of the last century. It was a period of general neglect and carelessness so far as the education and morals of the lower—indeed, it might be said of the middle classes, were concerned. The old Grammar Schools and "Free schools," so freely endowed in the first years of the Reformation, had been suffered to fall into decay, or, where they still flourished, it was owing, not to any general system of supervision, but to the accident of some efficient man having been appointed as Schoolmaster, as, for instance, Dr. Bayley at Midhurst, or John Grover at Brighthelmstone.

It was not likely that a very efficient man would be obtained at Mayfield (a parish at the north-eastern extremity of Sussex), where the salary was £16 a-year, until increased by the bequest of a house and garden which let for £18 a-year. No man could support a wife or bring up a family on such a miserable stipend as this; but this difficulty was got over at Mayfield by the election of a single man. The election lay with the Vicar and principal inhabitants of the place, and the first "principal inhabitant" who subscribed to Gale's appointment, John Kent, not being able to write, made his mark! The qualifications for the office were, to possess "a genius for teaching," write a good hand, and understand arithmetic well; in addition to which, he was " to be particularly careful of the manners and behaviour of the poor children (it was a 'free school') committed to his care."

How far Walter Gale acquitted himself of these duties, we shall have an opportunity of judging by and bye. The school must have been a poor place; for its master soon had occasion to note—"I found the greatest part of the school in a flow, by reason of the snow and rain coming through the leads." The scholars were 21 in number, "the third part of which are supposed to be writers" (that is, taught to write).

Walter Gale commemorated his appointment to his office by the commencement of a Diary, one of the first uses (?) of which is to chronicle a dream to the effect "that I should be advantageously married, and be blessed with a fine offspring, and that I should live to the age of 81, of which time I should preach the Gospel 41 years." There is no evidence in the succeeding entries that any of these prophetic intimations ever came to pass. But in this and other entries there are signs of the superstition of the times. One of Mr. Gale's earliest visitors at the school is "Mr. Hassel, the conjuror," and the worthy pair soon adjourn to Elliott's (the public-house, we presume) "where he (that is, the conjuror,) treated me (the schoolmaster) with a quartern of gin, and I gave him a dinner at Coggin's Mill" (Mr. Gale's place of abode.) "Having," he proceeds, "dined the conjuror, we returned to Elliott's, where he treated me as before."

"The conjuror," it seems, was at work on the map of a farm belonging to Col. Fuller, and Mr. R. W. Blencowe, who edits the Diary, remarks, "The profession of a conjuror a hundred years ago was by no means uncommon, nor does it seem to have been thought a discreditable one. A person of the same name was in full practice as a cunning man in the neighbourhood of Tunbridge Wells very recently. One of the best known of his craft was a man of the name of Saunders, of Heathfield, who died about fifty years ago. He was a respectable man, and at one time in easy circumstances; but he neglected all earthly concerns for astrological pursuits, and, it is said, died in a workhouse."

Of the credulity of Walter Gale we find many instances,—amongst them the following :—

"May 10th, 1758. Received a testimony of a death in our family within a twelvemonth, and, by the appearance of it, I suppose it to be myself."

"April 10th, 1759. My mother, to my great unhappiness, died in the 83rd year of her age, agreeable to the testimony I had of a death in our family on the 10th of May last."

What strikes one in the Diary of the Mayfield schoolmaster is the almost total absence of any reference to his school or scholars. He engages in a multiplicity of tasks,—from the drawing of quilts,—that is, the patterns of them,—to the drawing of wills; he measures land, engraves tomb-stones, paints public-house signs, designs ladies' needle work, &c., &c.; but as to the 21 scholars whom he undertakes to teach to read, write, and keep accounts, we hear very little; and that little is not of a very edifying character. Like Falstaff with his ragged soldiers, Walter Gale would not march through Coventry with them :—

"26th. Old Kent came, and I went with him to Mr. Baker; they said they should have a ragged congregation of scholars, who should sit together in the new gallery, and that they should insist on my sitting with them; to this I did not assent."

The very first reference to school duties,—"began my school at noon,"—followed by—"I waited on Miss Annie Baker, of whom I received a neckerchief to draw"—shows the "divided duties" that occupied Mr. Walter Gale's time and talent. He could not, indeed, live on the miserable stipend allotted to him as schoolmaster of the Free school of Mayfield, and had to eke out a revenue by other means, one of which (and it was permitted by the Trustees of the school) was to "enter on the assistant hop business at Rotherfield."

The chief opponent of Mr Gale in these multifarious money-getting pursuits was John Kent,—"old Kent," as Gale irreverently calls him,—the same who put his cross to the rules laid down for the management of the school; and no small part of the Diary is occupied with the quarrels between the two. Gale having accompanied a neighbour on what was evidently a drinking bout, and the worthy pair having lost their road, and Gale slipped from a high bank, "but received no hurt," "Old Kent came to the knowledge of the above journey, and told it to the Rev. Mr. Downall, in a false manner, much to my disadvantage; he said that I got drunk, and that that was the occasion of my falling, and that, not being content with what I had had, I went into the town that night for more."

And, shortly afterwards, "The old man entered the school with George Wilmhurst and Eliz. Hook, and said they should be taught free. I asked him how many I was to teach free; without any further ado, he flew into a violent passion. Among other abusive and scurrilous language, he said I was an upstart, runnagate, beggarly dog, that I picked his pocket, and that I never knew how to teach a school in my life. He again called me upstart, runnagate, beggarly dog, clinched his fist in my face, and made a motion to strike me, and declared he would break my head. He did not strike me, but withdrew in a wonderful heat, and ended all with his general maxim, 'The greater scholler, the greater rogue.'" A maxim worthy of the age!

The division of the scholars into free boys and such as were paid for by their friends, was one of the causes that ruined so many Grammar Schools and Free schools. The free boys—those on the foundation—were neglected by the Master, and came to be looked down upon by the other scholars, until at last many a public school, like that at Midhurst, had not a scholar on the foundation and was shut up altogether.

We have said that Walter Gale, in spite of his dream of advantageous marriage and fine offspring, remained a bachelor all his life. But it was not by reason of indifference to the sex. *Ex. gr.* : "I set out out for Frantfield Fair with a roast pig for my sister Stone. Came to her, and there drank tea with the ncomparable Miss Foster."

We are rather surprised that we do not hear any more of "the incomparable Miss Foster!" But she passes out of sight like a fairy vision, or

> "Like a snow-flake on the river,
> One moment seen—then lost for ever."

Admiration of a single lady might be allowed to the Mayfield Dominie even by "old Kent;" whereas it was scarcely fair to rouse the jealousy of a fellow-pedagogue, and he, too, so estimable a character as John Grover, of Brighthelmstone. Yet, by the following entry, Walter Gale seems to have been "guilty of as great a sin":—

"I set off for Brighthelmstone, and came at noon to Malling-street, and went to the Dolphin. Kennard told me that Burton's successor had had a great many scholars, but that their number began to decrease, by reason of his sottishness, and he offered, if their dislike of him should increase, to let me know of it. The rain clearing off at three o'clock, I set out for Brighthelmstone, passing through Southover, but being advanced on the hills, the rain returned, and drove me for shelter under a thin hawthorn hedge, and I was obliged to return to Grover's, where I drank tea, and discoursed merrily, but innocently, with his wife, notwithstanding which, Grover was so indiscreet as to shew some distaste at it, and to have great difficulty to keep his temper."

It did not take much to draw Master Gale from his school duties. Thus, "Left off school at 2 o'clock, having heard the spellers and readers a lesson a piece, to attend a cricket match of the gamesters of Mayfield against those of Lindfield and Chailey." This is a singular application of the word "gamesters."

No small part of the Diary is taken up with jaunts to fairs, &c., and convivial meetings, in which not a little beer, brandy, milk, punch, cherry brandy, elderberry wine, &c., is consumed, and Mr. Gale is none the better for it in health or reputation. There is not a total absence of reference to books; but the literary taste of Mr. Gale was not of so high a character as that of Thomas Turner. Here is the chief entry:—"Mr Rogers came to the school, and brought with him four volumes of *Pamela,* for which I paed him 4s. 6d., and bespoke Duck's *Poems* for Mr. Kine, and a *Caution to Swearers* for myself (!) He wanted to borrow of me the three volumes of *Philander and Silvia,* which I promised to lend him. I went to Mr. Baker's for the list of scholars, and found him alone in the smoaking-room; he ordered a pint of mild beer for me, an extraordinary thing. Left at Mr. Rogers' the three volumes of *Love Letters from a Nobleman to his Sister.*"

The majority of these works do not bespeak a very refined taste, and none of them have anything to do with scholarship. In fact, it is clear that Master Walter Gale's heart was not in his school, nor was his time given to his scholars. He took to teaching, like too many Masters of his day, to earn a living, and he was accepted for want of a better man and because little real interest was felt in the education of the people. A great many people believed, in the last century,—and the belief came down to our own times, though now pretty well extinct,—that the working classes were better without reading and writing—that such things did more harm than good. As then taught, perhaps, there was some truth in it. In one of the altercations between "old Kent" and the schoolmaster of Mayfield, the former said that " I (Walter Gale) spent my time in reading printed papers, to the neglect of the children; and that I was covetous * * * that the children did not improve, and that he would get an old woman for 2d. a-week that would teach them better." To which the Master replied, that "many of them (the boys) were extremely dull, and that I would defie any person that should undertake it to teach them better."

Altogether, the glimpse we have in this Diary of the Free School of Mayfield is not calculated to raise our ideas of the education of the people in the middle of the 18th century; and if it were general, as there is reason to believe it was, it cannot be a matter of surprise that at the beginning of the 19th century England stood, educationally, very low; that the great mass of the people did not know how to read or write, and that, morally and religiously, the nation was rather going back than forward.

Mr. Gale outlived his old antagonist, John Kent. But a day of reckoning was to come at last, and on the 18th of October, 1771, it was unanimously resolved by the then Vicar and four parishioners "that he be removed from the School for neglecting the duties thereof," and, on the 10th April following, that he "be not paid his salary due till he has absolutely put the schoolhouse in such a condition as to the form of it as it was at the time of his entering upon such house."

From which it may be inferred that neither the schoolmaster nor the school-house of Mayfield was very efficient in the years 1771-2.

That Walter Gale was not an exceptional teacher of youth in the 18th century, the Editor of his Diary (Mr. R. W. Blencowe) gives many evidences of; and he concludes with the following characteristic anecdote:—"Two or three years ago a friend of the Editor visited the school of —— in no distant part of England; and, observing some deep-coloured stains upon the oaken floor, inquired the cause. He was told that they were occasioned by the leakage of a butt of Madeira which the master of the Grammar School, who had grown lusty, not having had for some time any scholars who might afford him the opportunity of taking exercise, employed himself upon a rainy day in rolling up and down the school-room for the purpose of ripening the wine and keeping himself in good condition."

Upon which we may remark, with some degree of satisfaction, "These things are ordered differently in England" in the present day.

It may be questioned whether "Timothy Burrell, Esq., Barrister-at-Law, of Ockenden House, Cuckfield," who kept a Journal and Account-Book from the year 1683 to 1714, despite the excellence of his character, his good family, learning, and social position, deserves to be ranked among the diarists of Sussex. Most certainly the Journal and Account-Book on which his claims to do so rest, fall in interest far below the diaries of the Rev. Giles Moore, Anthony Stapley, Thomas Turner, and Walter Gale. It consists chiefly of bald entries of monies paid and received; of the presents which were sent to him (often, doubtless, in acknowledgment of legal advice) by his friends and neighbours, rich and poor; of the wages of servants, the price of grain, &c. Occasionally, however, Mr. Timothy Burrell enters into, to him, more interesting and domestic matters, and on these occasions, like the Rev. Giles Moore, he makes use of the Latin language. Thus (as rendered into English by Mr. R. W. Blencowe), "I severely reprimanded John Packham for his continual drunkenness, and at last I turned him out of my house, of which he had had the free run for five years: a drunken extravagant fellow!" And, touching on more delicate ground, he thus records a family trouble :—"My sister quarrelled with me, and was insolent to me, and I was somewhat, not to say too much, irritated with her; the consequence was, that for two days my stomach was at intervals seriously affected. I took Tipping's Mixture, and one or two doses of hiera picra" (still a favourite medicine, says Mr. Blencowe, who edited this Journal for the Sussex Archæological Society, with the common people of Sussex). And, if sometimes Mr. Timothy Burrell could call his sister to account for insolence, he also shows that he was not blind to his own defects of temper. *Ex. gr.:* "I was rather too impatient with my servant for having put too much salt in my broth."

The larger number of entries are, however, of the business-like and homely character we have adverted to, and one or two of these will serve to illustrate the rest. As showing the price of wheat, in October, 1709, Mr. Burrell enters, "I bought two bushels of wheat for 16s., and then two bushels more for 17s. The two bushels, with the bag, weighed 134lbs. Since that wheat has fallen to 8s. a bushel." And then he adds: "Query, what returned from the miller? 121lbs. So the toll paid was 13lbs., which was reasonable for double toll, which Sturt saith might have been 16d. the bushel."

"Bringing grist to the mill" is still a Sussex proverb; but the days of taking toll in this way for grinding small parcels of wheat are well-nigh gone; and the old jokes at the expense of "honest millers" are obsolete.

Mr. Burrell records the receipt, in 1698, of "the three first Flying Posts," the newspaper of that day, which was thus recommended to purchasers :—" If any gentleman has a mind to oblige his country friend or correspondent with his account of public affairs, he may have it (that is, the 'Flying Post') for 2d., of G. Salisbury, at the 'Rising Sun,' Cornhill, on a sheet of fine paper, half of which being blank, he may write his own private business, or the material news of the day." This offer of a choice between the news of the newspaper and that of the purchaser betokens, at least, modesty in the journalist of the age !

On one occasion, in 1699, Mr. Timothy Burrell, after visiting at the Comb or Highden, the residences of his relations, the Bridgers and the Gorings, records that he paid the following sums in "vails" :—" Mr. Johnson, 10s. 9d. (half-a-guinea); chambermayd, 10s. ; cook, 10s. ; coachman, 5s. ; butler, 5s. ; chief gardener, 5s. ; under cook, 2s. 6d. ; boy, 2s. 6d. ; under-gardener, 2s. 6d. ; nurse, 2s. 6d. Total, £3 0s. 9d." Rather a heavy price—the "vails" of those days—for the pleasure of visiting one's friends or relations !

In one respect the journal of Mr. Timothy Burrell surpasses those of his Sussex fellow-chroniclers. It is an illustrated one. Mr. Burrell evidently had a talent for pen-and-ink sketches, and there is scarcely an object named or subject referred to by him but it finds a "counterfeit presentment" in the margin of his journal. Pipes, spoons, fiddles, spades, rakes, hats, honey bees, horns, bottles, jugs of all sizes, pigs, cows, cocks and hens, horses, trees, tables, bells, barrows, carts, books, candles and candlesticks, and even neckties and shirts, figure on the margin of the Journal, and the likenesses of "Nanny West" and "Mary Slater" when he paid them their wages—all these and numerous other objects to which reference is made in the Journal are limned with a tolerably faithful and skilful hand. One of the most ambitious attempts at Art is a sketch of his own residence at Cuckfield, Ockenden House, which, by-the-bye, still stands—whether in its integrity or not, we cannot say—and was, up to the last two or three years, occupied by a member of the

Burrell family. Another pretentious flight, and with a touch of humour in it, is that of a barrel of liquor on its stollage, and with a vessel below the tap ready to receive the contents. This is in illustration of the Latin entry : "Nov. Pandoxavi." A fishing-net, with the captured fish, and two hind-wheels of the family coach, "made by Juniper," and the window on which the first window-tax,—a most objectionable tax then just introduced,—was paid, also find a place in this most original of journals.

Two of the most curious of the illustrations, and which Mr. Timothy Burrell could scarcely have intended for the public eye, accompany the following entries :—" For a payr of fine scarlet stockings for my girle, 3s." " I bought of a Scotchman a payr of pink scarlet stockings for my girle." To each of these entries is attached a representation of a very shapely foot and leg, which we may presume to be that of Miss Burrell, the draughtsman's only daughter—" my girle " ; the limb being carried to a little above the garter-line, and the garter itself made a very conspicuous object. The Scotch pair of stockings is distinguished by the tartan, very neatly drawn.

Mr. Burrell continued this practice of illustrating his journal up to the very last. Only a fortnight before his death an entry of a hog which was shut up to fatten is accompanied by a drawing of the animal, but which, says Mr. Blencowe, without the context no one would imagine was intended to represent it.

One of the most prominent features of Mr. Timothy Burrell's Journal,—and it marks the benevolence of his character and illustrates the closer relations which once existed between the higher and the lower classes in England,—is the lists of guests, from the humbler classes of society, whom he invited to dine with him at Christmas and the bills of fare that he provided for them. He commenced this custom in 1691, and he kept it up to the year before his death (1717). The following are the bills of fare for the Christmas dinners of 1706 :—

" 1st January, 1706. Plumm pottage, calves' head and bacon, goose, pig, plumm pottage, roast beef, sirloin, veale, a loin, goose, plumm pottage, boiled beef, a clod, two baked puddings, three dishes of minced pies, two capons, two dishes of tarts, two pullets."

"2nd January, 1706. Plumm pottage, boiled leg of mutton, goose, pig, plumm pottage, roast beef, veal, leg, roasted, pig, plumm pottage, boiled beef, a rump, two baked puddings, three dishes of minced pies, two capons, two dishes of tarts, two pullets."

It will be remarked that plum-pudding, without which no Christmas-day festivities would be now complete, does not figure in Mr. Timothy Burrell's bill of fare. Its place is supplied by "plumm pottage," (sometimes called plumm broth) which occurs thrice in each bill, and which, no doubt, stood in the place of and was the embryo of its more famous successor. Minced pies had arrived at maturity ; but plum puddings had yet to be invented!

The Journal of Mr. Timothy Burrell, Barrister-at-Law,— "Counsellor Burrell" was his more common title amongst his neighbours,—was brought to a close on the 25th July, 1715, when he gave over the cares of housekeeping to a Mr. Trevor, who had married his only daughter, Elizabeth. The death of this lady, after a short and very unhappy married life, hastened, it is believed, the death of her father, who expired on the 26th of December, 1717, at the age of 75, and lies buried in Cuckfield Church ; and with him we will bring this chapter of Sussex Diarists to a close.

THE SUSSEX IRON-MASTERS.

IT is not an easy task to call up again a picture of Sussex when its Weald was the seat of extensive iron works—when the ore was dug and smelted in Sussex, when the fuel was grown in Sussex, and when the iron was manufactured in Sussex. Let the reader try to conceive the activity and noise and bustle that must have attended the working of 42 forges or iron-mills, and the blowing of 27 furnaces, These existed little more than 200 years ago—in 1653—in the Weald of Sussex,—in a district where all is now as quiet and as peaceful as it was in Arcadia. As the modern traveller walks or rides through such villages as those of Waldron, Robertsbridge, Lamberhurst, Horsted Keynes, Ardingly, Mayfield, Maresfield, Ewhurst, and Ashburnham, or rambles through the remains of Tilgate and St. Leonard's forests, and as his eyes and ears take in only the sights and sounds of rural life—the slow-going plough, the browsing sheep, and the heavy-looking labourers, —how difficult is it to conceive that these places have known any other kind of life than that in which they now slumber! And yet these were the places which supplied " His Majesty's stores " with guns and shot in the days when Rupert and Monk and the Duke of York thundered day after day against Van Tromp and De Ruyter,—nay, it was the forges and furnaces of these Sussex villages which furnished the ships of the Drakes and Hawkins and Frobishers with the artillery which they used so well against the floating castles of the Armada.* Sussex was then the

---

* In the Inventory taken of the goods of the Lord High Admiral Seymour, when he was impeached for high treason (temp.—Edward 6th), are included a number of furnaces and forges possessed by him in the forest of Worth, Sussex, with the number of men—"founders, ffylers, coleyers, miners, gon-founders," &c., who worked them. One item will show the warlike nature of the manufacture :—" Ffyrste, a duble ffurnace to cast ordynaunce, shotte, or rawe iron, wt all implements and necessaries appertenyng unto the same :—*Item*, there ys in sowes of rawe iron, exij. ; *Itm*., certain pieces of ordynaunce, that is to say, culverens, xiv. ; dim culverens, xv. ; *Itm*, of shotte for the same, vi. tonne, v. ct. ; *Itm*., ordynaunce caryed from thens to Southwark, and remanyeth ther as foleth : sakers, xv. ; ffawkonr, vj. ; mynnyons, ij. ; and dim. culverens, j ; *Itm*., in shotte for the same delyvered at the h. std., xiij. toune ; *Itm*, in myne or ower at the furnace, redye receved, xvjc. lode ; *Itm*., in mync, drawen and caried, Mixx. lode ; *Itm*., in whode, viijc. corde."

Wales and the Warwickshire of England—the centre of the country's iron-works. Foreign countries sought eagerly for its cannon—its culverines and falconets. Its richly-decorated fire-backs and fantastic andirons or "dogs," as they were called in common parlance, were the pride of lordly mansions. London had to send hither for the railings that went round its great Cathedral; and Sussex ploughshares, and "spuds," and other agricultural implements and articles of hard-ware, were sent all over the Kingdom. Fancy the glare and noise and activity that must have gone on in and around these 42 forges and iron mills—the digging and carting of ore—the cutting down and dragging in of trees—the blowing of furnaces, the ding of hammers, the clatter of mill-wheels, turned by merry little streams; to say nothing of the building of workshops for the men, cottages for their families, and mansions for the masters.

Of all this busy and active scene, what remains to indicate to the passer-by that it once existed? Here and there a name, like Cinder-hill, at Chailey, or Mill-place, at East Grinstead, to raise a faint suspicion of uses of which no sign or vestige now remains. Nature has resumed her original rights. Ceres has driven out Vulcan. The only forge is that of the village blacksmith; the stream turns the wheel of no iron mill—raises no hammer— works the bellows of no furnace—only harbours a few meditative trout, which are persecuted by a few deluded anglers; the ore lies undisturbed in the ferruginous soil, and the forest is once more safe from the woodman's axe. The skies are unsullied, the air is pure. All is peaceful—rural—and very slow and sleepy. The fierce tug of life, the strife for gold in the shape of iron, has passed away, with its noise and smoke and dirt, to other districts, the denizens of which—that is, such as can afford it—escape as often as they can from their Pandemoniums to the peaceful, rural villages of Sussex, ignorant, perhaps, for the most part, that they are coming to the ancient homes of the mine, the furnace, the forge, and the mill.

But are there no records of these old Sussex ironmasters? of the Burrells, the Fullers, the Challoners, and the Gales? Are there no memorials of the life they lived, of the houses they built and the fortunes they made—of their ups and downs in life?

Thanks to the labours of modern archæologists, a few relics have been preserved, "few and far between." Of the works that existed at different periods,—and Mr. Lower believes that they date from the first century of the Christian era,—there are several lists, and in a few cases with the names of the families who owned them. But we only know of two Sussex iron-masters who left any personal records for the information of those who came after them: and these are Leonard Gale, and his son and namesake, the owner of Crabbett House, Worth.

From the journals of these two, contributed to the Sussex Archæological Society's Collection by Mr. R. W. Blencowe (to whom the MS. was lent by Mrs. Morgan, of Cuckfield), we will try to select a few facts that will illustrate an extinct class of men: the Ironmasters of Sussex.

Leonard Gale was not Sussex born or bred. "I was born," he says, "in the Parish of Sevenoaks, in Kent, in 1620." "My mother was the daughter of one George Pratt, a very good yeoman, living at Chelsford." There was a family of five sons and one daughter, and the whole of these, with the exception of Leonard and a brother, were swept off by the plague. The brother went to sea and died. Leonard, the sole survivor of this large family (and this is only a sample of the days of plague and small pox and other enemies of the human race) began life with £200, and in two years and a half "ran out £150 of it"—not, as he pathetically says, "with ill husbandage, for I laboured night and day to save what I had left to me, but bad servants and trusting was the ruin of me."

So that times have not changed in these respects, for could not many a man say the same thing now in 1878? But Leonard Gale had the true stuff in him. He was a deeply religious man— of the Puritan type. "Then," he says, "I was in a great strait and knew not which way to steer, but I cryed unto the Lord with my whole heart and with tears, and he heard my cry, and put into my mind to try one year more, to see what I could do, for I resolved to spend nothing but mine own, and I resolved always to 'keep a conscience void of offence towards God and towards men.'"

"Then," he proceeds, "I took a boy to strike and to blow for me, and a man to work by the piece, but kept no maid nor woman in my house; and then I so thrived that, within two years and a half, I got back all that I had lost before, so that, by the time I came to 21 years of age, I had lost £150 and got it again, and I began to be looked upon as a thriving man, and so I was, for all the time I kept a smith's forge I layd by £100 a-year, one with another, and being burdened with free quartering of soldiers, I left off, and came down into Sussex, after one Spur, who owed me between £40 and £50, and he being in a bad capacity to pay me, though he did afterwards pay me all. Before I went home again, I took St. Leonard's forge, and so kept a shop to sell iron, and let out the smith's forge. . . . I had not been in the country one year, but Mr. Walter Burrell, whom I looked upon as my mortal enemy, sent to speak with me, and when I came to him he told me he heard a very good report of me, and desired to be acquainted with me, and he told me if I would let his son Thomas come into partnership with me, he would help me to sows nearer and better and cheaper than I had bought before. I told him I wondered to hear such things from him, for I heard he was my mortal enemy, because I took that forge, and I told him that if he would let me go partners with him in the furnace, he should go partners with me in the forge. He desired time to consider of it, and he rode presently into Kent to enquire of me, and found such an account of me, that he told me I should go partners with him in all his works."

After a partnership of 15 years with the Burrells (the progenitors of the owners of Knepp Castle, West Grinstead, and Ockenden House, Cuckfield), Leonard Gale became the sole proprietor of Tinsloe forge, one of the best in Sussex. At 46 years of age, having made, in 30 years, about £5,000 or £6,000, he thought it time to marry, "and chose (to use his own words to his sons) this woman, your mother, the daughter of Mr.

Johnson, with whom I had £500 *and one year's board with her.*" A singular provision this, and which, we believe, is now unknown to newly-married couples in England.

Things now prospered so well with Leonard Gale that at 66 years he had improved his estate to at least £16,000, "which is," he remarks, " £500 a year, one year with another, which is a very great miracle to me how I should come to so great an estate, considering my small dealings, the bad times, and my great losses by bad debts, suits of law, and by building." A proof, this, that fortunes were not so rapidly accumulated, even by Sussex ironmasters, 200 years ago, as they are now.

Leonard Gale had five children, and, addressing his two sons, Leonard and Henry, he gives them some advice which throws a light on his own character and also on the times. "Be not," he charges them, "too familiar with your vile neighbours, as I have been, *and you now see how they hate me.*" It is clear from this that there was a Nemesis of prosperity 200 years ago; and that the man who rose from the lower classes, be his virtues what they might, had his enviers and detractors. "Next, suffer no man to inclose any land nor build houses on the waste." Here shines out the old spirit of resistance to encroachment, came it from high or low. " Next, I charge you never to suffer that lane to be inclosed by Woolbarrow or Sears, or anyone else, for you see I have made them take away the gates, but they leave the posts standing, thinking to set them up again when I am dead. But you may safely cut down the gates, for it was never inclosed but by old Sears, who took delight to damm up highways to his own ruin; and so it was observed by his own neighbours, for he never thrived after he took in Langley-lane, and turned the Crawley footway, and to my knowledge he never thrived after he took in this lane." A piece of rural superstition for which some allowance may be made, for it has doubtless kept open many a pleasant path.

And now comes another "sign of the times:" "Next, I advise you to have a great care of ill and debauched company, especially wicked and depraved priests, such as are at this present time about me, as Lee and Troughton, of Worth; never give any of them any entertainment, nor none of their companions, for they are most vile and wicked men to my knowledge."

And, returning to the same point, he says : "Next, my advice is, that whatever estate either of you ever attain to, yet follow some employment, which will keep you from abundance of expenses and charges, and take you off from evil thoughts and wicked actions; and observe the mechanic priests, which have nothing to do but to come to church one hour or two on a Sunday, and all the week besides they will eat and drink at such men's houses as you are; but avoid them; but love and cherish every honest, godly priest, wherever you find 'them; and, above all, hold fast the ancient Protestant religion, for a better religion cannot be found out than that is, only I could wish the abuses were taken away, and wicked men found out, and punished, or turned out."

There can be no doubt that there was much of the old Puritan spirit in Leonard Gale the senior. And he closes his parental advice as follows :—"Next, my advice is, that you avoid swearing, lying, drunkenness, whoring, and gaming, which are the ruin of all men's estates, that are ruined in this nation, and pride of apparel, which is a great consumer of men's estates in this kingdom."

Neither did Leonard Gale, in his last advice, lose sight of the "main chance":—"If you can get," he says, "one of the Cowden furnaces, it will be very well, for I do assure you that, if I were but 40 years old, I would, by God's help, get a good estate by this employment, for I have within these 20 years cleared near £300 per annum out of that very forge."

Leonard Gale died in 1690, leaving the larger share of his estate to his son Leonard, who had received a liberal education and was called to the bar, but did not practice. In 1698 he purchased the house and estate of Crabbett, in the parish of Worth, for £8,000, and took his position among the gentry of the County, the son of the blacksmith being, as Mr. Blencowe remarks, elected one of the Members for East Grinstead in 1710. He, too, like his father, was a deeply religious man, and he, too, had his annoyances in life—some of them proceeding from "those inferior beggarly fellows," as he calls them, who had been the plague of his father, and who, it appears, had brought about the ruin of the previous owner of Crabbett, Mr. John Smith.

At 52 years of age Leonard Gale had so far successfully carried out his father's precepts as to be "now worth, at Michaelmas, 1724, at a reasonable computation, £40,667, though," he adds, "I have been guilty of a great many oversights in missing good bargains and taking bad (particularly the Mayfield estate), and not for want of care, but of understanding ; but I will not look back upon what is passed, but with a thankful heart daily praise Almighty God for what I have."

He had married, and had a large family, and the terms in which he records this event of his life are very simple and touching. "I marryed with Mrs. Sarah Knight, my mother's sister's only daughter, after I had made my court to her two or three years; by her I had a plentiful fortune : we were marryed in the parish church of Charlwood, by Mr. Hesketh, the rector. She was truly my own choice, and I am extremely well satisfied with it ; and do verily believe that for truth and sincerity, kindness and fidelity, humility and good nature, she has few equals. I am sure none can exceed her ; and I pray God to continue us long together in health and prosperity, and to crown us with all those blessings which he has promised to those that serve Him, and walk in His ways." One of the entries of the journal tells us that on Nov. 18, 1703, "My wife went to London in the Ryegate stage-coach," and whilst there occurred the great storm chronicled by De Foe, and by which, amongst other places, Brighthelmston was "miserably torn to pieces," and many of its fishing boats lost, with their crews.

A considerable portion of Leonard Gale's journal is occupied with records of family calamities in the deaths of the children born to him. Indeed, in all these old diaries and journals a striking feature is the ravages of death amongst children and young people. The small-pox had something to do with it ; but there is good ground for concluding that bad drainage lay at the root of the mischief. Leonard Gale outlived all his sons, only one of whom, in fact, lived to man's estate. The family became extinct, in the male line, in the third generation from the Kentish blacksmith. In the female line there are still descendants of it, in the Blunt and Clitherow families.

The memoir of Leonard Gale closes with an account of the marriage of his daughter,—"A woman," he says, "of excellent accomplishments, and who will, I doubt not, prove an ornament to her sex, to her parents, and the family she is grafted in." She married James Clitherow, Esq., and received a portion of £8,000, and had £1,200 a-year settled on her and her heirs, "of which £600 per annum is for her jointure."

Though the bride was so well provided for, the wedding was a sober one, and offers a strong contrast in this respect to modern nuptials. As Mr. Blencowe says, "No carriage with four horses and smart post-boys in those days was waiting at the door to carry the happy pair away to Tunbridge Wells or the Isle of Wight; the bride and bridegroom returned quietly to her father's house, where they remained a week, and a fortnight after that her mother accompanied her to her new home at Boston House."

Leonard Gale died in 1750, and was buried in Worth Church. He left estates of the value of about £1,110 a-year, which were divided among his three daughters. One of the latest entries of his journal indicates the character of the man:—"I am now in the 58th year of my age, and my memory is sensibly growing worse, for I have made some mistakes in my accounts within the last three years of above £150, which I cannot possibly find out after my utmost endeavours."

The Gales must have witnessed the decline of those iron works to which they owed their fortune. The growing scarcity of wood, and the opening of coal mines in Wales and other parts of the kingdom, where iron ore was in close proximity to them, were fatal to the Sussex works, which gradually grew fewer and fewer, until the last of them, at Ashburnham, was closed in 1809, the immediate cause of it being the failure of the foundry-men, through intoxication, to mix chalk with the ore, by reason of which it ceased to flow, and the blasting was stopped, and it was never renewed again. So ended, ignominiously, the Sussex iron-works. Their very sites are now for the most part only a matter of tradition : the streams which turned the wheels by which the furnaces were "blown" are only visited by the angler; the pits from which the ore was dug are bosky dells, dear to the naturalist ; the furnaces are cold—the forges silent. The Sussex iron-works are, like the Gales, who assisted to work them, extinct. Whether they will ever be revived depends on the problem now in course of being solved: is there coal in Sussex?* If there be, perhaps some new ironmaster will write a journal for future ages like the Gales !

---

* Since the above was written it has been solved—fortunately for the lovers of the picturesque—in the negative : the attempt to find coal by boring at Netherfield, in East Sussex, leading to no result.

THE SUSSEX SMUGGLERS.

WITHIN little more than a century, Sussex has seen two classes of smugglers flourish on her coast. The first were *exporters* of an English production—wool—which English legislators were foolish enough to try to keep at home under the idea of "protecting" the woollen manufacturers, and so there was a regular war along the southern coast (encouraged, it was asserted, by members of the higher classes who owned sheep-farms) between the smugglers of wool to France and Holland, and the supervisors, "surveyors," and "riders" who were appointed to prevent the exportation of wool. The second and later class of smugglers were *importers* of foreign goods—chiefly tea, spirits, tobacco, and silk—the duties on which were so enormous as almost to prohibit the use of them,—indeed, some manufactured articles were prohibited altogether. If it had not been for the smuggler in the latter years of the last century and the beginning of the present century, a large proportion of the population of England would have had to go without a good many articles now looked upon as necessaries of life. The smuggler supplied the farmer with spirits, and the farmer's wife with tea. He supplied the fine lady with silk and lace, and the fine gentleman with Bandana handkerchiefs. Huskisson, who saw the folly of the system long before the days of Cobden and Bright, told the House of Commons once that the only way to put down smuggling was to take off duties; otherwise it would defeat all their supervisors and blockade men. " Hon. Members," he went on to say, " were well aware that Bandana handkerchiefs were prohibited by law, and yet," he continued, at the same time drawing forth a Bandana from his pocket amidst the roars of the House, " I have no doubt there is hardly a gentleman in the House who has not got a Bandana handkerchief."

So, from 1671 to 1787, all the severity of the law could not prevent the exportation of British wool. Calais was often full of it —40,000 packs at a time. A law was passed that no person living within 15 miles of the sea in Sussex or Kent should buy wool without entering into sureties not to sell it to any people within 15 miles of the sea. It was of no avail. In 1698 the Supervisor of Sussex and Kent (Mr. Henry Baker) wrote to the authorities to say that in a few weeks 160,000 sheep would be shorn in Romney Marsh, and that the greater part of their fleeces would be "sent off hot into France." Warrants were sent down to arrest the wool smugglers at Romney, and some wool was seized on the horses' backs; but the smugglers assembled—50 armed horsemen—attacked the supervisor, rescued his prisoners, and pursued him and his officers till they were glad to make their escape to Guildford. More officers were appointed, but with little or no effect. "Large gangs of twenty, forty, fifty, and even one hundred, rode, armed with guns, bludgeons, and clubs, throughout the country, setting everyone at defiance, and awing all the quiet inhabitants. They established warehouses and vaults in many districts, for the reception of their goods, and built large houses at Seacock's Heath in Etchingham (built by the well-known smuggler, Arthur Gray, and called "Gray's Folly"), at Pix Hall and the Four Throws, Hawkhurst, at Goudhurst, and elsewhere, with the profits of their trade."

"The illicit exportation of wool," says Mr. W. D. Cooper, in his paper on "Smugglers in Sussex," "was never stopped;" and when a new kind of "fair trade" commenced, and it became profitable to import as well as export, the men and machinery were ready for it in Sussex. The nature of the goods smuggled doubtless had some effect on the class of men engaged in it. The wool smugglers were men of substance, and landowners and farmers were interested in the illegal exportation of wool to France. But the smugglers of brandy, hollands, gin, tea, &c., into England, were a lower class; and a brutality showed itself in some of their proceedings which ultimately raised the whole country against them. As early as 1737 an engagement, with loss of life, had taken place at Bulverhithe, near Hastings, between the

Custom Officers and some of the murderous gangs with which the County was over-run, and for the next ten years there was a guerilla war between the smugglers of Sussex and Kent and the officers of the Government, in which for the most part the smugglers 'had the advantage, frequently making the officers prisoners, disarming and cruelly cutting them with their swords, and riding off triumphantly with their goods.

The state of the Sussex roads at this time will furnish some clue to this defiance of the law. They were all but impassable. "The foul ways in Sussex" were proverbial. In 1703, the King of Spain, who paid a visit to Petworth House—the seat of the Percies and the finest house in the County—was six hours in travelling the last nine miles. Gentlemen and ladies were drawn to Church by oxen; and so recently as 1818 Bishop Buckner advised a gentleman whom he had ordained in the November of that year as the curate of Waldron to lose no time in going there, for in the course of a very short time he would find it impossible to do so! By some true Conservatives of the times this state of things was rejoiced in; and it is a fact that when the highway from London to Brighton, through Cuckfield, was projected, it was petitioned against by the residents of Hurstpierpoint, and diverted from that place, on the ground that it would be the means of bringing down cut-throats and pick-pockets from London! The impassable roads were also looked upon by some Sussex people as a protection against foreign invaders!

This is a diversion; but it explains a state of things otherwise incredible: a guerilla war carried on within 60 miles of London, and an organised resistance to the Government, in which towns were besieged, battles fought, Custom Houses burnt down, and the greatest atrocities committed.

The gang chiefly guilty of the latter was known as "The Hawkhurst gang," Hawkhurst being a village in Kent. But its leaders were Sussex men, and some of them in a respectable station of life. Such was Perin, a native of Chichester, who had been a master carpenter in that city for some years, until, being deprived of the use of his right hand by a stroke of the palsy, he became a purchaser of French goods for smugglers, and was on board a cutter off the Sussex coast with a large quantity of brandy, tea, and rum, when the vessel was captured by the Revenue Officers and its cargo taken to Poole, in Dorsetshire.

Perin and the crew of the smugglers made their escape in a boat.

On Sunday, October 4, 1747, the smugglers of Sussex and Kent met in force in Charlton Forest (the Duke of Richmond's hunting ground, near Chichester), and resolved, upon Perin's suggestion, to attack and break open the Poole Custom House. A portion of the gang, under the same Thomas Kingsmill who now headed the attack on Poole, had shortly before attacked Goudhurst, in Kent, and only been repelled by a regular force of militia after having three of their men killed and several others wounded. Others were taken and executed; but Kingsmill escaped, and acted as the leader in the attack on Poole. Assembling at Rowland's Castle, in Hampshire, armed with swords and firearms, they marched on Poole, which they reached at 11 at night, and, receiving intelligence that, owing to the ebb tide, the sloop lying off the town could not bring her guns to bear, they proceeded to the Custom House, broke it open, loaded their horses with goods, and rode off, first to Fordingbridge and thence to Brook, where they divided their booty and dispersed.

Now follows the tragic part of the affair. A reward was offered for the apprehension of the perpetrators of this daring act, but for some months with no avail. At length, a man named Diamond was captured and lodged in Chichester Gaol. The chief witnesses against this man were a Custom House officer named Galley and a shoemaker of Fordingbridge named Chater. On the 14th of February these two were on their way to Major Batten's, a Magistrate at Stanstead, near Chichester, to have their evidence taken, when they were induced to stop at the White Hart, at Rowland's Castle, in Hampshire, for refreshment, and here something fell from them which led the landlady to suspect the business they were travelling on. It shows how strongly the popular feeling was in those days with the smugglers that this woman should have sent for two of the men engaged in the late outrage, named Jackson and Carter, and communicated her suspicions to them. They sent for others of the gang, and Galley and Chater being made drunk they were put to bed, and then, in the middle of the night, were woke up, brought out, and, having been placed on a horse, their feet were tied under its belly, and a journey commenced, which, perhaps, is unparalleled for barbarity in a civilised country. As they rode along, the smugglers lashed the unfortunate men with their long whips, until, in their agony, they fell with their heads under the horse's belly, and so the journey was continued, until Lady Holt Park was reached, and here Galley was taken from the horse in order to be thrown down a well. Changing their purpose, however, the brutes replaced the wretched man on the horse, and then, re-commencing their torture of him, whipped him to death on the Downs, and there dug a whole and buried him. Chater was still alive, and was reserved for further sufferings. Being taken from the horse and chained in a turf-house, he was here brutally cut about the eyes and nose with a knife; and then, in the dead of night, he was taken to Harris's Well—a noose tied round his neck by Tapner (a native of Aldrington, near Brighton), and he was ordered to get over the palings to the well. Having done so, his murderers tied one end of the rope to the pales, and pushed the miserable man into the well. The rope, however, was too short to strangle him,—so, after hanging some time and being still alive, he was drawn up, untied, and then thrown head-foremost down the well. Still he was not dead. His groans were audible, and, to stifle these and finish the horrible deed, the smugglers tore up the rails and gateway round the well and threw them and large stones upon their victim till he expired.

These atrocious murders were not long undiscovered; though the discovery of them was by accident. Whilst a gentleman named Stone was hunting on the Downs, his dogs unearthed the body of Galley, and six miles off, in the well, was found the corpse of Chater. Such a crime as this could not be allowed to go unpunished. Seven of the fourteen men engaged in it were cap-

ed before Christmas (1748), and a Special Commission was
ued for their trial at Chichester, in January, 1749. The whole
them were convicted, either as principals or accessories in the
irders, and six of them (namely, Tapner, two men named Mills,
her and son, John Cobby, and John Hammond—all Sussex
n—and William Carter, a native of Hampshire) were executed—
ne of them in chains, as Tapner, on Rook's Hill, near
ichester, and Cobby and Hammond on Selsey Island. The
enth convict, Jackson, escaped a similar fate by dying in prison.

The daring character of these men, and the danger which
vellers ran from them, is illustrated by a circumstance in con-
ction with these trials. One of the men executed, Richard
lls, had another son besides the one who suffered with him, and
s worthy, being at liberty at the time of the trial, actually pro-
sed to his associates to stop the Judges as they were travelling
er Hind Heath and to rob them! In company with the Judges
re officers of the Court and Counsellors, altogether enough to
six coaches, each drawn by six horses, so that the smugglers
)ught the risk was too great; and the Judges escaped this danger
1 the country a very great scandal.

So far, however, from the execution of these men acting as a
rning, a crime of the same character was, shortly afterwards.
nmitted with the same circumstances of brutality almost on
: same ground. The son of Mills above referred to, meeting one
twkins, whom Mills and a party of fellow smugglers suspected
stealing two bags of tea, they accused him of it, and, on his
nying it, they flogged and kicked him to death, and then, car-
ng his body to a pond in Parham Park, twelves miles off, sunk
there. Mills—the third of the family who so suffered—was
this crime hung in chains on Slindon Common, and others of
e gang were convicted at the same Assizes as highwaymen, and
ecuted.

Still there were some of the leaders in the attack on Poole at
ge—amongst them, Perin, the concocter of it, and Kingsmill,
e leader. Both of them were, however, betrayed by one of
eir gang and captured and convicted, with two others, named

Glover and Fairhall. Their behaviour at their trial was most insolent. Fairhall threatened one of the witnesses, and when Perin, whose body was directed to be given up to his friends, was lamenting the fate of his associates,—not so favourably treated,—Fairhall exclaimed : " We shall be hanging up in the sweet air, when you are rotting in your grave." The night before his execution, Fairhall kept smoking with his friends till he was ordered by his keeper to go to his cell, when he exclaimed : " Why in such a hurry? cannot you let me stay a little longer with my friends? I shall not be able to drink with them to morrow night." Kingsmill was only twenty-eight, and Fairhall only twenty-five years of age, at the time of their death.

The Hawkhurst gang was thus broken up,—some of its leaders " hanging up in the sweet air," and others seeking safety in flight to France or Holland. But the " trade" still went on ; its profits were too great to be given up, and to some wild spirits it had an attraction even in the perils that attended it. So for nearly another 100 years,—nearly, in fact, up to our own time, —smuggling was carried on, with more or less success, along the Sussex coast ; and there were few persons who, 30 or 40 years ago, were not brought, in some way or other, in contact with the men who carried it on. Stories of them and their adventures were a staple topic of conversation, and smuggling anecdotes—the good luck or ill-luck of former townsmen—still live in the memories of Sussex men of this generation. It is amusing to find Mr. W. D. Cooper, himself a Hastings man, whilst recording some of the doings of his smuggling fellow-townsmen, in the Sussex Archæological Collections, not 20 years ago, cautiously explaining that " it would be improper to enter into any details *which might involve the characters of those still alive*"*!* We ourselves have a vivid recollection of an incident which our immediate predecessor in the proprietorship of the *Brighton Herald* was in the habit of narrating. He was taking a stroll along the Shoreham-road somewhat late at night when he suddenly heard the tramp of horses and saw a long file of mounted men approach him. He stood still in wonderment, not unmingled with alarm, when one of the riders, quitting the ranks, rode up to him and presented a pistol at his head. At that moment the hero of the adventure recognised the horseman as an intimate acquaintance and uttered his name. At the same moment the leader of the smugglers,—for it was a large body of these men, engaged in "running" the contraband cargo of a vessel off the coast,—recognised him, and exclaimed, "By ——, if you had not spoken, ——, I should have shot you." They had taken him at first for a Revenue Officer, and if he had been one it would have gone hard with him. As it was, there was a laugh, a shake of the hands, and the party rode off.

It is difficult to say to which of the long lines of coast that lie to the west and east of Brighton the credit, or discredit, of carrying on the "Fair Trade" with the greatest daring and resolution should be given. Both were favourably circumstanced for it, in the ruggedness of the coast, the sparseness of the population, the badness of the roads, and the total absence of police. From Worthing to Selsey there was a long line of flat coast on which boats could be "beached" at any time, and their tubs or bales landed from a lying-off Dutch or French lugger, and there was a wild and almost unpopulated country lying behind the few small towns or villages which, like Steyning, and Shoreham, and Bramber, lay nearer to the coast. It was, as we have seen, in the wild country between Chichester and Worthing—taking in Charlton Forest, Slindon, Parham, &c., that the Hawkhurst gang organised their attack on Poole, and afterwards consummated their crime by the murder of Galley and Chater. But the signal punishment which these atrocities brought down upon the chief actors in them seems to have checked their proceedings for a time in this quarter,—at least, they were not carried on in the same daring spirit. The improvement, too, in the roads of the Western part of Sussex, about this time—chiefly by the agency of Sir Walter Burrell—may have had something to do in arresting smuggling. However that may be, in the latter part of the last century, and the beginning of this, it is in the eastern part of Sussex that we find the smugglers most active and daring. The Hastings men took the lead in it, and, following in the footsteps of the famous Viking from whom their town presumedly takes its name, joined piracy to smuggling.

In 1758 Nicholas Wingfield (Wingfield is still a good Sussex name) and Adams Hyde, masters of two Hastings cutters, had the audacity to board a Danish ship, on which was the Ambassador to Denmark from Spain, and carried off a portion of its cargo. For this they were tried, convicted, and executed as pirates. So far from the Hastings men being deterred by this example, for the next seven years vessels coming up Channel were exposed to the piratical attacks of a gang known as "Ruxley's crew," most of the members of which lived at Hastings, and who did not hesitate, when resisted, to add murder to piracy. Thus, the master of a Dutch hoy, called "The Three Sisters," was "chopped down" with an axe, and the perpetrators betrayed themselves by boasting "how the Dutchman wriggled when they cut him on the back-bone!" To put down this gang it was thought necessary to send a detachment of the Inniskilling Dragoons, 200 strong, to Hastings, and a man-of-war and a cutter were stationed off the town to co-operate with the military! If the town had been in the hands of the French, and about to be besieged, more warlike measures could scarcely have been taken. Nay, so fearful were the authorities of their unscrupulous fellow-townsmen who favoured "Fair Trade" and piracy, that the soldiers had strict orders to conceal the object for which they had been sent down; and because the Mayor of Hastings would not divulge this he was attacked, and ran considerable danger of being murdered. Then it was considered time to act. Several men were arrested, brought to trial for piracy, and four of them hung.

This was in 1769, and yet ten years afterwards we have the strongest proof that smuggling was carried on as actively as ever along the Sussex coast. A new Act had been passed against it, and, in a pamphlet issued by the authorities to enforce the law (called "Advice to the Unwary," 1780), it is stated that the practice of smuggling had made such rapid strides from the sea

G

coast into the very heart of the country, pervading every city, town, and village, that universal distress had been brought on the fair dealer. The quantity of spirit distilled at Schiedam, to be smuggled into England, was estimated at 3,867,500 gallons, and five or six millions of pounds of tea were yearly imported in the same way from France. For the management of the transactions connected with the "trade," the Sussex smugglers had regular resident agents at Flushing; and these official representatives of Sussex smugglers continued to be appointed up to 30 years ago!*

The exportation of wool had ceased, but the high duties on tea, silks, tobacco, and spirits left plenty of work for the smuggler in the introduction of those articles into the country without payment of duties; and, when successful, the profit was so great that plenty of men were ready to risk their lives for it. So the work went on, not only through the whole of the war with France, from 1793 to 1815, but up to 1840; and during that period scarcely an Assize went by without some trial taking place for more or less heinous offences arising out of it; whilst the loss of life in the constant conflicts between the blockade-men and the smugglers was incessant, and sometimes heavy on both sides.

"In May, 1826," writes Mr. W. D. Cooper in the paper on "Smuggling in Sussex," from which we have before quoted, "a smuggling galley, chased by a guard boat, ran ashore near the mouth of Rye Harbour, and opened fire on the guard. The

---

* The cool audacity of these men is illustrated by a piece of intelligence communicated to the *Chichester Journal and Hampshire and Wiltshire Chronicle* of October 6, 1783, under the head of "Lewes, Sept. 29." It is as follows:—
"One night last week Mr. Marson, Excise Officer at Newhaven, was seized by six or eight smugglers, who escorted him to their main body, composed of near 200, assembled at the sea-side, *by whom the Exciseman was tried for his life*, on a charge of aiding and abetting in wantonly shooting a smuggler some time since, when, happily for him, he was acquitted by a majority of ten and suffered to depart unhurt." This was, indeed, turning the tables! Only try to conceive the state of things when smugglers apprehended and tried for their lives Excise officers!

blockade-men from Camber Watch-house came to the spot, and seized one of the smugglers, when a body of not less than two hundred armed smugglers rushed from behind the sand-hills, commenced a fire on the blockade-men, killing one and wounding another, but were ultimately driven off with the capture of their galley, carrying off, nevertheless, their wounded. On another occasion, four or five smugglers were killed whilst swimming the military canal at Pett-horse Race, having missed the spot where it was fordable. On April 13, 1827, about twenty smugglers went down to the eastward of Fairlight; a struggle ensued; the smugglers wrested some muskets from the blockade men, beat them with the butt-ends, and ran one through with a bayonet. The smugglers at length retreated, leaving one of their number dead; another was found afterwards, having been apparently dropped by the smugglers; a third, some distance on the way to Icklesham, the body scarcely cold; the rest of the wounded men were carried off by their companions; and I have been informed that one of the party alone carried one of his fellows on his back from the scene of the conflict at Fairlight to his residence at Udimore, a distance of six miles at least."

It was, indeed, one of the best traits in these lawless menthat they always carried off their wounded comrades; and we will do them the credit to attribute it to a fellow-feeling on their part, and not to the fear of being "split upon" by their captured comrades.

One of the latest of the smugglers' battles,—for such they often really were,—in Sussex, was fought in 1828, near Bexhill. A lugger having landed its illicit cargo between that village and the little public house at Bo-Peep, a party of smugglers, armed with "bats" (large clubs), rushed down to the beach, and, placing it in carts, on horses, and on men's backs, made straight to Sidley Green. But here they were overtaken by a Blockade force of 40 men, and the smugglers halting, and drawing up in a line, a regular engagement took place. With such resolution did the smugglers fight on this occasion, that they repulsed their assailants, after killing Quarter-master Collins, and severely bruising several others.

In the first volley from the Blockade an old smuggler named Smethurst was shot dead, and his body was found the next morning, his "bat" still grasped in his hand, but almost hacked to pieces by the cutlasses of the Blockade-men. As usual, all the wounded smugglers were carried off.

For this fatal affair eight men were tried at the Old Bailey, and, pleading guilty, received sentence of death. But the sentence was eventually commuted to transportation.

Two smugglers were shot dead near Hastings in 1831, and another at Worthing in 1832, in an affray in which between 200 and 300 smugglers were engaged. In 1833, the Chief Boatman of the Blockade was killed at Eastbourne, and on this occasion the smugglers, forming in two lines down to the beach, kept up the fight until the whole cargo had been run, in spite of having several of their party wounded. On none of these occasions were any of the men engaged discovered. Indeed, as a rule, the smugglers were "true" to each other.

The last occasion on which life was lost in a smuggling affray on the Sussex coast was in 1838, when a poor fiddler named Monk was shot dead by the Coast Guard at Camber Castle. Since then no blood has been shed in smuggling transactions, and, in fact, smuggling may be said to have died a natural death. No farmer would now connive at a fraud on the Government by allowing his barns to be filled with kegs of brandy, or his horses to be "borrowed," —a frequent practice in the olden times,—or even by leaving his gates unlocked for their passage; all of which things were at one time usual. Nor would any respectable tradesman now buy lace or silk which had not come through the regular channels of commerce and paid the duty to which they are subjected. In fact, the smugglers, as a body of men acting to some extent in the interests of the public, by keeping open commercial dealings with other nations which would otherwise have ceased altogether, and who certainly were looked upon with a good deal of sympathy by the general community, belong to the past. Traditions of the spots where they concealed their goods (one of them, a hole near

Falmer Pond),* or where they suffered for their crimes, still remain, but every year they become fainter. It is difficult, indeed, in the present day, when, thanks to Free Trade, commerce has free scope, to form an idea of the extent to which illicit dealings with the opposite coast were carried on, even by the respectable classes, and how it perverted men's notions of right and wrong. The smuggler was a popular man, except where, as in the Chater and Galley case, he committed atrocious crimes; he had the majority of his fellow-subjects with him, though the law was against him. He was carrying on a hazardous game—that was all. If he was successful, people looked upon and talked of him as a fine fellow; he had "done" the Exciseman, nothing more. As for defrauding the revenue or gaining an unfair advantage over his fellow-subjects who paid duty on their goods, nobody thought of reproaching him with that or of denouncing him as a public robber, and thus respectable tradesmen entered into smuggling transactions in those days, as respectable people in these days gamble in shares. Fifty or sixty years ago some of the leading tradesmen of Brighton, Worthing, Hastings, Rye, and other towns along the coast took the goods that were "run" by the Fair Traders, and some of them made fortunes, and some of them — indeed, most of them — were ruined. The effect of this gambling, to call it by the mildest term, may be conceived. The very foundations of public morality were sapped; a war was carried on between the Government that acted, or professed to act, for the people, and the people themselves; and the sympathies of the public were against the Government. It was a fine thing in the estimation of

---

* Very curious places were sometimes chosen by the smugglers to conceal their goods in. The Vicar of a country parish not far from Brighton wanted to visit his Church rather earlier than usual one Sunday morning, and was met by all kinds of excuses and obstructions from the Sexton for not finding the key, until at last it came out that the sacred edifice was full of kegs of brandy! And they had to be cleared out before Service could be proceeded with. Of course, the Revenue Officers did not think of looking for spirits of this kind in the Parish Church!

numbers of men to defy it—to go out in armed bands to resist the officers of the Crown and to fight with, and sometimes to murder, these officers. Many of the men who did this were known and applauded as fine fellows, and were, in fact, men of great courage and resolution and talent, and who, acting in a lawful cause, would have won honour and fame. Their daring acts were talked of with a sort of admiration, and even when they were brought to justice, and deservedly suffered for such acts of brutality as those of the Tapners and the Mills and the Perins, they were looked upon in a different light from the ordinary criminal. Up to the present day it is held to be no disgrace to have had these men for your ancestors—rather the reverse! The smugglers are still heroes in people's opinion, though, fortunately, the race is extinct. Free Trade has put it down, and if we had no other cause to thank the men who, like Huskisson and Cobden, Gladstone and Peel, have given us Free Trade, we should thank them for this: that they have removed such a blot on the social body as the Sussex Smuggler.

THE SOUTH-DOWN SHEPHERD.

IF any class of men in Sussex have escaped the touch and changes of time, it is surely the shepherd of the South Downs. Not only is his occupation one that does not change, and does not admit of change, or of very little change, but the spot where he pursues it remains necessarily the same. Ages go by, fashions come and go, and revolutions sweep over him, and he takes no note or heed of them; and they have no word or work for him. No matter who is master in the land, king, or lords, or people, they do not want and yet cannot do without the shepherd. The sheep must be tended on the hills, and the man who does it is equally respected and disregarded by all parties. He is part of the flock. He does not constitute a class; his numbers are too few for that; he is but a unit in the great total of humanity. He stands apart out of the crowd—is an exceptional being, and retains his place and his characteristics—his peace and his solitude—when all around him is in a state of flux and mutation.

It would be a great mistake, however, to suppose that the shepherd of the Downs is like other shepherds, or rather, perhaps, we should say, that shepherds in other parts of the world, or even in our own England, are, or have been, like the Shepherd of the Downs. The shepherds of the East, like Abraham and Laban and Jacob, were, as their descendants are to this day in the oases of Arabia, the chiefs of great tribes—often warriors and kings, sages and legislators, with a wide and changing field of action, and an outlook upon the world. The shepherds of the Alps pursue their task beset by dangers of crevasse, glacier, and cataract—floods and landslips. The shepherds of South America and Australia are armed horsemen, who carry their lives in their hands and must be prepared for attack at any moment from savages or bushrangers. They are often the owners, too, as well as the guardians of the countless flocks which they drive over thousands of miles of almost trackless prairee, scrub, or desert, and often return to the life of cities, which they have left for a time, as millionaires and men of note.

In other parts, too, of Europe, and even of England and Scotland, the shepherd's or drover's life is one of varied change from place to place, of collision and dealings with other men, and has no small amount of incident and excitement and ups and downs in it, such as accompany the dealings of men with men.

But, with the shepherd of the South Downs, life must be as peaceful and unchanging—as like from day to day, year to year, and century to century, as one can well imagine it. Shakspeare has put into the mouth of Henry the 6th, when weary of the intrigues of Courts and the tragedies of war, a picture of the shepherd's life—a South-Down Shepherd, it must have surely been —in his day, which will serve to picture it just as truly now :—

> O God ! methinks it were a happy life,
> To be no better than a homely swain ;
> To sit upon a hill, as I do now,
> To carve out dials quaintly, point by point,
> Thereby to see the minutes how they run—
> How many make the hour full complete,
> How many hours bring about the day,
> How many days will finish up the year,
> How many years a mortal man may live.
> When this is known ; then to divide the time :
> So many hours must I tend my flock ;
> So many hours must I take my rest ;
> So many hours must I contemplate ;
> So many hours must I sport myself ;
> So many days my ewes have been with young ;
> So many weeks ere the poor fools will yean ;
> So many years ere I shall shear the fleece ;
> So minutes, hours, days, months, and years,
> Pass'd over to the end they were created,
> Would bring white hairs unto a quiet grave.
> Ah, what a life were this ! how sweet, how lovely !

> Gives not the hawthorn bush a sweeter shade
> To shepherds, looking on their silly sheep,
> Than doth a rich embroider'd canopy
> To kings, that fear their subjects' treachery?
> O, yes, it doth; a thousand-fold it doth;
> And to conclude—the shepherd's homely curds,
> His cold thin drink out of his leather bottle,
> His wonted sleep under a fresh tree's shade,
> All which secure and sweetly he enjoys,
> Is far beyond a Prince's delicates,
> His viands sparkling in a golden cup,
> His body couched in a curious bed,
> When care, mistrust, and treason wait on him.

Allow for the poet's exaltation of this life of the hill-shepherd, and it is as true a picture now as it was in the day that Shakspeare drew it. Still the same peaceful spot, with no shadow of danger on it which a dog or a crook may not ward off; still the same fleecy forms and innocent faces creeping up and down the hill-sides; still the same quiet buzz of insects in the wild thyme, that still gives out the same sweet scent, or the melancholy cry of the pee-wit as it sweeps with the wind over hill and dale; still the same softly-rounded horizon landward, or, seaward, a vast flat of waters until sea and sky meet, and close in the little world of the shepherd. For he has none besides this, and thinks of none and wishes for none. Sheep and dog, and birds and Downs, with the alternations of the seasons, and the flock-duties they bring, are to him the Alpha and the Omega of his existence. For generations it has been so,—how many we do not venture to say, for sheep did *not* come in with the Conqueror; he found them here, and that being the case, of course there were shepherds. In the Weald, most probably, the swineherd held sway, and many a Gurth fed his unruly herd on the fruit of the oak and the beech. But swine could find no mast or acorns, or such-like food, on the unwooded Downs of Sussex. Here there was, and is, nothing but the short sweet grass which has covered it since the day when the rounded backs of the ribbed chalk began to show themselves, " dolphin-like," above the waves, and to which the sweet breath of the south is as much the parent as Zephyr and Aurora were, in their May sportings, to the spirit of Mirth.

On these Downs, then,—these beautiful South Downs of Sussex,—must the first sheep that were brought from Spain by Carthaginians, or from Gaul by Celts or Romans, have been turned out to feed. And, allowing something for the difference of nationalities, we do not think the first guardian of them could have differed very much in garb or customs from those shepherds who now tend them. He must have had his toga—his warm great coat or mantle—to shelter him from the keen winds that sometimes blow eastward and northward over the Downs, and he must have had some kind of flopping head-gear—sombrero or cappello—to shade his eyes from the mid-day sun. And when he had these—Celt or Carthaginian, Roman or Saxon—he did not, probably, look so very unlike that figure that now meets our gaze on the Down side. Motionless, of course—the Down shepherd always is motionless, but erect, or just leaning on his crook, with his wallet at his side, and with his dog at his feet, looking up at him with that eager look, in expectation of a command, which sheep-dogs are born with. Not a young man,—who ever saw a *young* shepherd?—but of an age not easy to fix, nor with an expression of face easy to decipher. A blank, and yet not a blank; rather an unwritten page in which much may be read—an expression moulded by generations of men (for Down shepherds, as a rule, descend from father to son) who have looked daily on the same scene,—and that mainly made up of three great elements, —sky, and sea, and Down,—and with the same object in view: to feed that flock of sheep and renew it from year to year. Objects, these, uninterfered with by the outer world, and with as little intermixture of those personal elements of love and hope and fear —of desire to rise or fear to fall—as it is possible for human life to go on with. For as to those passions and that poetry which the Pastoral poets and Italian and Spanish novelists import into the shepherd-life, it may have been true of Arcadia or Andulasia, or in the vales of Tempè or Tivoli, but with these things the Down-shepherd has naught to do and never had. If he "told his tale," it was his tale of sheep, and not of love, and he did not tell it, as Milton sings, under a hawthorn tree,—there are few or no hawthorn trees on the South Downs,—but as the animals passed into or out of their fold ; and if he had his likes and his dislikes— his desires and his disappointments—they had reference to the masters into whose service he passed, the wages he received, the "guerdon" he got for successful lambing, and such-like business matters, and not to rages and jealousies and hates arising from the tender passion—the jiltings of mistresses (his "young woman" never thought of jilting him nor his "missus" of planting the "green-eyed monster" in his breast !) or the treasons of friends. If the human passions slumber anywhere, they do so in the heart of a South-down shepherd, and thus he seldom or never figures at a Police Court or in an Assize calendar. Even the Game Laws lose their terrors to him : he is no poacher, but fast friends with the sportsman, to whom a "shepherd's hare" is always a *dernier ressort*, and a safe one too, when the covers fail to supply sport.

The Down shepherd, too, has his own field of sport, or used to have. Wheat-ears, which once abounded on our Downs, were a little mine of wealth to him—he caught them with springes set in the turf—and plovers' eggs were another source of revenue. The capture of the first and the search for the second, the marking down of a hare's seat, or the watching of rabbits going in and out of their burrows,—these, doubtless, supply those varieties to the shepherd's life on the Downs without which it would be dull indeed, for days must sometimes pass with no other society but that of sheep and dog, and nothing more to do than watch the one and order the other.

"What a fine opportunity for study !" some contemplative reader, or some member of a School Board, eager for juvenile development, may exclaim. We believe that the class is as innocent of literary or scientific tastes as Audrey was of poetry. It is in the society of men, and not of sheep or beeves, that these cultivated tastes flourish—in England at least. Now and then there is an exception ; but they are few and far between. Scotland can boast of a poet and an astronomer who were shepherds, and

Sussex has one instance, and only one, of a shepherd who turned aside from sheep to letters. This latter was John Dudeney, a native of Rottingdean, and a descendant from a long line of shepherds, who, in a "plain unvarnished tale," has left us a chronicle of the life of a shepherd of the South Downs which is, in prose, as truthful a picture as Shakspeare's is in verse.

John Dudeney was born at Rottingdean on the 21st April, 1782, his father being shepherd to John Hamshaw, Esq. His own shepherd-life extended from his 8th to his 23rd year, when he exchanged his flock of sheep for a flock of children—in fact, became a schoolmaster at Lewes, and so spent a long and useful life.

"When I was eight years old," he tells us, in a communication made by him to Mr. R. W. Blencowe at an advanced period of his life, "I began to follow the sheep during the summer months; in winter I sometimes drove the plough. I was fond of reading, and borrowed all the books I could. When I was about ten, a gentleman (whom I afterwards found to be Mr. Dunvan, author of what is called Lee's History of Lewes) came to me on the hills, and gave me a small History of England and Robinson Crusoe, and I read them both with much interest. When he first came he inquired of the boy who tended my father's flock, while I was gone to sheepshearing, for a wheatear's nest, which he had never seen. These birds usually build their nest in the chalk-pits, and in the holes which the rabbits had made. I afterwards bought, when I came to Lewes fair, a small History of France, and one of Rome, as I could get the money; indeed, when I came to the fairs, I brought all the money I could spare to buy books.

"My mother sometimes tended my father's flock while he went to sheepshearing. I have known other shepherds' wives do the same; but this custom, like many others, is discontinued. I have not seen a woman with a flock for several years.

"The masters allowed me the keeping of one sheep, the lamb and the wool of which brought me about 14s or 15s a year, which I saved till I had enough to buy a watch, for which I gave four guineas, and which has now shown me the time of day for more than half a century. My father let me have the privilege of catching wheatears, which brought me in a few shillings. These birds are never found in great numbers so far from the sea-coast, and I very seldom caught a dozen in a day. The bird called the bustard, I have heard old shepherds say, formerly frequented the Downs; but their visits have been discontinued for nearly a century. I have heard my father say, that his father saw one about the year 1750; he saw that near to *Four Lords' Dool*, a place so called because at the tumulus or dool there four parishes meet—St. John's under the Castle, Chailey, Chiltington, and Falmer. When I was sixteen I went to service, as under-shepherd, at West Blatchington, where I remained one year. When the transit of Mercury over the sun's disc took place, on the 7th of May, 1799, my curiosity was excited; but in looking for it without due precaution I very much injured one of my eyes.

"In the winter of 1798-9, during a snow, my flock was put into a barn-yard, the first instance I know of putting the sheep into the yard, except in lambing time. There we caught more wheatears than at my father's. I used to sell some to the gentry on their excursions to the Devil's Dyke for 2s. 6d. or 3s. a dozen; at the beginning of the season sometimes catching three dozen in a day, but not often. At Midsummer, 1799, I removed to Kingston, near Lewes, where I was under-shepherd for three years. The flock was very large (1,400 the winter stock), and my master, the head shepherd, being old and infirm, much of the labour devolved on me. While here I had better wages, £6 a year; I had also a part of the money obtained from the sale of wheatears, though we did not catch them here in great numbers, a dozen or two a day, seldom more. The hawks often injured us by tearing them out of their coops, and scattering their feathers about, which frightened the other birds from the coops. During winter I caught the moles, which, at twopence each, brought me a few shillings. I could, therefore, spare a little more money for books. I still read such as I could borrow, on history, &c., for I never, after I was twelve or thirteen years of age, could bear to spend my time in what is called light reading.

"I had very little opportunity of reading at home, so used to take a book or two in my shepherd's coat-pocket, and to pursue my studies by the side of my flock when they were quiet. I was never found fault with for neglecting my business through reading. I have sometimes been on the hills in winter from morning till night, and have not seen a single person during the whole day. In the snow, I have walked to and fro under the shelter of a steep bank, or in a bottom, or a combe, while my sheep have been by me scraping away the snow with their forefeet to get at the grass, and I have taken my book out of my pocket, and, as I walked to and fro in the snow, have read to pass away the time. It is very cold on the Downs in such weather; I remember once, whilst with my father, the snow froze into ice on my eyelashes, and he breathed on my face to thaw it off. The Downs are very pleasant in summer, commanding extensive views of both sea and land : I very much wanted a telescope, and could not spare money to buy one; but I met with some lenses, and putting them into a pasteboard case, I contrived one, which afforded me much amusement in pleasant weather.

"In 1802 I began practical geometry from Turner's 'Introduction.' I bought some paper and a pair of iron compasses. I filed off part of one of the legs so that I could fasten on a pencil or pen, then, laying my paper on the greensward on the hill, I drew my circles, triangles, &c.

"On that part of the hill where my sheep required least attention, I dug a hole in the ground amongst the heath, and placed a large flintstone over it. No one would think of there being anything under it if they had seen it. In that hole I kept some books and a slate, which, when convenient, I took out, and went to work at arithmetic, algebra, geometry, &c. This under-stone library was on Newmarket Hill, not far from a pond, near to which a cottage and a barn have since been erected. For more than thirty years the place where the hole had been was to be seen ; and I have several times gone a little way out of my road to visit it, and offer up my thanks to that gracious Providence who has so directed my way ; but within these last few years the plough has passed over it, and I can no longer find the exact spot.

" My master, the head shepherd, at Kingston, had the keeping of twenty sheep as part of his wages ; and I have heard old shepherds affirm that, in the generation before them, some of the shepherds had nearly, or quite all, their wages in this way, and it seems to have been of very ancient practice. We have an instance in the case of Jacob and Laban ; and I think it probable that the wages of the labouring man were, almost of necessity, money being scarce, paid in this manner.

"At Midsummer, 1802, I went (at his request) to be head shepherd to James Ingram, Esq., of Rottingdean. Mr. Thomas Beard and Mr. Dumbrill had each of them sheep in the flock, but Mr. Ingram having most, he was my real master. The farm was called the Westside Farm, extending from Rottingdean to Black Rock, in Brighton Parish ; it was a long narrow slip of ground, not averaging more than half a mile in width. My flock required very close attention, as they had to feed so much between the pieces of corn, and there were no fences to keep them off. In such situations a good dog is a most valuable help to a shepherd, and I was fortunate in having a very excellent one.

" The farm extending along the sea-coast, I caught great numbers of wheatears during the season for taking them, which lasts from the middle of July to the end of August. The most I ever caught in one day was thirteen dozen; but we thought it a good day if we caught three or four dozen. We sold them to a poulterer, at Brighton, who took all we could catch in the season at 18d. a dozen. From what I have heard from old shepherds, it cannot be doubted that they were caught in much greater numbers a century ago than of late. I have heard them speak of an immense number being taken in one day by a shepherd at East Dean, near Beachy Head. I think they said he took nearly a hundred dozen; so many, that he could not thread them on crow-quills in the usual manner, but took off his round frock and made a sack of it, to put them into, and his wife did the same with her petticoat. This must have happened when there was a great flight. Their numbers now are so decreased that some shepherds do not set up any coops, as it does not pay for the trouble.

"I had a good father and mother, though they were poor, my father's wages being only £30 a year, and the keeping of ten or twelve sheep, having a family of ten children, yet we were never in want."

We doubt if John Dudeney has had any followers among South-Down shepherds in his pursuit of knowledge under difficulties, or in his exchange of the tending of sheep for the instruction of children. The life of the South-Down Shepherd is, at best, a "hard one," and presents few or no opportunities for self-improvement, and none of those degrees or steps in the social scale by which men mount Fortune's ladder. As a rule, once a shepherd, always a shepherd; and the shepherd's boy has nothing higher to look to than to be a shepherd. The opportunities of leisure and contemplation which, to minds already formed to study, may seem tempting to some, are more than counterbalanced by the absence, in a shepherd's life, of those incentives to exertion which are supplied to other men by closer contact and the fiercer competition of city-life. To those engaged in them, these seem to be evils; and doubtless they have their evil side. But let the theoretic lover of solitude—poet or philosopher—try a year or two of sheep-tending on the South-Downs, and those hills, so beautiful and delightful when seen in their summer garb, would soon disgust him by their barren solitude and bleakness. The shepherd endures all this with stolid patience; but it does not develop his mind or raise him in the scale of humanity. We question if the tendency in the life of the South-Down Shepherd. of modern days is not to sink, rather than to rise, in comparison with other classes of labourers. The latter move onward with the stream; *he*, almost necessarily by the conditions of his life, is stationary. His world of action is rather narrowed than enlarged. The wide-sweeping Downs are pressed upon by the plough on the one side, and by Building Societies on the other; the limit of the shepherd's domains is yearly narrowed, and he is brought more under the eye and within the ordinary control of the farmer, and is less his own master; has lighter responsibilities and less trust; and all this tends to make the Down shepherd a less important member of the rural community than he used to be in by-gone days. Still, he remains—perhaps more closely and truly resembling the figure that was seen on the same hills a thousand years ago than any other set of men, on mountain or plain, in this England of ours. And, of all spots so to see the Shepherd in his primitive state, the South Downs are the best.

"Shepherds," writes Richard Lower, of Chiddingly, Sussex (the father of Mark Antony Lower), in a paper on " Old South-Down Shepherds," " were famous for spinning long yarns; and if it chanced that two or three met together on some lofty brow, within sight of their respective flocks, stories of great length would surely be related. These, chiefly referring to their own calling, would beguile many hours, and sometimes concerned matters that happened ' fifty year agoo,' or very likely a ' hundud.' I once accidentally overheard two retired shepherds, who were sitting on a March morning under a sunny hedge, conversing in a somewhat disconsolate tone concerning the prosperity of bygone days. One was telling the other how he had known the time when, in a single year, from forty to fifty thousand sheep had been washed near the spot where they were sitting, and ' now,' he exclaimed, 'there be none!' The 'wash' had been removed to another locality, and this seemed to him almost a national calamity. ' As to *birding*,' he continued, in a still more doleful tone—' birding is now all auver; why, I used to make quite a harvest of my birds—twelve pound a year or more I have made of my birds ; and one year I made fourteen pounds eight shillings. We sent 'em ye see to Burthemson (Brighthelmstone—Brighton), and otherwhile we catched so many that the Burthemsoners coud'nt take 'em all, and I myself have sent some to Tunbridge Wells. That was the time o' dee, Old Boy, for shepherds.' For laziness the shepherd, in his every-day habits, had no equal. Wrapped up in his thick great-coat, impervious to rain, snow, or hail, he would throw himself backwards into a *hawth* bush, and snugly repose as on a bed of down for hours together. If a traveller, chancing to stray to the spot where he lay, enquired his road over those trackless, lonely hills, the shepherd, too lazy to rise to give the required information, would stretch out his leg, pointing with his foot, and say—' over dat yander hill—by de burg —down that 'ere bottom—and so up de bostle,' as the case might be, and drop again into his doze as snug as a dormouse."

THE SUSSEX SHEEP-SHEARER.

TO some readers it may suggest itself that the shearer of sheep ought to have been associated with the shepherd,—that it is one and the same set of men who tend the sheep and who shear them. But this would be to fall into a mistake. A shepherd may be, and indeed, usually is a shearer, but the great majority of shearers are not shepherds; and whilst the character of the shepherd varies with the locality in which he carries on his work,—and thus the shepherd of the hills may be a very different character from the shepherd of the plain or the mountain,—the occupation of the sheep-shearer knows no such variation. It is pursued in every county and country pretty much under the same circumstances and conditions, and gives rise to no special character in those who pursue it. It is, indeed, so to say, only an accident of rural life; occupies a few days' labour, and then is not needed until another year. So, sheep-shearing is not a vocation—a settled calling; there is no body of men who get their living solely by it, as shepherds get their's. A shepherd is always to be seen where there are sheep; but enquire for a sheep-shearer in any but the sheep-shearing months, and the only reply you would get would be to be shown a man who can shear, but whose settled employment is of a very different kind. And yet it is not every man that can shear—only here and there one; and so the sheep-shearer stands out from the common herd of agricultural labourers: he is, for some few days of the year, a skilled labourer—almost an artist—and as such he must be treated with some respect, and calls for our notice and attention.

Sometimes, indeed, a shepherd will undertake the shearing of his flock, and then we have the nearest approach to a pure sheep-shearer. But there is many a shepherd who does not shear, as there are thousands of shearers who are not shepherds,—not, indeed, agricultural labourers at all. It is the one province of rural industry, now that spinning is no longer carried on in the cottage, that approximates most closely to the work of townspeople. Not only may any hand on a farm take to shearing if he possess the necessary skill, and will be allowed by his master to shear for other farmers as well as for himself, but men who are not farm labourers at all—tailors and shoemakers and such-like as are skilful in the use of the scissors,—will join a "Company" of shearers and take a circuit of country, such circuits being mapped out and kept by the different sets of shearers with as much strictness as gentlemen of the long robe keep to their circuits—and some people may be malicious enough to insinuate, for the same object, namely, of shearing *their* sheep!

The arrival of these shearing "Companies" at a farm used once to be a very important event. Each Company had its Captain and Lieutenant, selected for their trustworthy character, their superior intelligence, and their skill in the shearing art. And, as a symbol of the authority with which they were invested, the Captain wore a gold-laced hat and the Lieutenant a silver-laced one. As soon as the Company was formed, all the men repaired to the cottage of the Captain, where a feast which was called the "White-ram" was provided for them, and on this occasion the whole plan of the campaign was discussed and arranged. They generally got to their place of shearing about seven, and, having breakfasted, they began their work. Once in the forenoon, and twice in the afternoon, their custom was to "light up," as they termed it; that is, they ceased to work for a few minutes, drank their beer, sharpened their shears, and set to work again. Their dinner-hour was one, but this was not the great meal of the day, their supper being the time of real enjoyment, and when this was over, they would remain for several hours in the house, smoking their pipes and singing their sheepshearing songs, in which they were joined by the servants of the farm; and sometimes the master and mistress of the house would favour them with their presence.

Some of these sheep-shearing songs still linger in the memories of old men and women, and may occasionally be heard at rural merry-makings, one of their characteristics being their interminable length. The following is a specimen :—

Come, all my jolly boys, and we'll together go
Abroad with our masters, to shear the lamb and ewe ;
All in the merry month of June, of all times in the year,
It always comes in season the ewes and lambs to shear ;
And there we must work hard, boys, until our backs do ache,
And our master he will bring us beer whenever we do lack.

Our master he comes round to see our work is doing well,
And he cries, " Shear them close, men, for there is but little wool."
" O yes, good master," we reply, " we'll do well as we can,"
When our Captain calls, " Shear close, boys!" to each and every man.
And at some places still we have this story all day long,
"Close them, boys, and shear them well !" and this is all their song.

And then our noble Captain doth unto our master say,
"Come, let us have one bucket of your good ale, I pray."
He turns unto our Captain, and makes him this reply :
" You shall have the best of beer, I promise, presently."
Then out with the bucket pretty Betsy she doth come,
And master says, " Maid, mind and see that every man has some."

This is some of our pastime while we the sheep do shear,
And though we are such merry boys, we work hard, I declare ;
And when 'tis night, and we are done, our master is more free,
And stores us well with good strong beer, and pipes and tobaccee.
So we do sit and drink, we smoke and sing and roar,
Till we become more merry far than e'er we were before.

When all our work is done, and all our sheep are shorn,
Then home to our Captain, to drink the ale that's strong.
'Tis a barrel, then, of hum cap, which we call the black ram ;
And we do sit and swagger, and swear that we are men ;
But yet before 'tis night, I'll stand you half a crown,
That if you ha'n't a special care the ram will knock you down.

The next specimen of rural minstrelsy is in a more tuneful spirit, but, we fear, is not such a genuine production of the soil as the foregoing. It was, however, frequently sung at Sussex sheepshearings in former days, and, for aught we know, may be so now :—

> Here the rose buds in June, and the violets are blowing ;
> The small birds they warble from every green bough ;
> > Here's the pink and the lily,
> > And the daffydowndilly,
> To adore and perfume the sweet meadows in June.
> 'Tis all before the plough the fat oxen go slow ;
> But the lads and the lasses to the sheepshearing go.
>
> Our shepherds rejoice in their fine heavy fleece,
> And frisky young lambs, with their flocks do increase ;
> > Each lad takes his lass,
> > All on the green grass,
> > Where the pink and the lily,
> > And the daffydowndilly, &c.
>
> Here stands our brown jug, and 'tis fill'd with good ale,
> Our table, our table shall increase and not fail ;
> > We'll joke and we'll sing,
> > And dance in a ring ;
> > Where the pink and the lily,
> > And the daffydowndilly, &c.
>
> When the sheepshearing's over, and harvest draws nigh,
> We'll prepare for the fields, our strength for to try ;
> > We'll reap and we'll mow,
> > We'll plough and we'll sow ;
> > Oh ! the pink and the lily,
> > And the daffydowndilly, &c.

Some of the toasts given on these occasions were very quaint and had their special ballads attached to them. One of these latter commenced as follows :—

> Our maid she would a hunting go,
> She'd never a horse to ride ;
> She mounted on her master's boar,
> And spurred him on the side.
> Chink ! chink ! chink ! the bridle went,
> As she rode o'er the downs.
> So here's unto our maiden's health,
> Drink round, my boys ! drink round !

The supper finished, and the profits shared, the members of the Company shook hands and parted, bidding each other good bye till another year, and each man bending his steps towards his own home, which, probably, lay widely apart from those of his late companions. Yet, year after year, the members of these Companies meet together, make their accustomed round, and carry out their compact with much goodwill and harmony. It is one of the few remaining instances which modern life affords of such voluntary associations for a common end. In the Middle Ages they were, doubtless, more common. The Masons of those days went about in Companies from city to city, and parish to parish, raising those wonderful and beautiful fabrics which are the admiration and marvel of later days. Other "craftsmen" did the same, and to the present day in Germany it is a part of the education, or apprenticeship, of the youth who desires to be a skilled workman, or "meister," thus to travel from place to place for a certain period.

But *we*, too, are wandering from our subject—our shearers, who, indeed, are lost to us as soon as the shearing feast is over. They disperse and resume their ordinary occupations. Neither are these merry meetings so common as they were wont to be. There has been an attempt to revive the harvest-feast, in another, and, doubtless, improved form; but we are not aware that this has extended to the sheep-shearing feast. As a consequence, the shearers take home more money to their families. The amounts they earn are, indeed, pretty considerable, and to be a good shearer is not only honourable, but profitable. The best sheep-shearer is a man known in his district, as the best swordsman or bowman used to be in former days. Some few years ago prizes were contended for at County competitions, and in one special instance the shearers of East Sussex were pitted against those of West Sussex, in Goodwood Park, and were beaten. But this, too, is a practice that has passed away. So

"The old order changeth,
Yielding place to new."

But, let there be what changes there may, there will always be shepherds and sheep-shearers in the land; they are two of those primeval vocations which remain unchanged and unchangeable in the midst of our changing civilization, and men must cease to be civilized,—cease to eat mutton and wear broadcloth,- before the shepherd and the sheep-shearer disappear from the ranks of labouring men. May they, then, flourish,—and in Sussex, and on the Sussex Downs especially, *esto perpetua!*

In the absence of any picture of a sheep-shearing feast, the following graphic description of a harvest-home one, given by Mr. Rock, jun., of Hastings, in the 14th volume of the Sussex Archæological Collections, as witnessed by him at a farm in Boreham Street, in East Sussex, twenty years previously, may be taken as closely approximating to it, especially in the gravity of the proceedings! The custom of "turning the cup over" was, doubtless, common to both occasions :—

"Towards the close of the meal we could hear a rather monotonous chanting proceeding from the kitchen. The effect, heard faintly, except when occasionally an intermediate door was open, was by no means disagreeable. Our host explained the ceremony of 'turning the cup over,' which was going on in the kitchen, and invited us to take part in it ourselves. Accordingly we all adjourned to the kitchen, which we found crowded with the labourers of the farm and the men who had assisted them in harvesting.

"At the head of the table, one of men occupied the position of chairman; in front of him stood a pail, clean as wooden staves and iron hoops could be made by human labour. At his right sat four or five men who led the singing; grave as judges were they; indeed, the appearance of the whole assembly was one of the greatest solemnity, except for a moment or two when some unlucky wight failed to 'turn the cup over,' and was compelled to undergo the penalty in that case made and provided. This done, all went on as solemnly as before. The ceremony, if I may call it so, was this :—

"The leader, or chairman, standing behind the pail with a tall horn cup in his hand, filled it with beer from the pail. The man next to him on the left stood up, and holding a hat with both hands by the brim, crown upwards, received the cup from the chairman, on the crown of the hat, not touching it with either hand. He then lifted the cup to his lips by raising the hat, and slowly drank off the contents. As soon as he began to drink, the chorus struck up this chant :—

> I've bin to Plymouth, and I've bin to Dover,
> I have bin rambling, boys, all the wurld over—
>   Over and over and over and over,
> Drink up yur liquor and turn your cup over;
>   Over and over and over and over,
> The liquor's drink'd up and the cup is turned over.

"The man drinking was expected to time his draught so as to empty his cup at the end of the fourth line of the chant; he was then to return the hat to the perpendicular, still holding the hat by the brims, then to throw the cup into the air, and, reversing the hat, to catch the cup in it as it fell. If he failed to perform this part of the operation, the fellow workmen, who were closely watching him, made an important alteration in the last line of their chant, which in that case ran thus :—

> The liquor's drink'd up and the cup *aint* turned over.

"The cup was then refilled and the unfortunate drinker was compelled to go through the same ceremony again. Every one at the table took the cup and 'turned it over' in succession, the chief shepherd keeping the pail constantly supplied with beer. The parlour guests were of course invited to turn the cup over with the guests of the kitchen, who went through the ordeal with more or less of success. For my own part, I confess that I failed to catch the cup in the hat at the first trial, and had to try again; the chairman, however, mercifully gave me only a small quantity of beer the second time.

"This custom of 'turning the cup over,' with its accompanying chant, was rather amusing at first, but, after hearing it, as I did on the occasion I have described, for at least four hours without intermission, it became at last rather tiresome. I could not get the tune out of my head for a long time after—indeed, I have not got rid of it yet."

SUSSEX CHARACTERS—SKETCHED FROM LIFE.

The Sussex Cottage-Wife.

HOW is it that all the Diaries have been kept by men? One would have thought this form of autobiography would have been better suited to women. Women have more leisure to jot down events as they occur; they are greater observers of the little matters that make up life and Diaries; they delight in gossip —in the passing scandal of the day—in what happens to Mr. This or Mrs. That. And yet no Diaries have been left to us by women, —only by men like Pepys and Evelyn and the Duc de St. Simon, who, doubtless, had a good deal of the woman in them,—at least, the first and last had,—but who were *de facto* men. What would we not give for a Diary by the wife of Anthony Stapley, or of Thomas Turner, or of the Rev. Mr. Moore ! But the good women only talked, and left their husbands to write, and when, as they perhaps thought, the Benedick was casting up accounts, or making out bills, or writing sermons, he was chronicling *his* peccadilloes and *their* infirmities of temper !

We can only now wish that the tables had been turned; that the wife, like the lion in the fable, could have told *her* story. What a light would be thrown on many phases of character that now lie hidden in obscurity, and can only be saved from total oblivion by the imperfect medium of the memory.

What would we not give, for instance, to set down in that freshness and sharpness which a Diary can only convey the features, moral, domestic, and physical, of that specimen of the old English cottage-wife whom we will try to introduce to our readers under the name of Mrs. Colly. She was a type of a class that was once common in Sussex, and which is still to be found in the little gable-end cottages with their open timber-work fronts and shelving thatched roofs, coming down at one end nearly to the ground, and little lattice-windows that look out so cosily from the eaves. Prettier pictures than these cottages for landscape painters, standing back as they generally do from the roadside, amidst apple, cherry, plum, and pear trees, it would be difficult to find in any part of the world. And inside, for the most part, they are as clean, and neat, and as carefully tended as their gardens are outside,—not without a touch of the ornamental, too, in gaily-coloured cups and saucers, and mugs and ornaments of quaint design, or even of the artistic, in engravings illustrating the adventures of Joseph and his brethren, or other Scriptural incidents, intermixed, probably, with adventures in the sporting field. But when thus much has been said for their cleanliness and neatness, not much remains to be added of a complimentary character. The brick floor is generally damp and uneven—the ceiling (often formed of massive oak beams, strong enough to support a Church and heavy enough to pull it down) is low; and the only place free from draughts full of rheumatism is the innermost corner in the huge open chimney—the place, according to immemorial usage, of the male head of the family. As to the female head, to judge by our typical cottage-wife, Mrs. Colly, we should say that she *never* sat down. She was always, like the sun, running her daily course of duty. Her place was on her feet, and the chairs of her cottage were for her visitors—not for her. As some good women are sure that they never should live " if so be they took to their beds," so Mrs. Colly was assured that her days would be numbered " if so be she took to a chair." Her legs were, to her thinking, made to be used as much as her hands, and as these latter were never idle, so were the former members never indulged in inactivity.

And yet their burthen was not very great. A body more spare than that of our Sussex cottage-wife is rarely to be met with—that is, in a sound healthy body, which, as was her boast, had never known a day's illness since it could take care of itself. Take care of itself? No, that won't do. Little care of itself had that little spare body ever taken, but a great deal of other people. In the days of crinoline, it was a wonder, and also to us a delight, to look at that little active body, as straight as a poplar, and as curveless. "Lines of beauty," physically, there were none; but, morally, in the absence of all thought of self, Mrs. Colly was a line of beauty from the top of her head to the soles of her feet. And at each extremity there was something to admire. Her hair, —and she was above 70 when we first knew her,—was raven-black, and there was plenty of it, too; her eyes matched with it, bright and quick, and with a kindly twinkle in them. If you could take your eyes off her's,—and it was not easy,—and give a glance at her feet, you saw that her boots, thick and leather-laced as they were, could bear the scrutiny. A tidy busy little soul was Mrs. Colly—one whose whole life had been spent in keeping the wolf from the cottage door and making good the adage that cleanliness is next to godliness. She had, of course, married young—all Sussex cottage-wives do marry young—and, equally of course, had had a large family of children, whom, to use her own expression, " she had brought up in the fear of God from a month up'ards." What they did in the month that preceded the "up'ards" we never could fathom. It was one of those mysteries of speech that went down to the grave with Mrs. Colly. But as to the after-months of the children's existence, there was no doubt about them. We knew all the children, sons and daughters, and they were all worthy of their mother, or nearly so. How she and her husband (a farm labourer) could have brought them up, as they did, and given them the learning they possessed, and which was Mrs. Colly's boast,—for they could all read and write, and she could do neither,—is another mystery that we must leave unsolved.

But there was a still greater mystery connected with Mr. and Mrs. Colly: a mystery that made at once the glory and the misery of their latter days. Nay, gentle reader! do not suppose we are going to indulge you in your love of the sensational. We have no tale of murder or robbery or treasure-trove to tell you. These poor peoples' lives were absolutely destitute of incident : and yet there was a tragical interest in what we are going to relate. It lay in this : Besides having brought up and educated a large family, without help from the parish, this Sussex cottager and his wife had "put by" a hundred pounds ! Do not smile ! You cannot, perhaps, conceive the amount of labour and privation that that £100 represented. You cannot imagine the depth of joy that it gave, or the magnitude of care and anxiety that it imposed on its possessors. The millionaire may be so rich that he could not if he wished cast up the sum of his riches, but he is not, nor ever will be, so rich as the Sussex cottager who has "put by" from his earnings one hundred pounds ! And then the care and trouble that attended on that treasure—where to keep it whilst it was being saved, and what to do with it when it was saved; who can sum that up ?

Well, our Sussex cotters, like richer people, found a way, or rather had a way found for them. The hundred pounds was disposed of—" invested, the wise it call,"—in plain language, was got rid of, chiefly through the medium of a favorite daughter whose husband was not well off, and partly through a Building Society, by the aid of which Mrs. Colly hoped some day to live in a house of her own.

We confess we could never understand the right and the wrong of the matter, though we listened to the history of it a hundred times, except to arrive at this conclusion : that the money was gone—irretrievably gone— as much as though it lay at the bottom of the sea—or more so.

And here lay the seat of Mrs. Colly's domestic mystery :— that hundred pounds, to her mind, was as much in existence as when it lay in good gold and silver at the bottom of a worsted stocking ! She had never spent that money—she had never thrown it away, or lost it, or been robbed of it, according to her notion of throwing away or losing or robbing. She had only lent it or invested it, and, accordingly, the hundred pounds was in existence, and was her's, and nobody else's !

It would have been a cruel thing to undeceive her, though we doubt if any one could have done that. The saving of that £100 had entered too much into her life—had been the centre round which too many joys and hopes and cares had grown, to be rooted up. And we verily believe the old lady died in the full belief that she—not her husband, though he survived her—not her daughter or daughter's husband, who had borrowed it—not the little building speculation that had swallowed up a good deal of it —was the owner of that £100, but she—good, honest, hard-working, simple Mrs. Colly!

Our Sussex cottage-wife was a woman of strong affections, or she could not have brought up that large family so well "from a month up'ards." And when boys and girls were grown up and were "doing for themselves," she turned her affections towards her cow. Her husband was a taciturn, eccentric old man—not unlike an old withered crab-apple tree—who never uttered a syllable if he could help it, and who had strange notions of dieting himself on horse-radish and such-like things. His wife did her duty by him; but as to love! There might have been a time for such a word; but it was gone, like the hundred pounds; and now the chief object of Mrs. Colly's affection was her cow. Yes, she *had* a cow, and not only lived by it, but for it. It was husband, children, friends, neighbours, all! She talked to it, kissed it, fondled it, fed it, and suffered no one else to milk it. She would lead it through the green lanes and let it browse on the roadside grass, lovingly watching it. Its shed was much warmer than her own cottage; and it was much better fed than herself. It was the one little drop of comfort in the domestic cup of poor Mrs. Colly, when the cottage had been emptied of its children and the stocking of its savings; and it was a happy thing that Mrs. Colly died first. She died quickly, as Sussex cotters and their wives are apt to do She had never had a day's illness until she was upwards of 70, and at that age she would walk long distances to take her milk to customers or little nosegays to friends. When sickness came, it came suddenly and sharply, and Mrs. Colly had not long to endure the misery, to her, of lying in bed doing nothing! She would have preferred, if her wishes had been consulted in the matter, to die on her feet, upright as a post, and talking, most probably, about that £100 and its whereabouts and wherewithals,—her thin bony hands crossed before her and her bright eyes looking sharply into your's.

One of her dying symptoms was a strange fancy,—it was only a fancy,—that her husband had been experimentalizing upon her with some of his strange vegetable diet, to which she had a strong aversion. She never suspected that she was out of health in a natural way. She never had been unwell—had a thorough contempt for doctor's stuff, and wondered why people's hair turned grey. She went down to the tomb with hers as black as ebony, and, to use one of her quaint expressions, "carried all her teeth with her to the grave." A harder-working woman, a better mother or cottage-wife, never slept the last sleep. Some may be disposed to ask what was a life so passed in drudgery, so limited in its sphere, so barren of what we call pleasure—what was it worth? But Mrs. Colly never asked herself such a question. No Sussex cottage-wife ever does. They have too much to do. A great modern philosopher has said that directly we ask ourselves if we are happy we cease to be so. And, certainly, Mrs. Colly never put her happiness to such a test! Perhaps she did not know what happiness was—certainly she had no knowledge of the enjoyments in which most of us place happiness. But neither did she ever ask herself if she was miserable, because she was as ignorant of that feeling as of its opposite. She had, of course, her pains and her pleasures,—her ups and her downs,—her bright days and her dull days. But she was, up to 70 years of age, a healthy, hard-working, children-loving, flower-loving, and cow-loving woman—fond of talking, but never sitting down to talk—fond of walking, but never "going out for a walk,"—fond of a little bit of wholesome meat, but seldom or never getting it. Altogether she was an excellent specimen of a class of women who have had much to do in the making of England's greatness for they have brought up and sent into the world not a few hard-headed, strong-fisted men, who have done many a good day's work for themselves and their country; and we doubt if England would miss many classes more than that of which we have tried to draw a sketch—a faint one, we know it is—a mere passing "glimpse"—in Mrs. Colly, the Sussex cottage-wife.

THE OLD SUSSEX RADICAL.

LET me try to draw out of the dim memories of the Past the features of a man who was one of the latest representatives of a class now passed away—of a class, indeed, which may be said to have passed away before he had closed his long life, and which is no longer remembered except by a few who, like myself in early life, were brought into contact with one of them.

I mean the men who used to be called Radicals, but whose principles were more nearly allied to Republicanism. I do not refer to the later Radicals who flourished in the days of the Reform agitation—the Hunts and Attwoods and Burdetts,—who, too, are now extinct and pretty well forgotten. The old Radical, or Republican, of my recollection was a contemporary of Fox and Philip Francis and Cartwright, and a member of the "Friends of the People" Society. He had, in his youth, read the "Letters of Junius" fresh from the pages of the *Public Advertiser*; he had execrated a kingly favourite in Bute, and sympathised with the fall and death of Chatham. He had, in middle life, shared with such men as Wordsworth, and Coleridge, and Southey in the enthusiastic hopes to which the opening scenes of the French Revolution gave birth in England—had watched its rapid passage from Constitutional reforms to democratic excesses, and had seen the Liberal ranks in England divide at this point: one section seceding with Burke to the Tory ranks; the other remaining true to their colours with Fox and Sheridan and Grey.

Clio Rickman,—for it is he of whom I write,—was one of these latter. Of his early life I know nothing, except that he was a member of the old Sussex Quaker family of that name, which still survives, and, I believe, flourishes, in this County. He must have early left the communion of the Friends, taking with him, however, that spirit of resistance to undue authority and that contempt of forms which used to characterise the followers of George Fox. But with the narrower and more ascetic spirit of Quakerism he had no sympathy, and he showed it by assuming that classical name of Clio—the Muse of History—which most certainly his Quaker parents did not bestow upon him,* but by which he was always known to his friends in after-life. It was in his latter days that I knew him,—and that was 50 years ago,— when he stood out of society like some old rock that carries down to later ages the evidence of a pre-existing world. How well do I recollect the mingled feelings of awe and wonderment with which I first encountered the heavy brow and severe-looking eyes that frowned from beneath a low-crowned, broad-brimmed straw hat! with what astonishment I looked at his quaintly-cut blue coat, with enormous brass buttons and square lappets, from the pocket of one of which peeped the corner of a silk handkerchief, at which many generations of London thieves had pulled and tugged, and never succeeded in extracting it ; and for a very good reason : it was securely sewn with stout pack-thread into the inner lining ! That handkerchief was for show and sport,—it was the fashion of the day so to show the handkerchief,—the fellow-one was for use, a huge coloured cotton one, and it lay safely inside the low-crowned straw hat that covered that capacious brow. That hat itself was a prodigy in the hat-way. It was a feat for us youngsters (I am speaking of days when I was a boy) to lift it, or to try to lift it; for its weight was enormous, and was yearly increased by a pound of solid paint bestowed upon it. It was the whim of its wearer so to freshen it up. But he had another reason : namely, to strengthen its powers of resistance to the blows of highwaymen (there *were* highwaymen in those days) or collision with mother earth. Men in those days, when they travelled, rode on horseback, like men, or in gigs, like travellers. Stage-coaches had not yet commenced their career, and removed the responsibility of travelling singly in your own vehicle. Clio Rickman was a

---

* His Christian name was Thomas.

I

great traveller, and he owed his life more than once to the strength of that straw hat, which had been shattered to pieces by a fall instead of his skull.

But to proceed with my description of Clio's outer man. To match the blue coat there were the yellow leathern breeches, showing a section of the manly calf above a pair of top-boots, such as the old stage coach-men used to wear down to our times, but which, years ago, were worn by Dukes, Earls, Lords,—nay, by Royalty itself. This was the garb, essentially English, which the Duc de Chartres (afterwards Philippe Egalité), Mirabeau, and other admirers of English institutions took back with them to France in the days of the first National Assembly, and it was adopted by the French patriots,—by the Girondists especially,—and is still to be seen in the French historical pictures of that day. Its adoption in France was a compliment to England and English freedom; but it passed away, like other fashions, with the stormy days that followed, when French Republicanism was swallowed up in Imperialism and English Republicanism was at a discount under Pitt and Dundas. Clio Rickman and a few others of the old school (Cobbett was one of them, though *he* came later than Clio) were faithful to the old garb, in spite of the gibes of little boys in the streets and the staring looks of older people.

The impression left by this old English garb now-a-days is a vulgar one; it smacks of stage-coaches and old-fashioned farmers. But, 100 years ago, it was the dress of gentlemen and wits and men of letters and *beaux;* and Clio Rickman was all these except the latter. He was a thoroughly well-educated man—well up in the classics—a good French scholar (I think he must have been a good deal in France, in the early days of the Revolution—probably because England was too hot and Pitt too hard for him), and had no small literary talent, which he exercised both in verse and prose. But he was a politician *avant tout*; and his opinions, like those of so many of the older English Radicals, verged on Republicanism. There was an excuse for it in those days, which does not exist now. At the close of the last century and the beginning of the present the Crown and Church and Aristocracy were all-powerful, and the excesses of the French Revolution had created such a strong feeling against popular concessions,—concessions now amply made,—that men might well be forgiven for thinking that liberty could only be secured by a Republic, and that Monarchy was another name for despotism.

Amongst those who so thought was Clio Rickman, and he did not conceal his opinions, either in speech or in writing, or, so far as that could indicate them, in dress. His favourite English heroes were Lord William Russell and Algernon Sidney,—his classical ones, Cato, Brutus, and Cassius. The education of men in those days was more classical than it is now; allusions to classical events by public speakers were more frequent, and the names of Greek and Roman patriots were much more common in men's mouths. In fact, there was a strong classical, and that signified Republican current, running through society and politics. We have worked out of that and beyond it in these days,—I mean as to the Republicanism. We have known how to erect Republican institutions under the forms of Monarchy, and it is a happy solution, which Sidney and Horne Tooke,—aye, and a greater than either of these—Cromwell,—would have rejoiced at, could they have achieved it.

Well, in Clio's days it was otherwise. A despotic government was "on the cards," and, therefore, men were Republicans. But Clio's Republicanism, at the time I knew him, was of a very harmless kind. It was more literary than political. It showed itself in quotations from Milton's Areopagitica and Addison's "Cato," and, above all, from Shakspeare's "Julius Cæsar." Men *did* quote in those days,—they seldom venture on it now, and, when they do, generally contrive to misquote. And we youngsters were made parties to the plot against Royalty. I was elevated to the rank of Brutus; my brother (being older and "leaner") was dubbed Cassius, and "so we played *our* parts." But, in the midst of all our honours, I never lost the impression that Clio himself was a Cæsar! If, in theory, a Republican, in practice he was a despot. He ruled us, or would have ruled us, with a rod of iron. He had been brought up in the old school, under a despotic *régime*, when boys were scourged up their "Gradus ad Parnassum," and girls were kept strictly to their samplers and spinets, and when they grew up into men and women they carried out the same iron discipline. Day, the author of "Sandford and Merton," was a dreadful old tyrant to his children, and we all know how old Sir Timothy Shelley treated his son Bysshe. I don't know but that we go too much the other way now : it is the children who tyrannise now, and the parents have to "knock under." All Spartan and Roman discipline has been thrown to the winds, and boys and girls "rule the roost."

Clio resisted this innovation ; he always turned Brutus and Cassius out of the warmest seats by the fire, and took possession himself,- unless a milder authority interposed in the maternal form, and then Clio retreated and discipline went to the wall. For Clio, under his rough exterior, and with much love of self, had the true spirit of gallantry. The old Radicals, or Republicans—the terms were almost synonymous—were *preux chevaliers* to woman ; they treated her with a degree of deference that is now almost unknown. They had no notion, indeed, of giving her the franchise, nor had she of asking for it ; but the influence of woman was great with them, and they loved to bow themselves before her. My mother's word or look—and yet there was nothing terrible in either —was law to Clio ; and it was a shield extended over Brutus and Cassius against the tyranny of Cæsar ! So we never had occasion to kill him in the Capitol ! He died in his bed, after the Reform Bill was passed ; and to the last he wooed the Muses, in lines to Clelia, Cynthia, and Celia, and set down in terse prose his "Reflections" on men and things. These appeared from time to time in the columns of the *Brighton Herald*, and must supply the place of that Diary which few men could have kept better than he, and which would have been invaluable had he kept it, but which, unfortunately, he never did keep. Else what scenes might he not have described with the Hones, the Horne Tookes, the Thelwalls, and even older Radicals than they, with whom he must have come in contact !

Clio lost a much-loved wife in early life, and, when I knew

him, had, properly speaking, no home—only a room in London, to which he retreated, like an old lion to its den, when he was too infirm to travel. The world was *his* home. He loved to call himself, and to hear himself called, "a citizen of the world;" he belonged to no sect of religion, and his political and social sympathies took in the whole human race and made light of the distinctions of classes or of nations or of skins. He had few family ties; but he had a good many friends, who, in his latter days, when he was somewhat out at elbows with fortune, showed their friendship by providing for those few wants or luxuries— snuff and tobacco were the chief of them—to which he was tributary. In his palmy days, he was always travelling from country to country, or from County to County. It was one of his boasts that no Englishman could be in his company half-an-hour without betraying to him by some peculiarity of speech the County to which he belonged; and of the customs of all these Counties he was a master. He was as much at home in Yorkshire or in Hampshire as he was in Sussex; and, at last, he was equally a curiosity in all! Adhering to the old garb and fashions of his youth and manhood, and to the old ways of thinking and speaking, he looked like a portrait cut from an old picture-frame, and he talked like a page out of Boswell's "Life of Dr. Johnson." He was an original man at all times, even in an age when men were more original than they are now, and, as men looking and thinking like himself dropped off, he became a representative man of a by-gone age and extinct class,—a strong age and a sturdy class, with more of iron in it, and less of tinsel, than the present; who had to contend as freemen with real dangers to liberty, of which we know nothing, and were prepared to "champion" their principles "to the outrance," though they led to the scaffold. Exile and imprisonment, if not worse, were always in the probabilities of the "old Radical"— Clio had undergone both — and for words and acts which now enter into our daily life. So no wonder they were a little stern and sour, and looked, as Clio did, with a certain contempt on the Radicals of a later age, who had never known a Pitt or Castlereagh, nor faced an Ellenborough!

More of the Roman had these men in them than our later race of Englishmen : and, looking back to Clio Rickman, as I do still, with something of a boy-like affection—for I never knew him but as a boy, as a Triton among the minnows,—I would not question his title to have inscribed upon his tomb-stone the Brutus-like epitaph :—*Ultimus Romanorum.*

THE OLD SUSSEX TORY.

THE present age knows no such being as the Old Tory—he is dead and buried; nor do I know that it would be desirable to resuscitate him or the world in which he lived. But he had his good points, and, at all events, he was a reality: something upon which you could lay your finger, and, in due course of time, fix your memory, with the consciousness that there *was* something to rest upon. Your Conservative is a mere name: the man who answers to it to-day was something else yesterday, and may be something else to-morrow. Nor does he even know to-day very clearly what he is. His is a transitory, uncertain state of being. But the old Tory never changed. My Uncle Mason never changed. The world—that is, *his* world—moral, political, literary—might fall to pieces around him; he, like the righteous man of Horace, remained erect and immovable. He was born a Tory; he lived a Tory; and he died a Tory.

How he came to be born a Tory, I don't know,—not having known his mother. But she must have been a strong-minded woman and very difficult to be turned from a thing when she had made up her mind to it. Her partner in life must have found her a great help—and a great hindrance. She must have exercised his patience and sharpened his temper. I hold to the opinion (and in this I, too, am a bit of a Tory, for I have no foundation for my opinion) that we derive a large share of what we call character from our maternal parent and that we suck it in with our mother's milk.* My Uncle Mason must have sucked very hard, for a more incorrigible unmitigated old Tory never breathed. His Toryism was in his flesh and bones. It was not an affair, as our

---

* Shakspeare makes Volumnia say to her son, Coriolanus,—
 "Thy valiantness was mine: *thou suck'dst it from me.*"

modern political opinions are, of reasoning and arguing and such-like slow processes. It was a constitutional (I mean physically constitutional) fact—bound up with blood and brain and nerve and muscle and associated with the insoluble mysteries of human nature. The idea that my Uncle Mason could have been anything but a Tory! Absurd! ridiculous! It would have been to deny his *raison d'être.* He was, I am sure, a little Tory in long clothes, and held to his mother's breast as Filmer did to the Right Divine of Kings! Whilst at school he must have had a foretaste of all his subsequent joy and pride at the spectacle which the schools of those days presented of unbounded authority and dogmatism on one side and a mixture of servility and brutal tyranny—over younger boys—on the other.

But these are mere surmises of mine as to my Uncle's juvenile Toryism—a re-construction of the boy from the man. It was as a man—as a formed and complete Tory—that I knew him, when his education was finished,—when the Tory principles of the age had poured into the matrix made by Nature to receive them, and had become as hard and infrangible as the bronze statues of stern-looking Imperators that are still dug up after ages of entombment. The man and the politician were then welded together, so that no fracture could be detected to indicate where the man ended and the politician began.

And yet my Uncle was no politician—that is, in the modern sense of the term. He never made a political speech in his life, and couldn't for the life of him have laid down a political axiom. He was a party man to the backbone; and his party was the Tory party. Never did any man give himself up more completely to his party, in a day when men *did* give themselves up to their party in a way they don't know now. It was his country—his religion —the pride and glory of his life. He would do anything for it. My Uncle was as moral and as kind-hearted a man as ever breathed. But when his party was in question—when there was a Tory to be returned for his native City, which was Chichester, or for his County—which was Sussex—he threw religion, morality, friendship, kind-heartedness to the winds with a fine disdain.

He meant his party to win; and *that* meant that he meant to stick at nothing which might make it win. He entered without scruple—nay, with a ready joy—into the most atrocious conspiracies against his fellow-citizens. He lured them away from the poll on the last day of polling by the most abominable devices—he locked them up in his own house until the poll was closed; and he boasted of it afterwards (I have heard him do so!) as though he had performed the noblest, most patriotic, and most meritorious action in the world. How he escaped fine and imprisonment for this defiance of the law, I never could discover, except it was that everybody else in those days did the same thing, or admired those who did; or perhaps,—and I think this is the better explanation of the two,—there were, as our neighbours in France say when a man has murdered half-a-dozen people, extenuating circumstances in his favour which saved him from the penalties of the law. For, if there was a man in his own City who was respected and beloved, it was my uncle Mason, not on account of his Toryism, but in spite of it. Everybody knew that he was a rank old Tory, and stuck at nothing to serve the Tory cause; but then, too, everybody knew that he was just as ready to serve anybody who needed assistance, whether he was Tory, Whig, or Radical. He was really a man who did not allow his left hand to know what his right hand did, for the latter was continually in his breeches' pocket in search of coin, which, certainly, when found, was not "made a note of." This, too, smacked of Toryism. It was profuse expenditure, without discrimination, and which often did as much harm as good. It was to gratify his own feelings, without reference to consequences: a kind of Timon of Athens bounty, in which pride went hand-in-hand with generosity. "What a liberal, free-handed man Mr. Mason is!" That was a bit of flattery he could not resist, and so, in his little way, he scattered a shower of silver on his path, and was an inexhaustible mine of wealth to beggars, impostors, flymen, railway porters, chambermaids, and all the fry who feed on the little weaknesses of humanity.

But this profuseness was a growth of his latter days, when he moved more freely about the County in an official capacity. In the earlier period of his career he was, like nearly all English tradesmen 100 years ago, a fixture in his shop. This fixity of tenure by the shopkeeping class was a characteristic—I might almost say a principle—of Toryism. When the middle-classes began to move about—that is, when fast-going coaches and railways came in—Toryism went out. Locomotion was its deathblow. The true old Tory shopkeeper never thought of stirring from his city—scarcely of going over the sill of his door. One shopkeeper kept watch over another, and if a truant were found out—and he was sure to be found out if he only went over to the other side of the street—the astounding fact was proclaimed to the community, and suspicions flew abroad as to the state of the truant's affairs. No man—that is, no man of the shopkeeping class—dared to leave his counter for an hour, much less a day, except on causes of paramount necessity, duly set forth, without danger of being thought mad or insolvent! This was a rule of the "good old Tory days," and need I say that my Uncle strictly adhered to it? In his house—his castle—he was supreme—his wife permitting, despotic : workmen and shop-boys were slaves, who had no will of their own. Out of his own house *he* was a slave : a slave to public opinion—that opinion being Tory.

Such restraint in the present day, when the middle-classes, and even those below them, have broken through every shackle on freedom of movement imposed by "the wisdom of our ancestors," would be intolerable. But it was not so to our grandfathers. We are the creatures of habit, and it was as easy to them to stay at home—never to stir from the street in which they were born—for months, and even years together, as it is for us to rush about the country in railway carriages, or fly from land to land—not to say Continent to Continent—in steamers. My Uncle, then, as a model Tory tradesman,—he was a bookseller,—never went from home for years together in the early days of his life except on duly-announced matters of business. His City was his world, and everything was measured by it. It was an old Cathedral City, ruled by the Clergy, and hedged in by great aristocratic families : the perfection of a Tory city ; and Toryism grew up to perfection in it. Nothing was good that was not old ; nothing respectable that was not sanctioned by the Clergy ; nothing to be admired that was not aristocratic. Age, the Church, the British Constitution (the latter being embodied in a Tory Government), these were the essentials of British liberty, prosperity, and orthodoxy, and they were summed up in one term : Toryism. It took in religion, morals, and manners—even literature.

I have said that my Uncle was a bookseller, and in that day a bookseller, and particularly in a City like Chichester, meant a man who understood books as well as sold them ; for books *were* books in those days, whereas now they are merely so much printed paper. Let me explain. *New* books, whether in the shape of newly-written works or new editions of old authors, were the rare exceptions; *old* books were the staple of a bookseller's trade : good old authors, weighty in subject, and printed and bound in the same solid fashion as they were written in ; Hooker, Stillingfleet, Chillingworth, Barrow, Tillotson, and such like. Now, my Uncle Mason was thoroughly up in his business ; he understood books, and especially books of Divinity,—for which, of course, there was a large demand in a City like Chichester,—as well as any man in England. I don't say that he knew their contents—that he had ever read one word of them. That was not bookselling knowledge. But he was perfectly conversant with all the mysteries of the trade—knew which was the first, or second, or third edition of such an author—which edition, by the mistake of a word, or the transposition of a letter, was worthless, and which, by the presence of a certain passage or print, was invaluable. It was a treat to see him handle such books as these—to see him seize on a ponderous old tome—fling it open at the title-page—give it a glance, and then fling it from him with contempt or close it with a certain air which, without disclosing too much to the ignorant outer world (that was, if it was a public sale), said as plainly as action could speak, " *That* book is mine. I know all about it, and you—the *profanum vulgus*—don't." I should have liked to see the auctioneer in that day who dared to gainsay my Uncle Mason in the matter of a book!

But it was only one class of books my Uncle cared about, as it was only one set of opinions that he had any regard for. And that was old, and chiefly theological, books. For new works, and even for new editions of old works, he had unbounded contempt. In a later day Bohn was his horror. In an earlier day he turned up his nose at the different " Libraries "—" Classical," " Scientific," " Standard," &c., &c.,—that were sent forth by Murray, Longman, and Bentley. He would not give a novel house-room. For years did he stand out against the rage for " The Great Unknown," until all the world hailed the writer as Sir Walter Scott, and I never exactly understood how he gave in to this violation of his principles and passed under the yoke of the Magician. It was too tender a subject to question him about, for my Uncle, as a genuine old Tory, never admitted that he had been wrong—never changed his course if he could possibly help it; was always ready to stick to his ship and go down with it if it was necessary. He was certainly a very obstinate man. He cherished prejudices where other men conceal them. He would not sit down to a table at which there were 13 guests. He would make anyone who upset the salt throw some of it over his or her left shoulder. He never started on a journey, nor would allow anybody else if he could help it, on a Friday. And everybody humoured him in his crotchets; such a dear, kind-hearted, jolly, plucky old gentleman was my Uncle the old Tory. He was a child in his opinions, but he was a hero in his acts; he did not know what it was to be " daunted ;" he had what Churchill calls a " matchless intrepidity of face ;" he would speak up like a man to my Lord Duke This or to the great Earl of That, if there was something to say for the public good or for a neighbour or a neighbour's son. He did not know what fear—I had almost said modesty—was. He was certainly a very impudent man. That is, there was nothing he would not ask for, and nobody whom he would not ask, if he wanted to get something for somebody. There was no shame-facedness in him. And that, too, was a characteristic of the old Tories! They thought they had a right to all they could get, which was pretty well everything that was worth having in this world! As to any body else, on the other side, wishing to get any thing—it was robbery, spoliation, high treason, revolutionary! Put the rascals in gaol—transport them—hang them up as high as Haman!

A terrible blow was the Reform Bill, and, after that, the repeal of the Corn Laws, to my Uncle Mason. They upset his politics, as Sir Walter had demoralised his bookshelves. He could not argue—what old Tory ever could?—but he knew it was all wrong, and that it would end in anarchy and destruction. It was too bad of us reforming youngsters to plague the old gentleman like so many picadores, and to make him rush, in defence of his beloved Toryism, into the very jaws of an absurdity! There was no difficulty in it. Like the great mass of his party, he knew nothing of principles: only men. Now, one of his men was Huskisson, whom he knew personally, and potently believed to be a Tory, whilst all the while that great statesman was working hard to bring about that Free Trade in commerce which Peel and Cobden and Bright afterwards achieved. It was glorious to hear my Uncle, in the innocence of his heart, launch into praises of the Statesman who had done all he could to consign the Tory party and its principles of protection in trade and intolerance in religion to the tomb of all the Capulets! It was too bad of us! But we gave over at last, as we grew wiser and he grew older, and the old Tory floated into the calm waters of consideration and respect which his fine qualities as a man—*passons* the politician—deserved. He never surrendered a single point; he was as obstinate, as superstitious, as proud of his party—which existed no longer—as contemptuous of Whigs and Liberals as ever— as fond as ever of telling what enormities he had committed for it. But he gradually grew less bellicose—would come down with less scorn upon the saucy Liberal "boys"—(his nephews were always "boys" to him)—submitted more and more to female sway—was milder in denunciation of political and literary revolutionists like Cobden and Bright, Dickens and Thackeray—troubled himself, in fact, less about the singularly perverse course which the affairs of the world in general, and of England in particular, had taken since he commenced his career, some 80 years before, as a Tory, and, at, last, amidst the general regret of all who knew him—Liberals, Radicals, Conservatives,—there were no Tories left,—took leave of a world he had so often doomed to destruction as peacefully and forgivingly as though he had not been the last of the Old Sussex Tories.

THE SUSSEX COUNTRY DOCTOR.

IN the present day, doubtless, men attain to higher points in particular branches of science than their forefathers; but it may be doubted whether they are so well informed " all round." At least, as I look back to the past, the memories of men start up, not in one, but in all departments of life, who were more varied in their learning—who could turn with greater ease than men do now from one topic of discussion or speculation to another—who, if they were professional men, were also literary men, and not only literary men, but politicians, and could, if need were, throw aside politics, and talk nonsense to a pretty or philosophy to a plain woman. Music was not cultivated to so high a point as it is now-a-days; but there were more men who could play an accompaniment on the flute or violin, or take a part in a duet or trio, a glee or a madrigal. No such things as Fine Art Exhibitions were known; but yet the engravings of Raphael Morghens and of Bartolozzi were generally to be found on the walls of such men as these, in town and country, and they were more appreciated, perhaps, than the expensive works of Art bought by millionaires for their Palaces in the present day, not because the buyers appreciate them, but because it is "the right thing to do," and also because they are a good investment.

Of all the men who partook of this rounded character,—and there were several within my experience,—40 years ago,—the one who came up to the highest point was Charles Verral, the " Doctor," by universal consent, of Seaford. I may proclaim his name without reserve, for he has long passed away, and no member of his large family, and few, if any, of his still larger circle of friends, are to be found at Seaford; and if his name and memory still linger there, it is probably because they are linked with the almost tragic troubles that clouded the latter years of his life.*

Charles Verral stood high as a medical practitioner in Seaford and its neighbourhood. I do not know whether he held a diploma as a physician, or whether, as is often the case in the country, he was called "Doctor" by custom or courtesy. His profession was that of a general practitioner. But he was much more than a doctor. He was a poet; he was a dramatist; he delighted in literature and music and Art; he was a keen politician, and could hold his own when brought, as he was, into contact with men moving in the highest political sphere, like Agar Ellis, and even, if I mistake not, Canning, the intimate friend of Agar Ellis, and a frequent visitor to his seat at Seaford. And then his general conversation and his manners with all men,—and women, too, and children, — were so charming, so genial and pleasant, so frank and natural—that in a moment, to whichever of these categories you belonged, you were at your ease, and gave all that you had to give of your little store and received with delight the larger measure he dealt out in return. And of this, on his side, there was no stint. He delighted to pour forth his full streams of knowledge and fancy; but neither did he overwhelm you with them. It was to him as great a pleasure to receive as to give—to encourage others to show their little stock of knowledge as to exhibit his own larger one. He never preached, like Coleridge, or talked for victory, like Johnson, but made conversation a pleasant mode of bartering thought for thought. He delighted in being one of a very happy circle, and drew into it young, middle-aged, old—male and female—all who chose to come. And few could resist the charm of his manners —the liveliness of his conversation—the pleasant play of his features. Not that he was a handsome man—far from it. His

---

* Several letters drawn forth from residents in Seaford and its neighbourhood by the appearance of this paper in the *Brighton Herald* attested to the fact that Dr. Verral was still, in 1876, remembered with strong affection and respect by many of his former friends and patients.

features were homely, but full of tender sensibilities, and they always kept tune with his thoughts. A deaf man might almost have held converse with him by watching the flash of his eye and the quick play of his mouth. Children would gaze upon him with open eyes that did not wander as he talked about what they could not understand, in tones which they liked to listen to, and which held in check for a time their natural restlessness. There was a spell in his manner which, whether he unbent himself to them,—and he often did so,—or whether he soared into regions beyond their comprehension, held them in rapt attention.

With all his attractive qualities for society, Dr. Verral delighted in the joys of his own home. Few kept a more liberal or hospitable table. Hospitality in those days, —and especially in the country, where travelling was difficult, and visitors were rare,—was a more common virtue in England than it is now-a-days. The table might not be so richly decorated or loaded with such delicacies ; but it was rich in a wholesome abundance, and the house was flung open with a freedom that is unknown in these days. Where, now-a-days, a man in the position of Dr. Verral,—that is, the Doctor of the Parish,—gives one dinner to his friends,—upon a sumptuous scale, doubtless, and with a show and heat and crowding that make half the guests ill, and at an expense that impoverishes the host for the remainder of the year,—the old-fashioned Doctor would give twenty—thirty—" parties." Nay, in the case of a man like Dr. Verral, so sought after and so ready to give pleasure, it was almost "open house" all the year round. His family was large, and additions to it did not seem to make much difference in the provision to be made for every-day wants. There were pupils, too, and sometimes in-door patients—nearly always friends—his own, or his sons' or daughters'—all, by whatever title they sat down at his table, certain to become, before they rose from it, admirers of "the Doctor."

Such households as these are now things of the Past, and the men who formed the centre of them seem to have passed away. A vigour of body and an elasticity of mind,—above all, a variety of gifts,—were demanded of them, which few possess now-

K

a-days. More is given to the hard work and routine duties of life; the line is stumped out, the rails laid down, and in the grooves of this the head of the family revolves—round and round—until he has completed his day's work, and then he goes home to oil the machinery—to eat and drink and sleep—perhaps to be amused, but certainly not to amuse. He is too "used up," or, more likely still, he has never acquired the art of amusing. It is "not in the bond." He can talk about his profession or business, or, if he has read his newspaper, on the news of the day, if there happen to be any. But as to heading a table, or leading the conversation, he is unequal to it, and, aware of his deficiencies, either declines "society" altogether, or calls in the professional singer and player,—above all, he relies on the "professed cook" to cover all home defects.

Where and whence such men as Dr. Verral (and they were once a class in country-towns) obtained the stock of health and spirits to fit them equally for business and for pleasure, I cannot say. But they *did* it. They made long rounds of calls on their patients—talked, read, wrote, aye, and studied too, and, when all was done, took the head of their table as fresh and as genial as though they had been getting themselves up specially for the occasion. Was it the lighter spirit in which they went to their work, with a happy unconsciousness of that rivalry that now propels a man along his narrow path, forbidding him to diverge to the right or the left, lest another should seize the opportunity, and rush past him in the race for life? Was it this? or was it the hardier constitutions of the men, often fresh from the farmhouse or the country rectory, and renovated by fresh air and a ride "after hounds?" Or was it the diversity of occupation—the passing from one pursuit to another, suffering none of them to become that engrossing toil of mind or body which grinds the intellects of a man to dust? One or other of these it must have been that gave such strength and elasticity to men of Dr. Verral's stamp, and made them men of society as well as of science, poets and politicians, writers and talkers and thinkers, and not unfrequently, as in Dr. Verral's case, inventors as well.

For, wide and active as were the Seaford doctor's pursuits, he sought to extend his practice by a mechanical invention, for the relief of patients afflicted by diseases of the spine, of great merit, and which has been of late years turned to good account. He himself did not live to see it brought into full operation. In his autumn of life a quick succession of terrible misfortunes fell upon him that would have shattered a man of less vigour, and did, most unquestionably, embitter and shorten his life, though he bore up against them with a courage that was heroic. His eldest daughter—a beautiful and talented young woman, and whom her father loved with almost more than a father's affection — the daughter who was a mother to his younger children when he was left without a wife—she faded and pined away, and at length died, under a home-sorrow that had thrown a dark shadow on her father's happiness and against which she could not bear up. The lines in which he poured forth his grief for her loss are now lying before me. They are amongst the most touching and beautiful, I think, that a poet has ever penned in the bitterness of a death-grief. They were written down at the house of an old friend in Brighton, whose daughter had been *his* daughter's dearest companion. I make no excuse for copying them from the columns of the *Brighton Herald*, where they appeared above 40 years ago :—

>We've lain her in the cold churchyard,
>   Beneath a mound of clay ;
>Lov'd as she was, we've left her there,
>   To loathsome worms a prey.
>
>And, lo ! the mist is on the hill,
>   The rain is driving fast,
>The evening skies are wild and dark,
>   And chilly blows the blast.
>
>And now this roof—for many a year,
>   In many a storm so wild—
>This humble roof has been a home,
>   A shelter for my child.

And now this roof, her father's roof,
  Can be her home no more—
How shall I close mine house to-night?
  How bear to bar my door?

To shut her out for whom so oft
  It gladly open'd wide !
To shut her out that was so long
  My joy, my hope, my pride !

We, in these sheltering walls, to-night,
  On beds so soft and warm,
Shall rest uninjur'd by the shower,
  And shelter'd from the storm.

But she is in her cold, damp bed ;
  And o'er her lonely grave
The driving shower will wildly beat,
  The ruthless whirlwind rave.

And livid fires will glare around,
  And pealing thunders roar ;—
How can I close mine house to-night ?
  How bear to bar my door ?

But wildly, idly flows my verse :
  How vain are thoughts like these !
She heeds not now the driving shower,
  The tempest, or the breeze.

In vain for her the Spring shall bloom,
  The suns of Summer glow ;
In vain the fruits of Autumn smile,
  The blasts of Winter blow.

Untroubled in the silent tomb
  She lies in peaceful sleep,
While I in this wide world am left
  To wander and to weep !

Clarissa ! thou hast been to me
  A blessing from thy birth !
And time, that added to thy years,
  Still added to thy worth.

A little lovely babe wert thou,
  Within thy mother's arms,
When first thy father used to gaze
  And doat upon thy charms.

And still thy form more lovely grew,
  And still thy mind improved;
Thou wert by all who saw admired,
  By all who knew thee loved.

And oh, when grief was at my heart,
  And care was on my brow,
My kindest, truest, comforter,
  My fondest friend, wert thou.

Nor was thy kindness unconfess'd,
  Thy fondness unreturned—
Living, how dearly wert thou loved!
And dead, how deeply mourned!

Some readers of these most beautiful and heartrending lines (I do not think they are excelled, if equalled, for pathetic beauty in all the range of English poetry) may ask how could grief so deep put itself into the trammels of verse? The reply is, that, to a poet, verse has no trammels; it is the natural channel of his thoughts and feelings—the form in which his emotions clothe themselves as they well up in his heart; it is to him what tears, and lamentations, and wringing of hands are to other men,—a relief and a consolation, and also a necessity; for if he did not so give vent to his feelings, they would break his heart or madden his brain.

The death of this beloved daughter was Dr. Verral's greatest sorrow in life, and yet it had its consolation in the memory of the affection and virtues of the lost one. For that which had preceded it there was no consolation, and in that which followed there was a sharper pang. Dr. Verral was walking in the streets of London with a younger child—a merry laughing girl. They had to cross a road, crowded with traffic, and, before they could do so, a heavy vehicle was upon them; they were struck down, and when he rose, the child lay dead at his feet. In his agony he threw himself on the corpse and refused to be comforted. What comfort, indeed, was there for a father so bereaved of his child?

Before the last of these terrible misfortunes had fallen on Dr. Verral, his home at Seaford had been broken up, and he had begun the world again in another sphere. Into this I will not follow him. It was as a country Doctor—the centre of a large circle of friends and patients—the adviser,—the comforter,—the friend of rich and poor,—the delight of society,—the authority in all matters of literature and Art and politics,—it was as the Doctor *par excellence* of Seaford that I knew him; and his memory is so connected with the place, though it knows him no longer, that I never hear it named without recalling him. Perhaps there are some few others who still do the same; for he was not a man, once known, to be forgotten. His place is not filled up. Nay, the place itself no longer exists. Here and there an old-fashioned " country Doctor " of the type of him of Seaford,—a man of varied parts—with much wisdom as well as of " infinite mirth,"— is to be found. But the race is fast dying out. The great towns— so much more numerous and so much greater than in times past— naturally draw to them men of such talent as Dr. Verral. The country cannot compete with them as it used to do,—aye, and successfully too. Lesser men will now do for country places: well qualified, doubtless, for their duties, but not such "all-round" men,—not philosopher, poet, politician, as well as physician—like the Doctor of Seaford.

SELF-EDUCATED SUSSEX MEN.

IN a few years there will be no such thing as an uneducated boy in England, and then the race of self-educated men will have disappeared. When the State left children to themselves,—and a great many parents followed the example of the State,—there was, no doubt, a great deal of ignorance—a large tract of brain that lay fallow. But then, as if to compensate for this, here and there a boy or man took the work into his own hands—educated him-' self; and of all modes of education this, if not the best, is the most fruitful in results. For it can only be done, to follow out my rural simile, on "strong soils," where Nature has been prodigal of her gifts, and has given a decided bent in this or that direction. As a rule, this bent is followed in self-education (in enforced education it is often neglected or even thwarted), and the consequence frequently is, such a crop as you only get from virgin soil.

These self-educated men, in times gone by, made some amends for the general sterility : they vindicated the goodness of the native stock—the natural richness of the soil. But they were not a happy race of men. They had to fight against circumstances, and the jealousy of neighbours, and the doubts and indifference of friends and relations; above all, against the pride and superciliousness of "Society," which sets its face against irregular and erratic outbursts of talent, and closes its ranks like a Macedonian phalanx against such as attempt to make a way by force of genius into its Sacred Band !

So I do not know that the amount of human happiness will be much diminished by the loss of the self-educated man—of those who attempted to mount upwards, not by the national staircases, the Public Schools and the Universities, but by a kind of hand-over-hand process, as boys climb trees and sweeps get to the top of greasy poles ! For, though the prize at the top of the pole may be carried off, it is seldom worth the pain and suffering which it costs,—to the sweep or to the self-educated man !

At least, that is the conclusion I have come to from my knowledge of self-educated men in this town of Brighton. I have known some,—who that has lived 60 years has not? They used to be more or less numerous in every town in England, and were generally as much known for their eccentricities and misfortunes as for their talents; for, doubtless, in the process of self-education, tares came up plentifully with the wheat; there is little time for weeding—it needs a very strong man to weed himself!—and so the penalty paid by the local genius—the poet, or the linguist, or the mathematician—was, too often, to be pointed out to strangers as a kind of *lusus naturæ* ; in Sussex phrase, a " main clever kind of chap," but as much to be laughed at and pitied as admired or rewarded.

If I had to exemplify this class of men, as it existed in Brighton some 40 or 50 years ago, I should choose two men whose names are still familiar in some ears, and whose features are not quite forgotten, but whose works are passing more and more out of fame and use. I mean George Frederick Richardson and Samuel Simes : the former a native of Brighton ; the latter of Lewes.

I am not going to write their biographies, nor to draw a parallel between them, after the manner of Plutarch, but simply to illustrate my theory of self-educated men. In some respects they agreed, as in local position,—for both sprang from the middle classes, and one, like De Foe, was a draper—the other, like Stowe, a tailor ; but in most other respects they were as different as men could well be whose tastes lay in the same direction—Literature— and who drew everything from their own resources.

George Richardson had an intellect that was fitted to go in harness—to be trained and cultivated up to a very high point ; to submit to the severest discipline. If it had been his lot to be born in Germany, he would have been a renowned Professor, and even if educated at Oxford or Cambridge he must have risen to high fame as a scholar. He had a prodigious memory and an aptitude for acquiring knowledge that has seldom, I believe, been surpassed in this country. With an education such as country tradesmen's sons received 60 or 70 years ago,—that is, in the three "r's"—reading, writing, and arithmetic,—and by his unaided efforts, he acquired a knowledge of Greek, Latin, Hebrew, and then, passing on to modern languages, he mastered French, German, and Italian, not only so as to read, but to speak them with ease and elegance. This, remember, was at a time when the Continent was closed to Englishmen — when the language of Germany was almost unknown to the English people, and when its literature was only beginning to be recognised in Europe. Richardson assisted to make its claims known by translating the poems of Korner and Schiller and other German poets. How he came to speak as well as to know the language, and also French and Italian—I think, too, Spanish—I know not,—or rather I do know a little ; it was by his indomitable courage and perseverance. Not a wandering native of Faderland or of Gaul or Italy came across his path—were it a Bavarian broom-girl or an organ-man or a Savoyard—but Richardson would accost him or her—and bring his book-knowledge to the test of proof. He did not know what shame-facedness was in the acquisition of a language. He "aired" his French and German on all occasions, in season and out of season, never forgetting a lesson or a hint, until he became the proficient he was—until his French had all the exquisite *netteté* and *finesse* of a Parisian, and his German was acknowledged to be classic. It was, doubtless, in languages that the bent of George Richardson's genius lay most strongly ; but he had tastes and talent in many other directions. and, as opportunities offered, he followed them out. He was devotedly fond of music, but had no voice—and little ear ; and yet he laboured to sing Mozart with the same assiduity, though not with the same success, that he did to recite Schiller or Korner. How well do I remember his singing-lessons !—and his pathetic entreaties to his instructress (a very patient, good-tempered young lady), after successive failures in " La ci darem " or " Nott' e giorno," for " just once more, my dear Miss ——— !—just *that* passage, if you please, once more : " that "once more" being as illimitable as space !

To the Graces, indeed, though our friend Richardson made tremendous sacrifices, his sacrifices were not altogether acceptable. He carried the same indomitable perseverance into his cultivation of them that he did into the severer studies of language, and, later in life, science, but not with the same result. In music and dancing (and, oh ye Gods ! how he did labour to dance !) he failed decidedly, and in acting he was not successful. He played Iago to, I think, Barnard Gregory's Othello on the Brighton stage, and I don't know which was the worst of the two ; but, between them, Shakspeare got terribly maltreated ! No, the Graces were not propitious to George Richardson, devoutly as he worshipped them. In literature, he was much happier. He wrote in many styles—in verse and in prose—as a translator and as an original author—as an essayist, a critic, and in a light pleasing polished style that recalled the social sketches of Addison and Steele in "The Spectator" and "The Tatler." A series of these, under the title of "The Visitor," appeared in the *Brighton Herald* between 40 and 50 years ago, and they contain matter that would justify a more permanent form of publication. Some idea may be given of the vein in which they were written by the following *jeu d'esprit* ;—

LETTER FROM MISS AMELIA JANE MORTIMER, LONDON, TO SIR HENRY CLIFTON, PARIS.

> Dear Harry,—You owe me a letter,
> Nay, I really believe it is two ;
> But to make you still further my debtor,
> I send you this brief *billet doux.*
> The shock was so great when we parted,
> I can't overcome my regret ;
> At first I was quite broken-hearted,
> And have never recovered it yet !
>
> I have scarcely been out to a party,
> But have sent an excuse, or been ill ;
> I have played but three times at Ecarté,
> And danced but a single quadrille !

And then I was sad, for my heart ne'er
   One moment ceased thinking of thee ;
I'd a handsome young man for my partner,
   And a handsomer still *vis-à-vis !*

But I had such a pain in my forehead,
   And felt so ennuied and so tired,
I must have looked perfectly horrid,
   Yet they say I was really admired !
You'll smile—but Mamma heard a Lancer,
   As he whispered his friend, and, said he,
" The best and most beautiful dancer
   Is the lady in white," meaning me !

I've been once to Lord Dorival's *soirées,*
   Whose daughter in music excels ; —
(Do they still wear the silks they call *moirés ?*
   They will know if you ask at Pradel's.) —
She begged me to join in a duet :
   But the melody died on my tongue,
And I thought I should never get through it,—
   It was one we so often have sung !

In your last, you desire me to mention
   The news of the Court and the Town ;
But there's nothing that's worth your attention,
   Or deserving of my noting down.
The late-carried Catholic Question
   Papa thinks will ruin the land ;
For my part, I make no suggestion
   On matters I don't understand.

And Pa says the Duke has not well done
   To put his old friends to the rout ;
That he should not have quarrell'd with Eldon
   Nor have turn'd Mr. Huskisson out.
And they say things are bad in the City,
   And Pa thinks they'll only get worse—
And they say the new bonnets are pretty,
   But I think them quite the reverse !

Lady Black has brought out her two daughters,—
   Good figures, but timid and shy;
Mrs. White's gone to Bath for the waters,
   And the doctors declare she will die.
It's all off 'twixt Miss Brown and Sir Stephen,
   He found they could never agree;
Her temper's so very uneven,—
   I always said how it would be!

The Miss Whites are grown very fine creatures,
   Though they look rather large in a room;
Miss Grey has gone off in her features,
   Miss Green is gone off with her groom.
Lord Littleford's dead, and that noodle,
   His son, has succeeded his sire;
And her Ladyship's lost the fine poodle,
   That you and I used to admire.

Little Joe is advancing in knowledge,
   He begs me to send his regard;
And Charles goes on Monday to College,
   But mamma thinks he studies too hard.
We are losing our man-cook, he marries
   My French *femme de chambre*, Baptiste;
Pa wishes you'd send one from Paris,
   But he must be a first-rate *artiste*.

I don't like my last new piano,
   Its tones are so terribly sharp,
I think I must give it to Anna,
   And get pa to buy me a harp!
Little Gerald is growing quite mannish,
   He was smoking just now a cigar!
And I'm fagging hard at the Spanish,
   And Lucy has learnt the guitar.

I suppose you can talk like an artist,
   Of statues, busts, paintings, *vertu;*
But, pray, love, don't turn Bonapartist,
   Pa will never consent if you do!
" You were born," he will say, " Sir, a Briton,"—
   But forgive me so foolish a fear;
If I thought you could blame what I've written,
   I would soon wash it out with a tear!

And pray, Sir, how like you the ladies,
  Since you've quitted the land of your birth?
I have heard the dark donnas of Cadiz
  Are the loveliest women on earth.
Th' Italians are lively and witty,
  But I ne'er could their manners endure;
Nor do I think French women pretty,
  Though they have a most charming *tournure*.

I was told you were flirting at Calais,
  And next were intriguing at Rome,
But I smiled at their impotent malice,
  Yet I must say I wish'd you at home;
Though I kept what I fancied *in petto*,
  And felt you would ever be true;
Yet I dreamed of the murd'rer's stiletto,
  Each night—and its victim was you!

I'm arrived at the end of my paper,
  So, dearest, you'll not think it rude,
If I ring for my seal and my taper,
  And think it is time to conclude.
Adieu, then, dejected and lonely,
  Till I see you I still shall remain,
Addio, mio caro—Yours only—
  Yours ever,—

AMELIA JANE.

P.S. You may buy me a dress like Selina's,
  Her complexion's so much like my own;
And don't fail to call at Farina's
  For a case of his Eau de Cologne;
And whate'er your next letter announces,
  Let it also intelligence bring,
If the French have left off the deep flounces,
  And what will be worn for the Spring!

The hit, too, at the fashionable mania which raged amongst the young swells of that day of driving stage-coaches ("The Modern Phæton"), with its classical allusions, is full of wit, as, at a later day, was the rhyming description of a geological walk with

Dr. Mantell. The lines he addressed to the young lady referred to as his occasional musical instructress, on her marriage day, have a tender grace in them that will justify quotation:—

TO MARIANNE FLEET,

On her Marriage,* March 25th, 1837.

And thou shalt be a bride to-day, thou young, and good, and fair,
And the ring is waiting for thy hand, the wreath is in thy hair;
The young, the gay, the glad, are met to hail the joyous scene,
And thy bridesmaids wait upon thy steps, like fairies round their queen.

Thy young life hath been only past in love, and joy, and bliss;
Thou but hast known a mother's care, a sister's love and kiss;
But thou shalt seek another now, shalt bear another's name,
And the love that we alone have shared, another now may claim!

For thou, fair girl, art like the bird that left her ark of rest,
To seek a dwelling-place on earth, and build herself a nest;
So thou hast left thy happy home, in other spheres to soar,
And, like the dove the Patriarch sent, shalt seek thine ark no more.

And sad our task will be, and long, thy mem'ry to retrace;
To see, in fancy see, thy form, and view thy vacant place;
To dwell with grief on every charm that bade us once rejoice,
And miss the magic of thy smile, the music of thy voice.

One thought the while shall cheer our woes and soothe our grief to rest:
It is the thought, where'er thou art, that thou must still be blest;
For howsoe'er thy lot be cast, wherever thou mayst be,
All gentlest hopes and kindest loves must live and die with thee!

And when before the sacred shrine thou standest shortly now,
To pledge thy faith to God and man, and breathe the life-long vow,
Our warmest loves, our fondest thoughts, shall all be with thee there,
And meet and mingle in the sky in blessing and in prayer!

---

* With her cousin, William Hayley Mason, a godson of Hayley, the Poet

But hark! they call—thy lover waits—no more must we delay,
We fain would hold thee ever thus, yet dare not bid thee stay;
These streaming eyes, these breaking hearts, the pain of parting tell,
And these faint sobs are meant to say, but cannot speak, farewell!

The following graceful lines illustrate the union in George Richardson of tastes usually so opposed as the poetic and the scientific :—

THE NAUTILUS AND THE AMMONITE.

The Nautilus and the Ammonite
   Were launch'd in storm and strife,
Each sent to float, in its tiny boat,
   On the wide wild sea of life.

And each could swim on the Ocean's brim,
   And anon its sails could furl,
And sink to sleep, in the great sea-deep,
   In a palace all of pearl.

And their's was bliss more fair than this
   That we feel in our colder clime,
For they were rife in tropic life,
   In a brighter, happier clime.

They swam mid isles whose summer smiles
   No wintry winds annoy,
Whose groves were palm, whose air was balm,
   Where life was only joy.

They roamed all day, through creek and bay,
   And traversed the ocean deep,
And at night they sank, on a coral bank,
   In its fairy bowers to sleep.

And the monsters vast, of ages past,
   They beheld in their ocean caves,
And saw them ride, in their power and pride,
   And sink in their billowy graves.

> Thus hand in hand, from strand to strand,
>   They sailed in mirth and glee,
> Those fancy shells, with their crystal cells,
>   Twin creatures of the sea.
>
> But they came at last to a sea long past,
>   And, as they reached its shore,
> The Almighty's breath spake out in death,
>   And the Ammonite lived no more.
>
> And the Nautilus now, in its shelly prow,
>   As o'er the deep it strays,
> Still seems to seek, in bay and creek,
>   Its companion of former days.
>
> And thus do we, on life's stormy sea,
>   As we roam from shore to shore,
> While tempest-toss'd, seek the loved—the lost,
>   But to find them on earth no more!

This and many more of his poetical effusions found a place in the best periodicals of the day, and were also published in a volume that is to be found in the Public Library of his native town.

But in the case of George Richardson, as in so many others, the truth of the saying was exemplified, that "a prophet is not honoured in his own country." George Richardson got little honour in Brighton, and less profit. His habits, indeed, were not formed for business. His spirit revolted against the selling of silks and satins behind a counter. I do not think he could always have been very pleasant to his customers. On one occasion, I know, he was not. A lady whom he was serving made an uncomplimentary remark upon his face or figure—in French or German—ignorant of the Admirable Crichton who was rolling out the goods; and Richardson, in his pride or vexation, replied to her in the same language, and, doubtless, with a much purer accent, and in much better grammar. Of course, that lady, the next time she wanted a dress, went for her silks or satins to Mills's or Hannington's! He was very absent, too—had fits of abstraction, in which he did strange things and became the butt of practical jokers, so that it was not to be wondered at that the business left him which he was so desirous to get rid of. He did not, indeed, get into his right place until comparatively late in life, when Dr. Mantell opened his Geological Museum at Brighton; and then there was no man so fit to explain and preside over its treasures as George Richardson, the ex-draper, the linguist, the lecturer, the writer of verse and prose—of touching lines and witty *jeux d'esprit*,—the reporter and journalist, the amateur actor and laborious student of music and dancing! Yes, this self-educated man, having carried his powers into all these and other lines,—amongst them, conversation and mimicry,—found himself at last a worshipper in the Temple of Science,—and a more devoted one never entered it. For the first time his powers were concentrated, —he had a fixed and sole aim and object, and his wonderful memory and organ of acquisitiveness came into full play. In a short time he had so mastered the facts and theories of geology and the kindred science of crystallography that he was able not only to edit—in point of fact, to write—the latest work of Dr. Mantell, founded on the Lectures which that talented man delivered in Brighton, and which, being delivered extempore, were reported by Richardson, but to write a work on the subject which has since become a text-book of geology. So thoroughly, too, did he master the contents of the Mantellian Museum that, when it was bought by the State and transferred to the British Museum, it was necessary to take its Curator with it, and he became a Sub-Curator of the national institution. There he was in his element, and was appreciated at his value by the *savans*, native and foreign, who resorted to the geological department of the Museum, and with the latter of whom, whether French, German, Italian, or Spanish, he was able to hold converse in their own tongues. He was on the way to higher things when his career was suddenly brought to a calamitous close. I have said that in business matters he was never an adept, trusting to others and neglectful himself. He now had to pay the bitter penalty of this indifference to common things—to pounds, shillings, and pence. He had put confidence in a friend, who, at a moment of need, betrayed

L

him—went off with a sum of money which poor Richardson depended on to meet an engagement, and, in the despair of the moment, he put an end to his existence. It was a melancholy termination of a career which was to be admired in many respects, especially in the love of knowledge, of literature and science and Art—indeed, of all that was intellectual—it displayed, and in the indomitable will with which the avenues to this knowledge were stormed and captured by a man who had nothing but his own resources to depend on—who, in the many accomplishments that he possessed, had had no instructor but himself. If at any time the history of the Worthies of Brighton should be written, the name of George Frederick Richardson, linguist, author, poet, and man of science, ought not to be omitted.

In many respects Samuel Simes, though equally a self-educated man—perhaps more so than George Richardson,—for Simes was, I believe, originally only a journeyman tailor, and Richardson was a master-draper and had some advantages in the acquisition of knowledge which Simes had not,—was the opposite of his contemporary. He, too, was literary in his tastes; but his tastes lay towards politics and theology, for neither of which had Richardson any inclination. Simes was, in fact, a "free-lance"— a Switzer of the Brighton Press. He was, in his heart, I believe, a Radical, if not a democrat; but he began by writing for a Tory journal, the *Brighton Gazette*; he then passed on to a Whig or Liberal one, the *Brighton Herald*; and he ended by editing a Radical one, the *Brighton Patriot*. When he died he was on the staff of the *Brighton Examiner*. But the prime of his intellect was certainly given to the *Brighton Herald*. It was not limited to politics, in which he was, of course, curbed in his extreme opinions by the traditions of the journal, but took in a wide range of literature—imaginative, historical, musical, and theological. He was an inordinate reader, and his memory was a tenacious one, so that he could write and talk (and talk well, too) on nearly all subjects. And, like Dr. Johnson, he talked—perhaps wrote—too often for victory's sake, and not from conviction. I almost doubt if he had any settled convictions! He had had no grounding in knowledge—had picked it up in snatches here and there, as birds do their food, and so it lay all higgledy-piggledy in his head, being handy for use in irregular guerilla warfare, such as is often carried on in newspapers; very formidable to the uneducated opponents whom he met in the "Free and Easies" where he reigned, a "Triton among the minnows"; oftentimes, too, very surprising and embarrassing to men more highly and regularly educated than himself, but whose reading had not been so wide, and whose intellect was not so robust as Simes's. But still he was imperfectly educated, and never, like Richardson, found the corner-stone on which he could build up the multifarious materials he had collected into one harmonious whole. For, of that gift of studying and acquiring languages which was Richardson's forte in early life, Simes had not a particle. He knew no language but English, and though he wrote that in a nervous, racy, fluent style, yet even there he occasionally tripped. He wanted some one to revise his "copy," thrown off as it was at a white heat. Nor was he a poet, though he could rhyme, and some of his political squibs, in verse, were excessively happy.

But it was in prose—strong, sterling English prose—which those who run could read, that Samuel Simes shone. He had read Cobbett's political works,—his "Register," "Peter Porcupine," &c.,—and studied Cobbett's grammar, as a young man; and they had not been thrown away on him. He had much imagination, too, though not of a high class, and he had a keen sense of humour. Some of his reports of meetings were masterly. He did not use shorthand,—nobody did in that day, and reports were often the better for it,—having more of the reporter and less of the speaker in them—to the great improvement of the speeches and not to the loss of the reader.

But Simes was not merely a *litterateur*. He had other and refined tastes. He was an enthusiastic lover of music; and here he had the advantage of Richardson. (It is curious how the two men differed!) Whilst the latter laboured in vain over "La ci darem," and murdered "Nott' e giorno" in particular, and the music of Mozart in general, Simes, with a rich mellow voice, could take a part in all the glees, madrigals, and part-songs which are the glory of our English School. He understood, too, something of thorough bass, and could put together a few bars of music. He threw himself into the Mainzer movement, and a work of his (taken from the columns of the *Brighton Herald*), on the management of the voice, had a considerable sale. Then he was a good fencer, at a time when fencing was a rare accomplishment; could swim I don't know how far (not quite over the Channel certainly!), did something with the gloves, and was generally an adept in athletics, and physically, as well as intellectually, a fine specimen of an Englishman. His face,—and here, too, he had the superiority over his contemporary,—was a very handsome one, with a strong resemblance to that of the first Napoleon in his later years: of classical mould and clearly cut, with curved mouth, straight nose, and well-rounded brow. He was surely intended by Nature for greater things than he ever accomplished. Had Fortune been kinder to him—could he have concentrated his powers, he might have left something behind him that the world "would not willingly let die," or, with his robust intellect, he might have sat on the Judicial Bench or been another Warburton in theology. But the common wants of life—the bread and cheese necessities—always pressed too closely on him. He could not wait for his powers to ripen: he wrote to demand; the Printer's devil was ever at his elbow. "It is a work," he once said to the writer of these reminiscences, "which pulverises the brain." It exhausted his, and brought him to the grave before his time, with nothing to mark his long—and, in many respects, able—day's work, except what the columns of a local newspaper contain. And yet I doubt if there be a man in Brighton, or many in all England, at the present moment, who can compare with Samuel Simes in the vigour and variety of his genius; in the ability to sit down, as he would sit down, at a moment's notice and dash off, ready for the printer, a stirring political leader, or an amusing essay, or a pungent report, or a cutting squib, or a clever musical or dramatic criticism. What, indeed, could he *not* do?

All that a newspaper man was called on to do 50 years ago for a local journal he could do; and that was—*every thing*.

I will end by repeating what I said in starting : By and bye there will not be an uneducated man in England; fools, *faineants*, dull men, and all, will be " coached up " to the educational standard. And then, perhaps, the self-educated man will be missed, and even perhaps called for, though, so far as he himself is concerned, I do not think it is to be regretted that he will not answer to his name.

THE LAST OF THE SUSSEX M.C.'S.

"THE Last of the Romans"—"The Last of the Mohicans"—"The Last of the Barons"—we have all read of these famous ultimate personages. And why, too, should not "The Last of the M.C.'s" be enshrined in the mirror of the Past and handed down to the wonder and admiration of succeeding ages?

But we must be quick, or the fleeting image will escape us. There is so little of the solid, of the real and substantial in it, that, as we write, we hardly know whether we are dealing with a substance or with a shadow—a thing that lived and breathed and had a being, or an automaton answering to the pull of a string, and set in motion by a wire.

Let us try and fix our memories. Yes; Lieut.-Col. Eld, the last of the M.C.'s of Brighton, *was* a substantial being, and not merely *vox et præterea nihil*. He really did live and breathe and have a being, though his virtual existence—the period during which he shone as a visible and luminous body above the horizon —was limited to a very small period of time, namely, that which extended from the first of the M.C.'s balls for the Brighton season to the last of those memorable re-unions. For these two or three months Lieut.-Colonel Eld came out of his chrysalis, wherever that might be, and sported a butterfly existence. He was the curious centre of a curious circle—a fast dwindling one even then, and now totally extinct,—of old maids, and dowager aunts, and antique *belles*, all marriageable and all unmarried, who flew and buzzed and droned round the last of the M.C.'s, as ghosts of moths may be supposed to buzz round the ghost of a candle! For wings they had none to burn—they had been burnt off years ago; and there was no flame to burn them! Yet to them he was still a luminary, because all other luminaries had gone out. He was a relic of that Past to which they, too, belonged; and he still kept a hold, feeble as it was, on the Present, to which they clung with a despairing grasp. For nobody could gainsay his title to his position. He *was* M.C. He held it by right of descent from a line of M.C.'s dating back to Heaven knows what point of History or Tradition; and he carried his title in his look, his face, his figure, his every movement! How recall these, except to the memory of those who have beheld them with their eyes?

Only to such as have gazed on the bodily presence of Lieut.-Colonel Eld,—the last M.C. of Brighton,—who have seen him walk down North Street or up the Marine Parade, or down the Marine Parade and up North Street, would we venture to limn that tall and erect and Quixotic-looking figure,—that body poised so exactly upon those parallel legs, which kept such perfect time upon the Brighton pavement! If Archimedes could have made a man, amongst his other marvellous machines, it would have been such a man as our last M.C. It would have so looked—so moved—so stood still; its head would have been so held, in a perfect geometrical line, upon its shoulders; its arms would have so swung, and oh! perfection of Art, its toes would so have pointed, at the only correct angles for toes, right and left! For, as every man has his strong as well as his weak points—as the strength of Samson lay in his hair, and the vulnerability of Achilles in his heel, here—in his toes—lay the strength of Colonel Eld. Here was the essence of the man. His soul, if he had one, lay, not, as some philosophers aver, in the *pia mater*, nor the heart, nor the pit of the stomach, but in the extremity of that member of the body which determines, in the last degree, the most important points in the life of a human being, namely, in which direction he shall go, or to what altitude he shall elevate himself. We mean the toe—the big toe. Other men ignore this great fact, and, consequently, it matters little which way they do go, or whether they go or don't go at all. But in our *ultimus Arbiter Elegantiarum* it was the all-in-all—the real starting-point in life—the summum bonum—the *to* kalon!

But to proceed with our portrait. As Lieut.-Colonel Eld stalked into your sphere of vision there was a something—a *je ne sais quoi*—that struck the imagination at once, and proclaimed to you, "Here is a character—a curiosity—a being that stands by itself, is a law and an example to itself, and is either the first or the last of its kind." It was a puzzle. And you searched in vain for the key to it until, from resting on that calm, imperturbable visage, that towered in the sky, and seemed to seek its natural aliment in the air—thin air—your eyes descended, by the waning medium of his attenuated waist, and the long spindleshanks of legs, to the sharply projected toes. And then you breathed again. Eureka! The problem was solved. *Aut Erasmus aut diabolus.* It was either the M.C. or a dancing-master; and as dancing-masters do not, as a rule, perform their *pas seuls* in the open air, why then it was the M.C. of Brighton, and nothing more nor less!

Let it not be thought that we are gasconading, or going beyond the fair limits of our subject. To show that we are not, we will call into Court a witness, whose evidence on such a point would be accepted by any Court in the world. Let Sydney Smith, the witty Canon of St. Paul's, " come into Court," and speak " the truth, the whole truth, and nothing but the truth," concerning the party in this cause.

" ' I never was in Brighton ' (we quote from the Journal of Julian Charles Young), ' till to day ; but, nevertheless, I have made acquaintance with a great local power,' said he of St. Paul's. ' Who may that be ?' asked Anderson. ' *Who* he is I know not; but I am certain *what* he is. It is that distinguished functionary, the Master of the Ceremonies. It could be no one else. It was a gentleman attired *point device*, walking down the parade like Agag, 'delicately.' He pointed out his toes like a dancing-master, but carried his head like a potentate. As he passed the stand of flies he nodded approval, as if he owned them all. As he approached the little goat-carriages, he looked askance over the edge of his starched neckcloth and blandly smiled encouragement. Sure that in following him I was treading in the steps of greatness, I went on to the Pier, and there I was confirmed in my conviction of his eminence; for I observed him look first over the right side and then over the left, with an expression of serene satisfaction spreading over his countenance, which said, as plainly as if he had spoken to the sea aloud, 'That is right. You are low-tide at present; but never mind, in a couple of hours I shall make you high-tide again.'"

If the whole order of M.C.'s, from Petronius downwards, had been called on to choose a man in whom, as the last of the race, their characteristics should be summed up and most visibly shine forth, they could not have made a better selection than in Lieut.-Colonel Eld. There was the stamp of office in his look and carriage—an imposing air, "as one having authority," that asserted his right to respect, and, in spite of the eccentricity of his manners, daunted the *profanum vulgus* and ensured him from insult. He carried, indeed, a good stout stick (it was the only stout thing about him!), and it was said that he was skilled in the art of using it. But it was not to that stick that he owed his perfect immunity from anything like impertinence. No! It lay deeper than that. It was his perfect adaptation to the part he was playing—the harmony that existed between the man and the office. It is incongruity—a falling short of the true standard—whether that standard be high or low—a hangman's or a king's—that provokes contempt and excites the laughter of "little vulgar boys." If a man play his part, whatever it be, with due regard to the degree and nature of that part, he is recognised as a real thing, and allowed to go by unquestioned and unassailed. Now, this was the case with Lieut.-Col. Eld. The man was made for the office. His body was cast in the M.C. mould, and he had a soul to match. So high, and no higher. You can but fill a vessel, and when Lieut.-Col. Eld was elected to the office of M.C. for Brighton he was filled, and he held all the liquor that there was to pour into him, or that he could hold. The whole world recognised it. How he existed previous to that moment, who can say? We are sometimes inclined to doubt if he did exist at all previous to it—if the occasion did not give him birth—so that, when the moment came, he walked forth, like Minerva from the brain of Jupiter, a complete and immaculate M.C. Who ever saw him under any other aspect?—in any other relationship? He had no wife—no sister, brother, cousins, aunt, or uncle—no relatives—no friends—no acquaintances—only his M.C. surroundings of spinsters, and widows, and "maids forlorn," and they only came forth on the occasion of his balls, to flit round him for a weary night or two, make their offerings (the price of a ball-ticket), and then fade away into the regions of single unblessedness.

They were ghostly assemblages, those M.C. balls. They began in nothing, except the announcement in the local papers that "such things would be;" they brought nothing to nothing—they ended in nothing. Did a single ray of love illumine them? Impossible. Did Hymen ever crown them? Incredible. Hope itself must have withered in such an atmosphere. There were but two elements in them: the M.C. element and the husband-hunting element; and the necessary link was missing! But they were the Avatars of the M.C. of Brighton—the occasions on which he made himself palpable to the senses of his followers, and was a Being. Did any one ever see his name except when appended to the yearly advertisements in the local papers which announced to the Brighton world the fact of the recurring M.C.'s ball? Did anyone ever hear of his doing, saying, suffering anything except as M.C.? Did he ever change in his "outward man?" We never noted it. Did he ever laugh, cry, joke, rage—do anything but walk? One would think that it lay in his office to dance; but he did not. He was the medium by which other people danced, flirted, fell in love, married—or tried to do so—and repented. But none of these things did he do himself. Was he ever merry, angry, sorry, glad, depressed, exalted? We doubt it. He was above, or beneath, "those natural shocks" that flesh is heir to. He wrote on his door, and on his cards, "M.C.," and they passed him by, as exempt from them by virtue of his office. Was he ever ill? He *must* have died, or we should still rejoice in an M.C. But, to ensure ourselves from error on this point, we would prefer to say that he ceased to exist—that he disappeared—that with him closed the dynasty of the Brighton M.C.'s. If he *did* die, only such a pen as that which described the last moments of the Knight of La Mancha could do justice to the scene. But as we have no credible record of his coming in, neither have we any trustworthy report of his going out. Like Arthur, that *flos regum*, *our* flower of M.C.'s may be only hiding his pedal extremities in some Vale of Avilion—behind the faded curtains of a deserted ball-room—until the propitious moment returns when the glories of the olden times shall be revived. Until then spinsters may wail and widows lament: ladies of a certain age and uncertain position may look round with despairing eyes for "help meet for them," and even younger ones may learn the fatuity of balls without partners and take to Rinks! For they have lost their last, best, truest friend, who for "a consideration," would run down their game and bring to their arms a partner. Lieut.-Col. Eld, M.C., walks on earth no more, and Brighton has seen "The last of the M.C.'s."

THE LAST OF HIS KIND.

ACCORDING to physiologists, the sense for which there is no need—no field of exercise—soon grows feeble, and eventually dies out. There is an analogy to this in society. Classes which have lost their uses die out and disappear. Even within my limited experience, I can recall individuals belonging to a class, —formerly, I have no doubt, a numerous one, but which has entirely disappeared in this part of the world,—as much as the great bustards on our Downs. They have not been destroyed like these; but they have ceased to exist because there is no longer a place or a demand for them.

I do not know but that the last representatives of these extinct social classes are as much to be pitied as the last Red Man or Black Man of America or Australia—perhaps more, for their susceptibilities, as belonging to a higher and more cultivated race, must be keener; and their fate is quite as inevitable: there is no escaping from it. They must die out and leave no trace behind them, or only such a trace as survives in the memory of some old friend or acquaintance.

To such a doomed, and now, I believe, extinct class, did Edmund Osmond belong. It would be impossible to find a substitute for him in the present day; and yet he had no place— no defined, fixed place—in society. He could fill up an immense number of little gaps in the social life of his day, but could supply no positive social want; and so Society gradually found that it could do without him, and did do without him, and he pined and withered away like a disused faculty.

And yet there are few men at the present day who can do all the things that Osmond did. He belonged to an age, or, rather, he ought to have belonged to an age,—for when he was born it had gone by,—in which the division of labour had not become a law of society—in which it was not a necessity of existence that a man should be proficient in at least one thing—useful or amusing, as the case may be, to his neighbours—no matter how simple or humble or even how humiliating. Osmond was one of the most handy men in the world, but it was in a way that was not positively wanted. He could draw and paint—he could handle the plane and the saw, the axe and the hammer; he could fish and shoot and skate; he could put a horse into a gig, and drive it when it was in, or groom it when it was out; he could dance and take a part in a glee—even play a little on the flute; was a first-rate ally of mothers in getting up a pic-nic, and could do a little flirting with the daughters, when the mothers were away, or nobody better was at hand. If a gala was to be planned or an anniversary to be celebrated, or honour done or pleasure given to somebody—Osmond was sure to be called in. He could "put his hand to any thing," and was ever willing to do so; and when all was over, there was no unpleasant reminder of his work in the shape of a bill! It was all done for the love and pleasure of the thing.

It is quite certain that there was a day in England when such a man as Osmond was a valuable member of society, and there are still, doubtless, societies in which his various gifts would come into play. He would have been able to "shift for himself" in a new country, or in a half-civilised country, much better than men more highly trained and developed, but only on one side. He would also have been invaluable as an appendage to a great family who could have afforded to support such a man—let him be called the Master of the Revels, or Jester, or what you will—with nothing particular to do — no particular department to overlook, but ready for anything or for nothing, as the occasion demanded, or didn't demand. But times are altered, and men of this kind are not needed now, even in "great houses," in which every officer has his function sharply mapped out—in the household, or in the office, or in the field. Only the Head of the family,—and not always he,—is allowed to give a broad look-out over the expanse of life, and say whether he will work or play—walk or ride or drive—

do much or little or nothing, and in what style he likes. Few Heads of houses, perhaps, can do this now,—they are tethered down too strictly to their duties. And so they have no need of anybody else to assist them in doing—well, I suppose I must say, in doing nothing!

The world into which poor Osmond was born—"an age too late"—persisted in regarding all that *he* did, much and various as it was, as nothing, or next to nothing—counting as nothing, and worth nothing in exchange for it. He was always active; and yet he had the reputation of being an idle man. He was always in request; and yet he was never wanted—in the way in which now-a-days men expect to be wanted—"for a consideration." He had plenty of services to give away, and was ready to give them, and people accepted them; but he had nothing to sell, or exchange, which people cared to pay or barter for. If they wanted to play, or to do anything that was unprofitable, Osmond was the first man to rise up in their thoughts. He had a profession—the shadow of a profession; but it never seemed to stand in his way, and so his friends never thought of it as an obstacle when they wanted him; and he seemed to think still less of it when he was wanted. He was deemed to be a kind of social *flotsam* and *jetsam*, carried by the tide of life here and there, and which any man or woman could pick up and turn to their use without cost to themselves. He was a "gentleman at large," without a groove to run in, but with a certain capacity for moving freely in every direction, as the wind listed or the fancy took him or his friends. He could not "settle down"; it was not in him. He was like a child in this respect, but, unlike a child, he could not be taught and he did not grow older. In face and form he might age; but his nature remained the same—youthful, volatile, anti-utilitarian. As different generations sprang up, they seemed to take him up, use him in their joy and flush of youth, and then leave him—where they had found him. *They* went on to work, in thought or action —to make money, perhaps achieve fame. *He* remained behind— in the play-ground which they had left—a boy-man. I never met with any of his friends, whatever difference there might be in their years, whose memories did not recall him in the self-same light and form—as the best of play-fellows—the quickest to turn his hand to all unprofitable kinds of labour. Who could organise a gipsy-party like Osmond? Who could "get up" a cricket-match or a boating-party, or an angling or shooting excursion like him? Who could paint transparencies for general illuminations (it was then the day of general illuminations), or design pretty devices for coloured lamps, or light them when they were up, or turn carpenter, or blacksmith, or groom, or anything else, " for the nonce," if he were required to do so? His presence was the signal that people were enjoying, or going to enjoy, themselves—that they were taking a holiday—a "red letter day" for themselves in life's almanac, to which, in all probability, they would look back in future years with a certain melancholy pleasure. "Ah, yes, I remember him well. How we did enjoy ourselves that day. What fun we had! Poor Osmond (people got to call him so after a time), poor Osmond was there. What a famous fellow for a party! how handy he was! how clever, how good-tempered! how ready to help everybody and do everything; What's become of him?"

And then, without waiting for a reply, with a half-smile, half-sigh, they put themselves into their groove again, and "move on" in the great daily journey of life.

What to them had been a halt in life—a pull-up—a jaunt—a stroll—was to Osmond life itself. It was a series of halts and jaunts and strolls. He had no power of continuous work. Light loads—for the hour or the day—he delighted to carry, especially when they had to be taken to some pleasant spot, where happy, merry faces were to meet him. But for the heavy loads of life, such as men take up now, his shoulders were quite unfitted. Life had no terrors—scarcely responsibilities—for him; he did not know them or seek to anticipate them as we do. We combat the Future as a deadly foe, and throw the Present to it as a bribe for its favors: because we know it has no mercy for those who do not so propitiate it. To him it ever seemed to wear the face of a friend. Certainly he did not tax it heavily—not, at least, at first. A batchelor, with no encumbrances and a small independence besides what his profession brought him in, perhaps he had no occasion to "look a-head." He certainly did not do so, until it was too late—until he was amongst the breakers. He had been all his life—up to middle-age—like a child playing on the edge of a precipice. He might have gone on until the end, and never known his danger—never known that he was a man born out of date—a remnant of a by-gone class that ought to be and must be extinguished—a doomed man, as much as the Mohican or the Iroquois of the New World; lacking as he did the power to keep up with the pace of the day. He *might* have so escaped, as, perhaps, many another doomed man or animal has done for a time, by a lucky chance. But it did not so fall out. In middle age, Osmond's foot slipped, and he fell—into matrimony. It was like a great bustard coming from some remote spot, where there was just a chance of its escaping the fowler, into the vicinity of a town, or, better, like some old whip driving a stage-coach on to a railway, and thinking to escape being run down. From out of his little bye-way of butterfly life, Osmond came into the eager and crowded highway of life, thinking to make his way like other men. Had they not wives and children, and why not he? Why not, indeed? There were thousands and hundreds of thousands of men, his inferiors in many things, who "got on," and lived, they and theirs, after a fashion. The only difference was, that they belonged to the age in which they lived,—had a place in the "great scheme," higher or lower, perhaps very low and very unpleasant, but still *a* place, which they could hold against the world, and which the world could not or did not wish to deprive them of, for it was of *use* to it. He did and could not make such a place, not for one—for himself—much less for two or three, dependent on him. He should,—so an old naturalist friend of his comically put it,—have done what the insects did which he somewhat resembled in his light-hearted, erratic, day-for-day kind of life: he should have spun a cocoon, beneath a pleasant shady tree, and gone to sleep, to wake up again in a brighter world than this old working-day one of our's has become. As to doing as other men did — taking unto himself a wife — hoping to continue such a race as his—to take his place in the ranks of daily plodders, and to provide for the growing wants of the morrow, it was absurd to think of such a thing. Osmond had never known what to-morrow was in its true sense—in its beef-and-mutton aspect—only in its promise of fruit and flowers, play and pleasure. The responsibilities of the future had never been realities to him—only to this extent : would the wind be in the right quarter for the trout to rise? or would the sky be cloudy enough for the harriers to run? or would the ice bear on Falmer Pond? or would the snow prevent his going to Mrs. Such-an-one's ball? These were the contingencies which chequered Osmond's future—which made it bright or gloomy—gay or sad. It was the simple unreflecting life of a primitive age and race, drawing all its joys and griefs from the surface. Of the complex, artificial life that makes up Society of the 19th century—of its numerous demands and necessities—its checks and safeguards—its provisions and sacrifices, he knew little or nothing. He had never cared much for himself—his wants had been few and inexpensive. He would do anything to give pleasure to others, and there he had not been unsuccessful. But to take up that position in Society which Society expects a man to take when he marries and has children—to be the head of a family—the master of a household —to have such things as servants, tradesmen, landlord, bills, rent, tax-papers, and all the multitudinous appendages of a man who "settles down" in a respectable sphere of life,—all this to Osmond was as strange as knives and forks, bolsters and pillows would be to a Cherokee or a Pawnee, fresh from his forest or prairie ! He had left all these things during his holiday life to his poor old mother (of course, he had been petted and spoilt by her), and she was gone. His wife—well, his wife was as in-experienced as himself and had to learn everything. Before she could do so the lesson was useless : the children's doll-house,—it was nothing more,--was broken up—the last holiday of Osmond was over. He did not die : it would have been better had he

M

done so: he went about the world some time longer, with a bewildered, dazed look, as if he had just woke up, or scarcely woke up, out of a sleep and was trying to remember the dream he had dreamt. Had he been dreaming all his life? And was this the waking up? He, who had always been so trim in his attire—of so smiling an aspect—so cheery in speech—whose thoughts, if not deep, were so fresh and sweet with the freshness and sweetness of the fields and the sky and the water—he now became, as at the touch of a wand, a seared and shrivelled figure—of dingy aspect, with a timid look that shrank from recognition, and a hesitating speech that only echoed with meaningless repetition the commonest sounds that fell from the lips of those who accosted him. His life—such as it had been—had gone out of him. He was now only a shadow of a shadow. Coming from the pleasant bye-ways of life in which he had played, into the crush of the highway, he was at an utter loss what to do. His light wares had been taken readily enough when he gave them, and looked for no return; but there was no one willing to buy them in the heavy-goods market. *Here* he was outbid — fore-stalled — ridden down by stronger men — browbeaten, roughly-elbowed—finally, heart-broken. He must have felt, poor fellow, that he was *de trop*—in the way—an impediment and an encumbrance even to those whose pillar and prop he should have been. They left him, or he left them—I don't know which. He again reverted to his original state of bachelorship—the life of irresponsibility,—uselessness, if you will,—for which alone he was fit. But it was stript of all its little joys and delights: its ornaments and attractions. The boy-man of a former age had attempted to become the full man of this, and had failed. He, a mere skirmisher on the skirts of life, had sought to enter the ranks of the heavy-armed disciplined army, and had found that he could not wield its weapons or bear its armour or even keep his place in its serried ranks. So, like the wounded deer (his heart *must* have been wounded), he sought the old covert and lay down and died.

The world did not miss him; and yet he was the last of a

class that made the world more pleasant; and those who knew him in his early days may in vain look round for a successor to him. At first, perhaps, they do so with a kind of regret—for did he not give and take much pleasure?—but, as they recollect his fate, and how inevitable that fate was, they must end with the hope that the world—the busy, hard-working, use-exacting world—may never know another Osmond—that he may be "the last of his kind."

THE SUSSEX REGICIDES AND THEIR CONTEMPORARIES.

IF we are to judge by the number of Sussex men, or men from Sussex, whose names appear on the High Court of Justice which tried and condemned Charles I. for treason to his people, or even of those whose names are attached to the warrant for his execution, this County took its full share in the guilt or glory of that act. In the Ordinance passed by the House of Commons for the trial of Charles Stewart for a "wicked design totally to subvert the ancient and fundamental laws and liberties of this nation, and in their stead to introduce an arbitrary and tyrannical Government," 131 persons were nominated to sit at Westminster as a High Court of Justice, and of these 131 persons (headed by Fairfax, Cromwell, and Ireton) eleven were Sussex men, some of them members of families which still stand high in the County. Thus we find in the list Peregrine Pelham, Abraham Burrell, Roger Gratwick, Herbert Morley, Anthony Stapley, James Temple, Gregory Norton, John Fagg, William Cawley, William Goffe, and John Downes, all either members of Sussex families or sitting for Sussex Boroughs. The 131 members of the High Court of Justice, as it was called, embraced a large proportion of the then House of Commons—itself a remnant of the famous "Long Parliament"—with a small infusion of the Upper House, which, as a body, had refused to join in the vote for the trial of the King, and had been then set aside. Of these 131 Commissioners, however, a large number shrank from the odium and the risk of such a daring act, and never took their seats at all. Such a defection was provided for by making twenty members of the Commission sufficient to form a Court; and the prudence of this step was soon seen. At the first meeting of the Court, in the Painted Chamber, there were only 52 members present; on the second occasion, when the Court entered upon its functions—when the

King was arraigned before it, and when every Commissioner present rose to his name, there were 65 present. Upon this critical occasion there was a considerable defection in the ranks of the Sussex members; but six of them, namely, Peregrine Pelham, Gregory Norton, William Goffe, William Cawley, James Temple, and John Downes, answered to their names, and Anthony Stapley and Herbert Morley joined on future occasions. John Fagg rather assisted, we are told, in making preparations for the trial than attending it as a Judge; and his name does not appear in any of the sittings.

The highest number that sat on the Court at any time was 69. But the number of those who actually signed the warrant for the execution of the King was 59; 44 signing their names at once in the Painted Chamber, and 15 afterwards. These 59 were the Regicides; the men who took on themselves the responsibility of an act which struck Europe with dismay and called forth, perhaps, a greater amount of horror than any deed involving the fate of an individual which stands recorded in the history of this country.

Amongst these 59 Regicides seven Sussex Members are to be found, namely, Peregrine Pelham, Anthony Stapley, James Temple, Gregory Norton, William Cawley, William Goffe, and John Downes.

As one of forty Counties, and that by no means the largest in extent or population, Sussex thus bore its full proportion of responsibility for the execution of Charles the First.

Public opinion is still divided as to the justice or iniquity, the wisdom or folly, of the act by which Charles was brought to the block. But few, we take it, will now join in the hue and cry raised against his judges after the Restoration, or approve of the ruthlessness with which they were hunted down and handed over —some to the executioner, some to the assassin's knife, and some to perpetual banishment from their native country. As the acts and motives of men are weighed in the impartial balance of history, and the consequences of those acts stand out distinctly in relief, very different judgments are pronounced upon them at different periods. Without any desire, therefore, to include the

Sussex Regicides among the Worthies of their County, they may, at least, in the present day, claim to figure among its remarkable men and to have that veil drawn aside beneath which it has been the fashion to conceal them.*

The Regicides did not belong to the scum of the land. In social position the majority of them were of the landed gentry class. Indeed, as we read the Sussex records of the struggle between King and Parliament, we are surprised to find how large a section of the upper classes took part with the latter, and how many of them even adhered to the fortunes of Cromwell and the Commonwealth. Among those Sussex Members of the Long Parliament who took the Covenant,—one of the most decisive acts of resistance to the King,—or were in the military or civil service of the Parliament—were a Pelham, a Shelley, a Stapley, a Temple, a Morley, a Parker, an Onslow, a Goodwin, a Selden, a Gratwick, a Middleton, a Courthope, a Fagg, a Gerrard, an Apsley, a Hay, a Baker, a Marlott, a Springett, an Eversfield, a Trevor, a Boord, and a Challoner. These, with others of the same rank, were a fair representation of the gentry and richer burgesses of the County. On the other side were the Gorings, the Lewkners, the Alfords, the Lunsfords, the Coverts, the Bisshopps, the Bowyers, the Culpeppers, the Fords, the Morleys (a different branch from that of Colonel Herbert Morley, of Glynde), the Sackvilles, the Howards, the Ashburnhams, the Carylls, and the Campions.

As early as 1642 Sussex had sent up a petition praying "for a thorough reform of religion." The middle-classes of the County, —now coming to the front,—were decidedly with the Parliament ; Rushworth remarking of Sussex, as of other Counties in the south and east of England, that, though many of the chief gentry were for the king, " Yet the freeholders and yeomen being generally on the other side, as oft as they (the chief gentry) attempted to show themselves, they were crushed, and their endeavours de-

---

* Not one of the Regicides finds a place in Lower's "Worthies of Sussex," although Jack Cade stands among them !

feated." For "chief gentry" we might, perhaps, more correctly read "nobility" in the above quotation.* The majority of the gentry, as also the great body of yeomanry and townsmen, were with the Parliament. Many, doubtless, like the Pelhams, the Gratwicks, and the Eversfields, fell off from the popular cause as it partook more of a Republican character. But others, like Col. Herbert Morley, Sir John Trevor (who married Hampden's daughter), Herbert Springett, Sir Gregory Norton, Anthony Stapley, and Sir John Fagg, adhered to it to the last, and it is in the ranks of these men that we must look for those who sat on the High Court of Justice, and, still more, who signed the death-warrant of Charles the First.

Perhaps the most prominent and active man on the Parliamentary side in Sussex was Col. Herbert Morley, of Glynde, and Member for Lewes and the County of Sussex. Of a good family and large possessions, he was one of the first to accept a Commission from the Parliament and to raise a regiment in Sussex ; he aided Waller in the capture of Arundel and Chichester, and maintained the military supremacy both of the Parliament and of the Commonwealth in Sussex up to the era of the Restoration. Twice he was nearly performing very memorable deeds. It was his soldiers who stopped and questioned Charles the 2nd when that Prince was on his flight from Worcester to Brighthelmstone,—a danger from which the ready wit of the King assisted to deliver him,—and Evelyn, his old schoolfellow and his friend to the last, thinks Morley might, with a little more decision, have anticipated the part of Monk in the restoration of Charles II., or spoilt that General's game, if he had been so minded. But, though an honourable and a consistent man, and a steady friend to liberty,—probably because he was such,—Morley shrank from extreme courses, and thus, though he was appointed one of the High Court of Justice and attended three of its sittings, he did not sign the warrant of execution. It has also been surmised that

---

* In the first Royal array there were only two Sussex names : Col. Ashburnham and Capt. Ford.

he favoured the escape of Charles II. from his soldiers. So, at the Restoration, he was leniently dealt with, and got off with a fine of £1,000. He died in peaceable possession of his Sussex estates, and lies buried in Glynde Church.

Abraham Burrell and Roger Gratwick (Member for Hastings) never attended the High Court of Justice at all, though nominated on it, and, therefore, may be concluded to have disapproved of it.

We now come to the Regicides Proper—to those men who did not shrink from putting their hands to that deed which stands out so prominently in the history of England,—nay, of Europe— and which, they well knew, sealed their fate if the tide of fortune ever turned against their cause. Both the gentry and the burgess class were represented amongst these men. To the former belonged Anthony Stapley and James Temple, Peregrine Pelham and Gregory Norton, and to the latter William Goffe, William Cawley, and John Downes.

William Cawley has many titles to be placed at the head of the Sussex Regicides, whether they be looked upon with a favourable or unfavourable eye. He belonged to the burgess class. His father, John Cawley, was a brewer of Chichester, was thrice Mayor, and his monument and effigy are still to be seen in St. Andrew's Church of that City. His son and heir, William Cawley, who was born in 1602 (his father died in 1621) was, there is no doubt, the most popular and influential man of his day in Chichester. He sat both for Midhurst and Chichester in Parliament, and his name appears as taking the Covenant on the same day (June 6, 1633) as his fellow-Sussexian, John Selden, and a still more famous man, Oliver Cromwell. He was appointed by the House as one of the Commissioners "for demolishing superstitious pictures and monuments" in London, and he was selected to return thanks to the Divines who preached before Parliament on August 28, 1644—a fast day—" for their pains in their sermons." At a later date he was empowered to pay to "three able preaching Ministers" in Chichester £100 a year each out of the estates of the Dean and Chapter. In all probability he was, like Cromwell, with whom he is said to have been on terms of close friendship, an Independent in religion; and, when war broke out between King and Parliament, he, like Cromwell, joined the army and received a Commission, though we hear nothing of him in a military way. But he was active and zealous in other directions. In 1642, when the Royalists of Chichester rose and wrested the City from the newly-appointed Parliamentary Mayor, imprisoning some of the train-band, with an intention to make Chichester the rallying-point of their cause in Sussex, it was Cawley who sent intelligence of their doings to Colonel Morley, then in attendance on Parliament, in London, and this led to the successful expedition into Sussex of Sir William Waller, who, having taken Arundel (the first time) by a *coup de main*, proceeded to besiege Chichester, and captured the City after a not very vigorous resistance by the Royalists of eight days. The fact was, as Clarendon confesses, the Royal cause was unpopular with "the common people of the County," and, to use his own words, "their (the Royalists) number of common men was so small that the constant duty was performed by the officers and gentlemen of quality, who were absolutely tired out." From this moment up to the Restoration, William Cawley's influence in Chichester was paramount, and it was exerted steadily, first for the Parliament and then for the Protector. Once, indeed, in 1647, he had occasion to ask for military assistance, and Sir Arthur Haselrig, who had taken part in the siege and capture of the City in 1642, was sent down to him. But, on the whole, Sussex was staunch for the Commonwealth, and gave little trouble to the Protector. William Cawley was much trusted by the latter. He was appointed one of the Council of State in 1650-1 ; he acquiesced in the assumption by Cromwell of the Sovereign power, and the Protector made him one of his Commissioners for the County of Sussex. His name also appears with those of Sir T. Pelham Anthony Stapley, Colonel Morley, John Downes, James Temple, &c., as one of the Sequestrators for Sussex. The Chichester brewer was, without doubt, all-powerful in that city during the

Protectorate, and such was the estimation in which Cawley was held in his native city that he was one of the few Regicides able to obtain a seat in the Convention Parliament called to smoothe the return of the Stuarts. But the tide was now running strongly towards Monarchy, and against the recent upholders of a Republic. Cawley had to conceal himself; and being absolutely excepted, with the other Regicides, from pardon both as to life and estate, he fled—first to France, and thence to Geneva and Lausanne, where, under the protection of the Lords of Berne, he passed the remainder of his days--in, as Noble observes, "the constant fear of detection, the loss of all society with those he loved, and with a scanty income." " He and some others implicated with him," continues the historian of the Regicides, " lived as if they wished to be forgotten even whilst on earth, and were spectators, as it were, of being cut off from the land of the living. A more melancholy situation cannot be conceived by the mind of man."

Bad enough, no doubt; but, most certainly, there are many infinitely worse situations. For these men did not hold themselves to be criminals, but rather martyrs for what they looked upon as a great and holy cause ; and some of them, at least, lived to see the principles they had espoused brought to a successful issue in the Revolution which placed William of Orange on the Throne by a Parliamentary title.* This Revolution, however, though it could not fail to bring consolation to such of the judges of Charles I. as still lived, did not better their condition. Macaulay tells us how one of them, Edmund Ludlow, who, like Cawley, had found a refuge in Switzerland and escaped the assassins by whom another of Cawley's companions, John Lisle, fell, made the

---

* Macaulay says, "The leaders of the Roundhead party in 1642 and the statesmen who, about half a century later, effected the Revolution, had exactly the same object in view. That object was to terminate the contest between the Crown and the Parliament, by giving to the Parliament a supreme control over the executive administration. The statesmen of the Revolution effected this indirectly by changing the dynasty. The Roundheads of 1642, being unable to change the dynasty, were compelled to take a direct course towards their end."

experiment of the public feeling towards the Regicides in 1689—the year following the Revolution—by coming over to England, and with what result. He was compelled to make a speedy flight to his old asylum on the banks of the lake of Geneva, and there, in the churchyard of Vevay, he lies buried.

William Cawley is characterised by Ludlow as "an able and ancient Member of Parliament." He was certainly a consistent politician, and, it would also seem, a charitable and pious man, for he founded and endowed a Hospital for ten poor persons in his native city, and had a Chapel erected in it and duly consecrated. The Hospital still stands, but is now converted to the use of a Workhouse. A portrait of its founder, at the age of 18, is still preserved there, and the house which he occupied in that part of Chichester called the Pallant is to this day called "Cawley Priory." It is a proof of Cawley's sagacity and insight into the character of men that he alone opposed the proposition to give Colonel Monk, when a prisoner as a Royalist in the Tower, a Commission in the Parliamentary Army.

Cawley left a son, who, in 1660, petitioned for himself and wife to have the estate of his *late* father restored to him, on the grounds that most of it had been settled on him at his marriage, and that his wife's father had been sequestrated for loyalty, and himself threatened with disinheritance because he, with tears and prayers, attempted to dissuade his father from "entering the detestable plot" (the King's trial). Of Cawley's wife all we learn is from a letter written by one Robert Johnson, and dated Jan. 7, 1663, stating that "Mrs Cawley, whose husband was one of the King's Judges, and is not yet discovered, lodges at her brother's in Red Cross-street, London, and is intimate with the wives of Ludlow, Goffe, and Whalley." So that at this time at least these unfortunate men were alone in their hiding-places; and it is very doubtful if Cawley ever saw his wife again. John Lisle, his companion, we know, did not; for *his* wife, Dame Alice Lisle, remaining in England, was sentenced to death by the infamous Jefferies, and cruelly executed—murdered—for concealing in her house some of the unfortunate fugitives from Sedgmoor.

Cawley's property, including some land at Rumboldswyke, near Chichester, still known (says Mr. Blaauw) as "Cawley's Lane," was granted to the Duke of York—afterwards James II., and who, by another turn of fortune, had to taste, in his turn, the bitterness of exile, and died, like Cawley, in a foreign land.

John Downes, member for Arundel, sat by the side of William Cawley during the whole of the King's trial, and voted and signed the death-warrant with him. He was evidently closely connected with the Cawley family, for, in a petition to Charles II. from Henry, Bishop of Chichester, the Bishop states that since April, 1643, he has been deprived of his whole estate, the chief actor being Henry Cawley (a brother, perhaps, of William) and John Downes. The latter is described by Noble as a Londoner of mean family, which, very likely, he may have been, but his connection with the Cawleys and with Chichester and Arundel would lead to the assumption that he came of a Sussex stock. Certainly he was a Sussex Member, and as such sat on the High Court of Justice and signed the death-warrant. His name, like those of other Regicides, was excepted from pardon, and, giving himself up, he was tried in October, 1660, and condemned to death, but pleaded so hard for his life that he was reprieved, and died in prison.

Anthony Stapley was a Sussex man *tout pur*, and belonged to the landed gentry class. He was the son of Anthony Stapley, of Framfield, by a daughter of another Sussex family, the Thatchers. He is sometimes described as of Patcham (near Brighton), to which place the family removed from Framfield between 1620 and 1630. Another branch of the Stapleys was settled at Hickstead Place, Twineham, and the Diaries left by some of its members have been already referred to in this volume. But the Twineham Stapleys inclined to the Royal cause. Anthony Stapley, of Framfield and Patcham, early took sides with the opponents of the King in the Long Parliament; refused to contribute to the war against the Scots; and, on the breaking-out of hostilities, received a colonel's commission in the Parliamentary army. His standing in Sussex must have been high, for he was returned both for

Lewes (with Herbert Morley) and for the County, and elected to sit (in the Long Parliament) for the latter. Appointed one of the High Court of Justice, he attended nearly all its sittings, and signed the death-warrant. He was appointed on the Councils of State that preceded the Protectorate in 1649-50-53, and was for some time Governor of Chichester. His wife was a Goring—a sister of that Goring Earl of Norwich who took so active a part for the Royal cause. Dying before the Restoration, he escaped both the fate of the other Regicides and the shame that the conduct of his two sons would doubtless have caused him. Both these young men, John, the eldest, and Anthony, had tendered their service to the Protector and were put by him on the Commission of Sussex. But in 1658 they engaged in a plot (referred to, but very cautiously, in the Diary of Anthony Stapley, of Hickstead Place), with the Marquis of Ormond, for the restoration of Charles II. The plan was, that the King should land on the Sussex Coast, and that that County, and Kent and Surrey, should rise and march upon London, and six blank commissions were received by John Stapley to fill up and distribute as he pleased. But, whilst this plot was going on, Cromwell's Secretary of State, Thurloe, was kept informed of every step of it, and at the very moment when the parties to the plot thought all was ripe for action, and the Marquis of Osmond had crossed over to France to persuade Charles to make a landing, the bubble burst and the Stapleys were arrested—John at Whitehall, where he was in personal attendance upon Cromwell. Nothing could then exceed the baseness of these brothers. Anthony was a witness against John, and John, to save his life, gave such evidence as ensured the conviction and execution of his chief confederates, Sir Harry Slings by (the head of an ancient Yorkshire family) and Dr. John Hewitt, of Norfolk. Not only did John Stapley betray his friends to death, but he wrote a pitiful letter to Cromwell. "For the future," he said, "I do promise, by the assistance of the Almighty, I will not only live peaceably, but will, with the utmost of my endeavours, stand by your Highness with life and fortune, to preserve your Highness's person, interest, and dignity, and if ever Charles Stewart should in my dayes make any attempt against your present Government, I will personally appear against him, though it be but in the capacity of a private trooper, if I may not be intrusted by your Highness, or your successors, with better preferment." Cromwell granted the traitor his life; but, we may be sure, gave him no "better preferment." At the Restoration, however, he met with better luck. Not only was the paternal estate at Patcham, which ' had been forfeited by the attainder of his father, restored to him, but he was first knighted and then created a Baronet by Charles II., and, to borrow the words of Mr W. H. Blaauw, in his "Passages of the Civil War in Sussex"—"Sir John Stapley, Baronet, lived to a good old age, very loyal, and very well satisfied to have expiated the sins of his regicide father by such prosperous loyalty." It was fortunate for him that the letter he had written to Cromwell was not discovered till later days. His wife was a daughter of Sir Herbert Springett, of Boyle Place, Ringmer, and he left four children, who, we are told, all married well. So treachery, it would seem, sometimes *does* prosper!

Peregrine Pelham, like Anthony Stapley, belonged to the class of landed gentry. He was a scion of the great Pelham family, several of which sat in the Long Parliament, and took part with the great leaders of liberty, Eliot, Pym, Hollis, and Hampden; but he was the only one who followed the cause to the "bitter end," and sat on the High Court of Justice. He was absent from only one of its sittings, and signed the warrant of execution. But little is known of him personally, though he was a man of family, fashion, and fortune, descending from that Sir William Pelham who was Lord Deputy of Ireland in the reign of Elizabeth, and being one of the Commissioners for conserving the peace between England and Scotland in 1646. Fortunately for him, he died previous to the Restoration, but his name was inserted in the exception clause of the Bill of Indemnity,

Sir Gregory Norton, Bart., was another of the Regicides residing in and connected with Sussex, though he came originally from Hants. He sat for Midhurst in the Long Parliament, and his name appears on nearly all the sittings of the High Court and on the warrant of execution. Noble, in his History of the Regicides, accuses him of being actuated by sordid motives—doubtless from the fact that he bought a portion of the furniture of Richmond Palace at a low price; but Noble never fails to put the worst construction on the acts and motives of the men whose lives he attempts, from very imperfect materials, to chronicle. Sir Gregory Norton died before the Restoration. His name was attainted and his property escheated to the Crown.

James Temple sat for Bramber in the Long Parliament, and, like so many of its younger and more active members, became a Colonel of the Parliamentary army. Though a member of a noble family, several of which took part with the King, he, like Peregrine Pelham, steadily adhered to the popular cause, and being put on the High Court was present at all its sittings and signed the warrant of execution. When the Regicides were excepted from the Bill of Indemnity, James Temple surrendered himself and was tried at the Old Bailey, October 16, 1660. At first he pleaded "Not Guilty," but eventually acknowledged his crime and begged for mercy. He was sentenced to death, but was not executed, and is supposed to have died in the Tower. His relation, Peter Temple, who served, it is said, an apprenticeship to a London draper, but who sat in the Long Parliament, served as a Captain in the army, sat on the King's trial, and signed the death-warrant, shared the fate of the Member for Bramber. He was sentenced to death, but died in prison.

William Goffe was a man springing from another class. He was a son of the Rev. Stephen Goffe, the Puritan Rector of Stanmer, Sussex, and, it is clear, imbibed the rigid principles of his father. His original vocation was that of a dry-salter in London, but, on the breaking-out of the war between King and Parliament, he left trade and became a soldier, and was doubtless a brave and able one, for he rose to the rank of Major-General, and was one of the officers most trusted by Cromwell, and who adhered faithfully to his fortunes and those of his son. His name occurs frequently in the long struggle between the Royalists and Cavaliers, and he was sent into Sussex by Cromwell, in 1665, to report on the state of feeling in that County, writing frequently to Thurloe, Cromwell's Secretary, on the reception he met with from Morley, Fagg, &c. He married a daughter of his fellow-Regicide, General Whalley. He sat on the High Court of Justice (though not as a Sussex Member), and signed the death-warrant. When Cromwell resuscitated the Upper House, General William Goffe was named as one of the new Lords, and was a person of weight and authority until the return of the Stewarts. He then fled, with his father-in-law, Whalley, to North America, where Noble represents them to have spent "40 years of as great misery and wretchedness as can be paralleled." In a very maudlin strain, Noble proceeds:—"Dreadful as their sin had been, none can read their sufferings without commiseration, and the endearing softness—the firm yet gentle constancy of his amiable wife to her parent and her husband, in their years of captivity, must melt any heart that is not impenetrable to pity, and ought to be a lesson written in brass to deter men from enormous vices that have only the wretched alternative of a painful and ignominious death or a life of infamy, dread, and misery, separated from all those connections that render existence desirable, that here have no hopes, that hereafter can have no prospect but of still greater infliction, unless their crimes are redeemed with the severest and sincerest repentance."

Modern history looks at what Noble calls "the enormous vices" of Goffe and Whalley—that is, their opposition to and punishment of regal tyranny—in a different spirit from his: and, whether we approve or disapprove of some of their acts, it is not as men expiating infamous lives that we contemplate them in the forests of North America or their hiding-places in Holland and Switzerland, but rather as political martyrs—the victims of their efforts to carry out principles in advance of their day, but which are recognised in the present age as constituting the very basis of our liberty and our national greatness. The tribute to the "gentle constancy" of Goffe's wife and Whalley's daughter is in better taste; and we shall see by and bye that there were other women of the Puritan class who could bring to their cause as many feminine virtues as any Royalist could claim for his. The real life of Goffe and Whalley in North America is not to be found in Noble. Hardships, doubtless, they endured, like other early emigrants to those Colonies—like the Pilgrim Fathers themselves. But they had their freedom of thought and action; and doubtless in that, and in the knowledge of the ultimate overthrow of the Stewarts and their despotic notions of government, they found some solace for the privations which they had to endure.

We have exhausted the list of the Sussex Regicides proper. Of those Sussex men who sat on the High Court of Justice, but did not sign the death-warrant, Herbert Morley and John Fagg were the most prominent. We have already spoken of the former. After the death of Cromwell, he was one of the most influential officers of the army which held the fate of the kingdom in its hands. His services to the popular cause during the previous conflict with the King had been great; he was the first to form a regiment in Sussex, doubtless out of his own tenants at Glynde and his friends and his constituents at Lewes, of which he was the Member in the Long Parliament, and he rendered valuable service to Sir W. Waller in the siege and capture both of Arundel and of Chichester. In 1643, he beat back the forces of Lord Hopton, who was laying siege to Lewes, and preserved that town to the Parliamentary cause. He assisted his fellow-Sussexian, Col. Norton, at the siege of Basing House, and, as we know by an interesting correspondence between himself and Sir W. Campion, he was with Fairfax when that General took Borstall House, of which Campion was the Governor. His treatment of Campion's young wife was most honorable to him, and, indeed, in every passage of his life he always behaved like a soldier and a gentleman. He sat three days on the High Court of Justice, but refused to sign the death-warrant, and in the ensuing Protectorate he was somewhat of a mal-content, and retired from active life to his house at Glynde.

Writing from Lewes, to Thurloe, in November, 1655,

General Goffe, Col. Morley's old fellow-soldier, says, "I intend (if the Lord please) to give Colonel Morley a kind visitt this day, his house being within two or three miles. I hope such a civility, whatever he thinkes of my business, will doe no hurt." It appears that Morley told Goffe he would assist him in any matter as a Justice of the Peace, but hinted that in any other things he wished not his name to appear. Col. Morley was returned for Sussex, and also for Rye, in the Parliament which Cromwell called in September, 1654, and which, after it had resolved, by 200 to 60, not to make the Protectorate hereditary, was dissolved on July 22, 1655. He was also again elected for the County and for Lewes in the Parliament of September, 1656, and which, refusing to recognise the "other House," was dissolved by the Protector in February, 1658. It was the last Parliament called by Cromwell, who died in September, 1658. Again, in Richard Cromwell's Parliament, of January, 1659, Col. Morley was returned both for the County and for Lewes, and, on its dissolution, and the revival of "the Rump,"—that is, the remains of the Long Parliament,—he acted as the champion of that resuscitation of the more moderate party, now verging towards Royalism, and, when the Rump was violently dispersed by General Lambert in the interests of the more extreme party in the Army, Col. Morley and Sir Arthur Haselrig, who, with three others, had been appointed to organise the Army, in order to guard against Lambert's violence, restored it (December 26, 1659),* and, at this stage of affairs, he seemed to hold, and perhaps for a few days did hold, the fate of the country in his hands. He was appointed Lieutenant of the Tower, which gave him the command to a great degree of London, and Evelyn, his old school-fellow, believed he might, if he had chosen, at this period have played the part of Monk. "I went this afternoon" writes Evelyn, on January 22, 1660, "to visit Col. Morley. After dinner, I discoursed with him; but he was

---

* Whitelock says Haselrig, Walton, and Morley came into the House in their riding habits, and Haselrig was very jocund and high. They all received the public thanks of the House, and its cordial approval of their conduct.

jealous, and would not believe that Monk came to do the King any service. *I told him he might do it without him, and have all the honour.* He was still doubtful, and would resolve on nothing yet, so I took leave."

It is probable that Morley shrank from betraying the men with whom he had been associated all his life.* And whilst he hesitated Monk was acting. This General had come up to London from the North on February 3, 1660, and Morley, with whom he was joined in the control of the army, being unable to penetrate his intentions, broke off his correspondence with Evelyn, and inclined to the party of the Commonwealth. Ludlow, a thorough Republican, assured of his support, proposed that 2,000 soldiers " should be ordered to march to the Tower, to join with Colonel Morley's regiment, which was already there and would be ready to receive them;" adding, " he (Morley) having sent to me to let me know that the Tower should be at my command whensoever I please to desire it." Yet, at this very time, Whitelock declares that " Col. Morley, Lieutenant of the Tower, concurred with Monk," so that both sides believed that he inclined to them, the truth being, perhaps, that he, like many an honourable man at that time and since, felt it impossible to approve altogether of either party, and would, if he could, have adopted a middle course. But that was impossible. The current was always running too violently in this or in that direction—now against and now in favour of Monarchy. At this moment, when Morley hesitated, it was running in favour of the King, and Monk took it at its flow,

---

* Ludlow characterises Morley as "of a temporising spirit," which, in a resolute Republican like Ludlow, meant, perhaps, a man of moderate opinions. Ludlow owed his escape at the Restoration to Colonel Herbert Morley. After a period of hazardous concealment in London, he made his way to Lewes, where an open vessel was waiting for him, but from which, on its passage down the Ouse—the wind blowing hard—he removed to another which had just returned from conveying over Richard Cromwell, ex-Protector, to France. The change of vessels was a most fortunate one for him, for the one he had just quitted was searched soon afterwards for fugitives, whilst the one he was in escaped suspicion because it had stranded; and getting off the next morning it got safely to Dieppe, whence Ludlow hastened to Switzerland and joined Cawley.

and, by one bold stroke, handed the country over to the Royalists. There was no longer a choice for Colonel Morley. He did not even attempt resistance, like his old companion in arms, Col. Cockeram, whose regiment rose in mutiny at Gravesend, and had to be put down by Monk's troops. He submitted, gave up the Tower, and in the ensuing May besought the intercession of his old school-fellow for his life. "Came to me," writes Evelyn, "Colonel Morley, about procuring his pardon, now too late seeing his error, and neglect of the counsel I gave him, by which, if he had taken it, he had certainly done the same work with the same ease that Monk did it, who was then in Scotland, and Morley in a post to have done what he pleased, but his jealousie and feare kept him from that blessing and honour. I addressed him to Lord Mordaunt, then in great favour, for his pardon, which he obtained at the cost of £1,000, as I heard. O the sottish omission of this gentleman! what did I not undergo of danger in this negotiation, to have brought him over to his Majesty's interest, when it was entirely in his hands!"

Yet it may well be doubted, with all due deference to Evelyn, whether the part taken by Col. Morley was not more honourable than that of Monk. He at least did not buy rank and wealth at the price of his colleagues' lives and the risk of his country's liberties.

Having procured his pardon, Morley retired to Glynde, and there ended his days peaceably in 1667, dying in the 52nd year of his age, and being interred in the Parish Church. His only son had married a daughter of Sir John Trevor, a grand-daughter of Hampden, and by this alliance the Glynde estate came to the Trevors, and, through them, to its present holder, the Right Hon. H. Brand, Speaker of the House of Commons. Sir John Trevor himself, it may be added, who married Hampden's daughter, Ruth, supported both Oliver and Richard to the last, but was, in spite of this, taken into favour by Charles, and sent as Ambassador to France in 1667.

John Fagg, though not so active a soldier as Col. Morley, ran, in many respects, a parallel course with him. They were, indeed, closely connected, Fagg marrying Morley's sister, Mary. He represented Rye, of which he was a native, in the Long Parliament; received a Colonel's commission in the Parliamentary Army; and sat on the High Court of Justice, but rather assisted in making preparations for the trial than acted as a Judge; above all, he did not sign the death-warrant. He was made one of the Commissioners for Sussex by Cromwell, but does not appear to have been a zealous supporter of the Protector, for Gen. Goffe, writing from Lewes to Secretary Thurloe, on Nov. 7, 1655, tells him that he had not put in Mr. Fagg's name, " as he appeared gracious with disaffected men, and would not stir a hair's breadth without Col. Morley." And in the following year (1656) he was precluded from sitting in the Parliament then summoned by Cromwell as not approved by the Protector's Council. At the death of Cromwell he, like Col. Morley, came again to the front. He was put in command of the Sussex Militia by the Council of State, directed to secure Chichester and Arundel, and to hold correspondence with the forces in Surrey, Kent, and Wilts. During the struggle between the Presbyterian party in the Rump and Lambert at the head of the Republicans, Fagg was made Governor of Portsmouth, and, probably, his acquiescence in Monk's plans for the Restoration obtained for him that immunity which he subsequently enjoyed for the past, and even favour in the future; for he was made first a Knight and then a Baronet by Charles II., and was secured in all his possessions. Amongst these was Wiston House, the old residence of the Shirleys in West Sussex, which the father of " the three Shirleys " had been compelled to sell from poverty, and which Dr. Thomas Shirley, a descendant, attempted to recover by law from Sir John Fagg, but failed, and was unlucky enough to be committed for breach of privilege in proceeding against the new Courtier and old Republican, Sir John. We are told that Sir John Fagg had a family of 16 children; but the male line seems soon to have failed, and Wiston passed, by the marriage, in 1743, of the heiress, Elizabeth Fagg, to Sir Charles Matthews Goring, to the Gorings. The name of Fagg is not now to be found amongst the gentry of Sussex, any more than are those of Culpepper, Challoner, Covert, Caryll, Springet, Boord, and a score more of once familiar Sussex names.

The close connection of Sir John Trevor, and, through him, of Col. Morley and Sir John Fagg with the great patriot, John Hampden, explains to some extent the support they gave to the Parliamentary cause, and, though not in the same degree, to the Protectorate. Hampden himself, it will be borne in mind, was a cousin of Cromwell, and so Cromwell was connected by family ties as well as political sympathies with these leading men of Sussex. The blood of Cromwell and of Hampden still flows in Sussex veins.

We have named the Springets as one of our extinct Sussex families. Their seat was Broyle Place, Ringmer, near Lewes, and here we have an instance, amongst many others, of the extent to which the rigid opinions of the Puritans had penetrated the ranks of the English gentry as well as of the bourgeois and yeoman class in the earlier part of the 17th century. One of the brothers of Sir Thomas Springet in the first Charles's day was a lawyer, but very strict in religion, and dying early of consumption, his widow (a sister of Sir E. Partridge, of Kent) brought up his son in the father's principles, sending him to Cambridge to "a Puritan College called St. Katherine's Hall, for he declined Bishops and Common Prayer very early." At home he was not less carefully looked after, his mother having a "Minister" to preach thrice a week to her friends and spending half her fortune in daily compounding and dispensing medicines to the poor. All these particulars we learn from the lady whom young William Springet married at the early age of 20, in Kent,—" without a ring," as she tells us, "and many of their formal dark words left out." She was a daughter of Sir John Proude, Knight; and she is worthy to take her place by the side of Lucy Hutchinson and with the daughter of Whalley and wife of Goffe for the devoted affection she showed to her husband and for her constancy to the principles in which it is evident she, like her husband, had been brought up in one of those "God-fearing households" then so common in England. On a son being born to them, her husband, she tells us, carried the child five miles off in order to avoid baptism in a Church, and to obtain it from the chosen hands of Master Wilson, of Otham, one of the Orthodox Divines of Kent.

On the breaking-out of hostilities between King and Parliament, the young Sussex Puritan was not long in choosing sides. He took the Covenant, and received a commission to raise a regiment of horse. He must have done his work promptly, for he was soon at the head of 800 horse, and was employed with it in suppressing a Royalist rising in the vale of Kent, and afterwards, in Surrey, besieged and took Lord Craven's house, fought at Edgehill, and was wounded at Newbury, for which and other services he was thanked by Parliament. He is supposed to have been early knighted by Essex, for, in a despatch from Arundel, Sir William Waller entitles him " Sir William." It was here—at Arundel—that his short career (he was but 22 years of age) was brought to a close. After the capture of the place by Waller, the custody of the Castle was committed to Sir William Springet and to Colonel Morley. Soon afterwards the garrison was attacked by a fatal sickness called calenture, or sun-fever, brought on by exposure to unwholesome night air,* and Col. Springet was one of the sufferers. His wife, then in London, was sent for, and, though far advanced in pregnancy, she immediately set out. The reputation of the Sussex roads in those days, and for many a long year afterwards, was very bad, and it was with great difficulty that Lady Springet succeeded in hiring a coach, at a very high price. She took a physician with her, and her husband's messenger escorted her on horseback. But the frost, which had

---

* In the delirium peculiar to this fever, says Mr Blaauw, "surrounding objects assumed the aspect of verdant meadows to the eyes of the sufferer, who, when at sea, would madly throw himself into it, as if seeking the refreshment of a cool walk on land. Dryden and Swift have made fine poetical use of this delusion. Probably Falstaff died of it, for Mrs Quickly, describing his last symptoms, after lamenting that he was "so shaked of a burning quotidian tertian," as Springet also was, says : " After I saw him fumble with the sheets and play with flowers, and smile upon his fingers' ends, I knew there was but one way, for his nose was sharp as a pen, and 'a babbled of green fields." Hen. V., Act 2.

been so useful in the siege of Arundel, was now broken up, and the poor lady was "forced to row in the highways in a boat, and take the things in the coach with her, and the horses to be led with strings tied to their bridles, and to swim the coach and horses in the highways." She was afterwards "benighted, and overthrown in the dark into a hedge," close to a very deep precipice. The colonel of a garrison which she passed invited her to stop for repose, but she gallantly says, "I was resolved not to go out of the coach, unless it broke, until I came so near the house that I could compass it on foot. . . . When we came to Arundel, we met with a most dismal sight, the town being depopulated, all the windows being broken with the great guns, and the soldiers making stables of all the shops and lower rooms." After passing through the dreary town, she was at last obliged to fulfil her resolution of walking, for, within a quarter of a mile of her husband's residence, "the horses came to a stand, the wheel of the coach being pitched in the root of a tree." This unexpected arrival at midnight did not allay the feverish excitement of the overjoyed husband, who had been now sleepless for five days. When his friends insisted upon quiet, he had covenanted with them for the liberty "to shoot birds with his cross-bow out of window, which he did till the fever took his head." . . "He was an artist in shooting and fishing," and had been employed from his boyhood with horses, dogs, guns, cross-bows, bullets, feathering arrows, and, a curious amusement, "pulling his watch to pieces."

The devoted wife now watched him incessantly for two more days of ebbing life, hanging upon his parched lips, to cool them with her own, unterrified by the danger of infection, and rewarded by his faint entreaty, "Oh, don't leave me." The next morning, after he had thus breathed away his love and life, in his 23rd year, Feb. 3, 1644, his body was carried in his own ammunition-waggon to Ringmer, his native place. Having always provided at his own expense both his tents and ammunition, and having kept a table at Arundel open to the volunteers of his own regiment, it was not surprising that only £12 was now found in his chest, and he left debts of £2,000, partly by having advanced loans for what he thought the good cause.

In addition to this he had spent the whole of his wife's fortune (£1,600) in fitting out his regiment, and, it is evident, was one of the most earnest spirits of that earnest age. He would never lodge in the sequestrated mansions of the Royalists, not even in that of his uncle, Sir Thomas Culpepper, and, as Mr. Blaauw (to whom we are indebted for these particulars) remarks, " his character, cherished in the fond memory of his widow, and traced by the hand of love forty years afterwards, may serve as a type of the strong feelings of that turbulent age, though indeed even she quietly laments his not having embraced the whole truth, as she complacently considered herself to have done."

Mr. Blaauw refers to the adoption by Sir W. Springet's widow of the tenets of the Quakers. This she did on her marriage with Isaac Pennington, son of the Regicide of the same name; and it was, doubtless, owing to this connection that her daughter, Gulielma, became the wife, in 1672, of the celebrated William Penn. But, though thus weaned (and wedded) from the vanities of the world, the widow of Sir William Springet never forgot her first love; and in her letters to her grandson, which she wrote in 1680, and which have been published, she dwells upon his virtues, and does not fail to initiate the young man into the secret of his Sussex and Springet ancestry.

Two Chaloners, Thomas and James, were nominated upon the High Court of Justice, and one of them, Thomas Chaloner, signed the death-warrant. But neither of these was a member of the Sussex family. The head of the Sussex Chaloners, Robert Chaloner, of Kenwards, Lindfield, was, however, engaged in the same cause. He was a Major in the Parliamentary army, and an active supporter of the Protector. In the Parish Register of Lindfield, about 1655, his name frequently appears attached to the entries of marriages which were performed by " Ye Major,' not at the Parish Church, but at Kenwards, his mansion at Lindfield. His possessions in East Sussex were very extensive;

but the Restoration was fatal to him and his family, and from this period the Sussex Chaloners declined till they disappeared altogether from the gentry of the County. Of the fate of Robert Chaloner, "Ye Major," of Kenwards, Lindfield, we are ignorant, but the tradition in the neighbourhood of his estate is, that he had to fly the country and died abroad. His house at Lindfield was dismantled, and the only part of it that now remains is the stables, which have been converted into a farmhouse. It seems to have been the fashion of the officers of the Puritan army to perform the marriage ceremony, for in the Framfield Register there is an entry to the same effect as those in the Lindfield Register, to which the name of Capt. Stapley is appended. Doubtless, however, in each of these cases, the military performer of the contract was a Justice of the Peace.

Samuel Gott, who sat for Winchelsea in the Long Parliament; for Rye in the Parliament summoned by Cromwell, in 1656; and for Hastings in the "Rump" Parliament of 1658, was a staunch upholder of the Republic, but he did not sit on the High Court of Justice, and we are ignorant how he closed his career. Perhaps, like many of the men who took an active part in the Protectorate, he was happy to seek safety in obscurity.

It will be remarked that, though several of the Sussex Regicides, like James Temple and John Downes, were tried and condemned to death, none of them was actually executed. James Temple and John Downes died in prison; William Cawley and William Goffe in exile; Anthony Stapley, Gregory Norton, and Peregrine Pelham died before the Restoration. Of those who sat upon the Court, but did not sign the death-warrant, Sir John Fagg was forgiven and came to honours and dignity under the Stewarts; and Colonel Morley died in peace at Glynde.

It is impossible to go through the records of families engaged in the conflict of King and Parliament, and follow all their vicissitudes, without being struck by the contrast of those troubled days with the present age, when "Harry follows Harry" in such peaceful succession, and the most exciting events of country life, in the way of war or peace, are a lawsuit or an alliance—a review or a ball! How easy, then, is it for us now-a-days to scatter praise and blame on the actors in the great events of the 17th century!—how impossible to realise the sacrifices made by the men who fought in those days for what they held to be the right and truthful cause! Good men and true there were, most certainly, on both sides, as well as, without doubt, men of a lower character. But as for the theory which sets down all the men on one side as rogues and rascals, knaves and hypocrites, we have passed beyond that; and it is no longer necessary to make an excuse for giving some particulars of the men in this County, who, like Colonel Herbert Morley and Sir William Springet, entered zealously into the conflict with the King, or even of those who, like Anthony Stapley and William Cawley, went a step further and put their names to the death-warrant of that unfortunate, but not the less most unscrupulous and untruthful king. Let us rather thank the good fortune which has reserved happier days for us, when the principles of hereditary Monarchy and of national freedom are reconciled to each other, and when the most zealous advocates of liberty may accept Constitutional Government and the Commonwealth as synonymous terms. We owe it not a little to the men who fought and suffered, in Sussex and elsewhere, for liberty in the 17th century.

SUSSEX TRAGEDIES AND ROMANCES.

SUSSEX is not distinguished, like Yorkshire, as the scene of *a tragedy* ;* but, like most other parts of the world, it has had its share of the tragic acts of men, and one of the earliest, if not *the* earliest of these on record, is the trial and execution for murder of Lord Dacre, of Hurstmonceux Castle. The title still survives in a Sussex family—the Brands—a member of which is the "first Commoner of England"—in other words, Speaker of the House of Commons, and the picturesque ruins of Hurstmonceux Castle still form a feature of the eastern part of Sussex.

The trial and execution of Lord Dacre for murder is one of the strangest stories of the Tudor times, and stands out as prominently in English jurisprudence as does the execution of Earl Ferrers, the head of the Shirleys, another Sussex family, at a later era, and for a similar crime.

The family name of the unfortunate nobleman was Fynes or Fiennes,—an ancient Norman family who had acquired Hurstmonceux in Sussex by marriage with the equally ancient family of Monceux; but the title by which he is known in the history of crime was derived from the famous Lords Dacre of Gillesland, the heiress of which family was married in 1440 by Sir Roger Fynes, and brought by him to the fine Castle he had built at Hurstmonceux, in Sussex. In right of his wife he was summoned to Parliament as Baron Dacre "of the South," in contradistinction to the Lords Dacre "of the North," then still flourishing in Cumberland. He was succeeded, in 1484, by his grandson Thomas, who, though Constable of Calais and distinguished for his services in the field against the Scots, got into trouble, and was imprisoned in the Fleet and fined for "harbouring of suspected felons," and

---

* "The Yorkshire Tragedy," a play of the 16th century, sometimes assigned, but incorrectly, to Shakspeare.

"for remysness and negligence in ponyshement of them." But the delinquencies of this Lord Dacre, whatever they may have been, shrink into insignificance when compared with those of his grandson, another Thomas, Lord Dacre of the South, the hero of our story. This Lord Thomas, like his grandfather, was left an orphan, in 1525, at the age of 17, and came into possession of one of the finest estates and Baronies of the kingdom. He married, too, a lady of noble birth, a Neville, daughter of another Sussex nobleman, Lord Abergavenny, and had every advantage which wealth, rank, and connection could give him. But his education had been neglected; his habits were dissolute; his companions were, it is evident, of rank far below his own, and, doubtless, selected by him for the congeniality of their tastes and habits. What these were can be guessed from the deed which involved him and three of them in the terrible fate which overtook them.

It would seem, from the legal documents found in the Record Office in our days, and published by the Deputy-Keeper of the Records, that, on the 20th of April, in the 32nd year of the reign of Henry the 8th, a party of fourteen men, including Lord Dacre himself, met at his mansion at Hurstmonceux, "and did there illegally conspire in what manner they could best hunt in the Park of Nicholas Pelham, Esq., of Laughton, in the County of Sussex, with dogs and nets called buckstalls, and bound themselves by oaths, &c., for such illegal purpose, and also to stand against all the lieges of the King, and to kill any of the King's lieges who might oppose them."

A list is given of the names, occupations, and late residences of these so-called conspirators, and whilst none of them was above the rank of gentleman, several are entitled yeomen, and one was a smith, of Fletching. With the exception of two, who are "late of London," and two others late of places in Kent, all are set down as being lately of places in Sussex, several of Hurstmonceux, and, doubtless, in the service of Lord Dacre; one (Thos. Duffield), of Framfield, and another (John Shelley, a well-known Sussex name), of Patcham. The meeting on the 20th of April broke up, we may presume, without any definite result. It led, at all events, to no immediate action; for ten days afterwards, on the 30th April, the same parties met again at the same house, and on this occasion the meeting was followed up by decisive acts. The conspirators, or, as we should call them in the present day, poachers, divided themselves into two bands; one led by Lord Dacre, and the other by Henry Fitzherbert (of Ringmer, Sussex), and so entered the Park of Sir Nicholas Pelham, at Hellingley, on two sides, with intent, doubtless, to drive the deer, as Earl Percy did at Chevy Chase in "the brave days of old." The only difference between the Percy and the Dacre driving was, that the deer in the latter case were those of a neighbour, and that it was not in the border line of Chevy Chase, but in an enclosed Sussex Park that they lay; and, above all, that these were the days of the Eighth Harry, who kept a strict hand over his Barons, and, if they over-stept the limits of the law, made very little difficulty of cutting off their heads!

It would seem that Sir Nicholas Pelham, like his prototype, Earl Douglas, had been warned of young Lord Dacre's design. At all events, his keepers were on the look-out for intruders, and at a spot called "Pykehay," in the Parish of Hellingly, the party headed by Lord Dacre had the misfortune to come upon three of these men, named John Busbrydgge, James Busbrydgge, and Richard Somener. What words passed between them (and, doubtless, there were some, for a quarrel is said to have ensued) is not stated, but it is declared in the old pleading that "for fear lest they (the poachers) might be known by them" (the keepers), they attacked and wounded them, and gave certain mortal wounds to John Busbrydgge, in consequence of which he died on the 2nd May then next following.

For this tragical act an indictment for murder was laid against three of the party—John Mantell, John Frowds, and George Roidon, described as "gentlemen," in the ordinary course of law, and they were found guilty by a Grand Jury, which is described as meeting first at Hellingly—the place where the crime was committed—and afterwards, by adjournment, at Maresfield, in the vicinity of it, before Sir Humphrey Brown, Knight,

Sergeant-at-Law, and Robert Oxenbridge and Thomas Darell, keepers (Justices) of the Peace, and they were sentenced to death and executed—by hanging, we presume—at a spot called "St. Thomas Waterings," the usual place of execution within the Sheriffdom of Sussex and Surrey, situated near the 2nd milestone on what is now called the Old Kent Road, by which, in former days, pilgrims travelled to the shrine of St. Thomas à Beckett at Canterbury.

Thus three of the conspirators were soon called to a bloody reckoning for their night's frolic. Nor was the head and chief of it,—at whose great house it was planned, and under whose direction it was carried out,—to escape. A few years before, such an act would doubtless have excited little or no attention, amidst the license and disorder of the Civil Wars, or in the times preceding them, when great men did pretty well as they pleased. But the Tudors had brought in a new state of things; and a striking example was now to be given that laws were made both for high and low—for Peer and peasant. As a Peer of the Realm, the legal procedure against Lord Dacre was different from that taken against the three commoners. On the 27th June (33 Henry 8) a Commission was issued, by which the Lord Chancellor Audley was appointed Lord High Steward and Judge, and, upon his precept, a jury of Peers was summoned for the trial of Lord Dacre, at the head of which was Henry, Marquis of Dorset, and on which also sat the Earl of Sussex, the Earl of Derby, the Earl of Rutland, Lord John Russell (High Admiral of England), and others of the highest nobles of England. Before these Peers on the 27th June the hapless young Noble, brought from the Tower (the Constable of which was his Sussex neighbour, Sir John Gage, of Firle) for the purpose, was arraigned on a charge of murder. To this he at first pleaded "Not Guilty," as not being the actual murderer, and put himself upon his Peers; but "sufficient and probable evidence" having been adduced, he reversed his plea to "Guilty," and put himself upon the King's mercy. The judgment of the Court was, that "he was to be hanged"—neither time nor place, however, being named; and this judgment was carried out, at the instance, it is said, of certain Courtiers, "who gaped after his estate,"—not an improbable thing, though there is no proof of its truth.

The execution took place two days after the judgment: on St. Peter's Day, the 29th day of June; so quick a despatch of justice that the King could, indeed, have had little inclination for "mercy." Was he not the 8th Harry, who "spared no man in his wrath, and no woman in his lust?" There was something terribly painful as well as ignominious in Lord Dacre's death; for to the last, it would seem, he was tantalised with a hope of escape. In the words of the old chronicler, Holingshed, "And afterward, the nine and twentith of June, being St. Peter's daie, at eleuen of the clocke in the forenoon, the shiriffs of London, accordinglie as they were appointed, were ready at the Tower to have receiued the said prisoner, and him to haue led to execution on the Tower hill; but, as the prisoner should come forth of the Tower, one Heire, a gentleman of the Lord Chancellor's house, came, and in the King's name commanded to staie the execution till two of the clocke in the afternoone, which caused manie to thinke that the King would have granted his pardon. But neuertheless, at three of the clocke in the same afternoone, he was brought forth of the Tower and deliuered to the shiriffs, who led him on foot unto Tiburne, where he died. His bodi was buried in the church of Saint Sepulchers. He was not past foure and twentie yeeres of age, when he came through this great mishap to his end, for whom manie sore lamented, and likewise for the other three gentlemen, Mantell, Frowds, and Roidon. But for the said yoong Lord, being a right towardlie gentleman, and such a one as many had conceiued great hope of better proofe, no small mone and lamentation was made; the more, indeed, for that it was thought he was induced to attempt such follie, which occasioned his death, by some light heads that were then about him."

When, indeed, the character of the times is considered, the punishment seems out of proportion to the offence, which was rather that of homicide than of murder; and in these days the penalty of manslaughter would, probably, be deemed sufficient for the purposes of justice. But in Henry the Eighth's day the kingly hand weighed heavily on the noble ; noble heads were cut off for very venial acts ; and the mere protext of "standing against all the lieges of the King," even if only to kill a buck, was sufficient to bring down the most dread vengeance of the law.

In his paper on this tragical event, the late Mr. M. A. Lower says the scene of it is still known. Pick-Hay, as it is now called, is an arable field of ten acres on the Horselunges Farm, in the Parish of Hellingly, adjoining a field called "The Cabins," on the Broad Farm, rather less than a quarter of a mile south-west of Hellingly Church on the road to Horsebridge. The river Cuckmere is the boundary of the two fields. The actual scene of the murder (writes a local archæologist, Mr. T. Horton) is near the bottom of the two fields and near the river. "In my youth (he adds) the tradition of the murder was current ; and I may add that a *ghost* has always been about the place." Whether of Lord Dacre, "of the South," or of John Busbrydge, "deponent sayeth not."

This is the earliest on record of what may be called our Sussex domestic tragedies.

We pass over a long space of time before we come to anything like a parallel to it ; for Sussex is not a County of great crimes. Poaching and smuggling have both flourished among us, and Lord Dacre may be included among the victims of the former class of misdeeds; but more heinous crimes have been "few and far between." The Jack Shepherds, Dick Turpins, and Claude Duvals belonged to other parts of the kingdom. Still we have had our highway robbers, or, as Sir John Falstaff lovingly calls them, " Diana's foresters, Gentlemen of the Shade, Minions of the Moon." In this class figure very prominently two brothers of the name of Weston, Joseph and George, who, in the years 1781-2, astonished the good people of Rye and Winchilsea by taking the mansion at the latter place known as "The Friars," and living there in great style and at lavish expense under the names of William Johnson and Samuel Weston. They passed themselves

o

off as persons of standing, and dressed, rode, and, above all, eat and drank like gentlemen. They were, in fact, forgers, horse-stealers, and highwaymen, carrying on their operations over a wide extent of country, and bringing their booty to the remote Sussex town of Winchelsea, to live a "jolly life." They were at length apprehended in London for robbing the Bath and Bristol mail on the morning of January 25th, 1781, between Maidenhead and Hounslow, and for this they were committed for trial to Newgate on the 17th of April, 1782. But, the day before the trial came on, they succeeded, with three other felons, by the aid of their wives, in breaking out of gaol. It says something for the rascals that the Mistress Westons thought they were worth saving! But it was not for long. George was soon after re-captured in Smithfield, and his brother Joseph in Cock Lane. This latter defended himself desperately, and wounded one of his captors in the cheek with a pistol. Strange to say, on being arraigned, four days afterwards, for the robbery of the mail, they were acquitted. They were, however, immediately tried on other charges: George for forgery and Joseph for firing the pistol; and this time they were convicted and sentenced to death. They were identified on this occasion by a witness from Draycott, Staffordshire, who had known them from their birth as the sons of a farmer named George Weston. They were executed at Tyburn on September 3, 1782, and, according to a writer in the *Gentleman's Magazine*, "made a good ending," receiving, as Catholics, the consolation of their faith. But the same account fails not to tell us that they were "two of the most artful villains that have ever appeared at any time in this country, and have robbed the country of an immense sum." It was the career of these men that supplied Thackeray with some of the incidents of the novel which he was writing when his life and the story were suddenly ended. The scene of it, it will be recollected, was laid at Rye, and an attempt to rob the London coach of a large sum of tax-money gives the hero an opportunity to distinguish himself at the expense of the highwayman, who receives the contents of the lad's pistol in his face.

It seems "a little too bad" to give Lord Dacre "of the South" such companions as these; but crime, like poverty, "has strange bed-fellows."

We have said that Sussex had no Dick Turpin or Claude Duval. But the foot-pad who, early in the present century (1807), infested the roads between Arundel and Chichester, and eased graziers and farmers of their heavy purses as they returned home from market, until he became a word of fear to the western part of the County, may well compare with any highway notoriety in daring acts and in his tragic end. His name was Allen, and he had been a footman in the service of the Lennox family; but this was not known until he had made the country so "hot" by his numerous robberies that, at length, the militia were called out to effect his capture. He was pressed so closely that at length he took refuge in a pond at Graffham, near Midhurst. There, however, he was followed, and espied by some of his pursuers—among them a son of Mr. Sargent, a neighbouring gentleman of large property. Unfortunately young Sargent—a fine young man,—a captain in the 9th Regiment of Foot,—recognised the highwayman, and called upon him by his name to give himself up. The only reply was a shot from Allen's gun or pistol, which laid the unfortunate young man dead on the spot. The soldiers who accompanied him immediately fired on the robber, and so gave him a better end than he deserved. The nieces of young Sargent were co-heiresses of the Lavington Estate, and it was their fate to become the wives of two remarkable men: Samuel Wilberforce, Bishop of Oxford and of Winchester, and Henry Manning, Cardinal of Rome.

Sussex soil, we have said, is not stained by many atrocious crimes. But one of the most atrocious crimes ever committed on it, and which, by the wholesale extermination of a household, closely resembles the Mars and Williams tragedies which terrified London at the commencement of this century, and have been so terribly described by De Quincey, was committed at Ditchling in 1734. The perpetrator of it was a Jew pedlar named Jacob Harris, who, whilst travelling the country with his wares, put up his horse at a public house in that lonely part of the country, Ditchling

Common, and whilst his host, named Miles, was engaged in cleaning the animal in the stable, seized the opportunity to attack him, and, as he thought, deprive him of life by cutting his throat with a razor. Leaving him for dead, he entered the house, and, meeting the servant-maid, who, it is supposed, had been alarmed by the noise of the struggle in the stable and was descending the stairs to see what was the matter, he attacked her too and murdered her. Then, mounting the stairs, he entered the room where the wife of the landlord was lying on a sick bed and destroyed the poor woman by cutting her throat. He then plundered the house, which, it would seem, was the motive for these wholesale murders, and made his escape. But only for a short time. We have said that he left Miles for dead; but he had not carried out his barbarous act so effectually in this instance but that Miles was able, with the little life left to him, to give information which led to a speedy pursuit and to the capture of his murderer, at Turner's Hill, and also to his identification. Harris was tried at Horsham Assizes in the following August,—the murders were committed in May,—and being convicted and condemned to death, he was hung at Horsham and his body then transported to the place of the crime, Ditchling Common, and hung on a gibbet near to the house in which the murders had been committed. A portion of the gibbet still remains,—it is, we believe, the only relic of the kind in Sussex, —and is known as "Jacob's Post."

Whilst in the Ditchling tragedy a pedlar was the perpetrator of the crime, in the succeeding instance he was the victim. The scene of it lay in the adjoining parish.

One of the many woods which lie scattered on every side of Lindfield is known by the name of Costell's Wood. It lies on the left-hand side of the road from Lindfield to Lewes, in the Manor of South Malling, and forms part of a large farm called Wallstead. Above 400 acres of this farm are covered with oaks —once famed for their girth and height. But these old giants of the forest have fallen before the axe, and Costell's Wood now consists chiefly of young trees, planted pretty closely together, in order that they may attain a greater height than oaks do when growing singly in hedgerows. The space between them is grown over with fern and underwood, but not so thickly as to bar a passage through the trees.

There are, however, too many woods round Lindfield, and too few people in it, to make Costell's Wood a common place of resort, as it would be near a town. With the exception of the woodreeve, who occasionally goes in to lop off an exuberant branch or so, perhaps months pass without any one being tempted to get over the gate which leads into it from the Lewes Road. It holds forth no attractions even to school boys in the shape of nuts or blackberries, or to the sportsman in the shape of game. In Costell's Wood the trees are left pretty much to themselves to grow in peace and quiet, with only the sun and the breeze to keep them company.

But at the time we are about to refer to—some 38 years ago —they had another visitor,—a poor idiot boy was their constant frequenter, and would wander about among them all the day. Being perfectly harmless, to himself and to others, his mother was in the habit of giving him his day's food, and with this he wandered forth, hiding himself in the woods all the day long, amusing himself in his own unintelligible way, and returning home at night mumbling forth his adventures in his own gibberish, which few could understand and nobody ever paid attention to. So, when, after his usual rambles, one evening he came home to his mother with a scared face and an agitated manner, and made strange motions with his hand across his throat and uttered something in his imperfect language about "man—man dead," "man in the wood," and pulled at her dress as though he wished her to go somewhere with him, she paid no more heed to him than she had a hundred times before, when he had returned home after seeing a pig killed,—a sight, it seems, of which he had a peculiar horror,—and it was her belief that a spectacle of this kind had caused the terror under which the boy was now evidently labouring. So no attention was paid to his gestures and mumblings, and the next day he was allowed to go out again upon his rambles; but still, day after day, it was remarked that he went in the direction of Costell's Wood; and from time to time, too, on coming home to his mother, he returned to the old subject, only with some variation in his tale, and, instead of its being "man dead," "man in the wood," it was now "birds—birds peck man's eyes" "dogs—dogs eat man," and other strange expressions of this kind.

At length a neighbour, who had noticed the boy's visits to the wood, and had heard him utter some of his strange expressions, took the trouble to follow him in one of his rambles, and having got over the gate and entered the wood some twenty or thirty yards from the road, following in the wake of the idiot boy, a spectacle presented itself which was sufficient to stagger the stoutest nerves; for there, in a comparatively open spot, among the long grass, lay the body of a man, but so decomposed by the elements, and so torn and mangled by birds and beasts, that, but for its clothing, there was nothing to denote humanity about it. The skull was separated from the trunk, and the coat only hung on a heap of bones. The man instantly reported his fearful discovery to the authorities, who went to the spot and took possession of the remains, and of an open razor that was found lying beside them. Active enquiries were set on foot to ascertain the identity of the body, and by what strange fate it had come in such a spot, and lain there so long; for the opinion of the medical men who examined it was, that the body had been in the wood some four months. Had no one disappeared about that time? or was there no recollection of any stranger having been seen in the neighbourhood—passing by or through it, or stopping at a village inn or beer-shop? None. Every inquiry was made in the neighbourhood, but no traces of a missing man were found. The clothes were searched, and three halfpence in copper and a bunch of keys were found in the pockets. The clothes themselves indicated that the deceased had been,—at one time at least,—in a respectable sphere of life, for the coat on his back (he had no waistcoat) and the boots on his feet were well made. His linen was marked "T. H." Then came the question, had he destroyed himself, or had he been murdered? The evidence produced at the inquest was inconclusive on this point. The razor found beside him might have been the means of destruction in his own hands, or those of others. Decomposition left no traces for medical science to raise even a surmise upon. All that could be done at the time was to return an open verdict of " Found Dead," to take possession of the keys, clothes, &c., and to advertise the facts as extensively as possible. These steps were taken; but they never led to the identification of the dead man. From the time he was found in the wood by the idiot-boy (who was examined at the inquest, but from whom nothing intelligible could be gathered as to the state in which he first found the body—though that must have been early after death) up to the present moment, his name, country, occupation, whence he came or whither he was going, are a mystery. No eye had marked his approach to the spot on which he was so suddenly and so mysteriously to close his existence; by what terrible means there can be little doubt, for upon this evidence did rise up sufficient to remove all moral doubt that the man was foully dealt with. " Just after the inquest," said a party who had taken an official part in the inquiry, in answer to our questions, "just after the inquest, I was telling an old man, who is very deaf, all about it; and when I had done, ' Ah, yes,' he said, ' I remember very well seeing the blood along the road about that time;' "and," continued my informant, "no sooner had he uttered the words than I, too, recollected seeing a line of blood along the road by the gate, and others even said they recollected seeing blood on the gate itself." " How long," we enquired, "was this before the body was found?" "About four months, which must have been the time of the man's death. I supposed," continued my informant, "at the time that somebody had cut himself, or had bled at the nose, and took no further notice. But of the fact I had a perfect remembrance, and it left no doubt upon my mind that the man had been murdered—attacked in the road most probably, and dragged over the gate to the spot where he was found."

Another circumstance strengthens this opinion, and at one

time seemed to give a clue to the discovery of the murderer. A pedlar's box, stripped of its contents, was found in a low part of Southover, and was sent to the Lindfield authorities, who still have it. The keys of the deceased did not fit this box; but it seems to point to the occupation of the man and to explain both the motive for the crime, and the reason why the body was never owned. The man was a wanderer—perhaps a foreigner; he travelled from place to place, late and early. In his journey to Lindfield he was either tracked, or had bad companions. The road by Costell's Wood is lonely—there is no house within a quarter of a mile in any direction, and high trees on each side darken the path. He was doubtless attacked at disadvantage, robbed, and murdered, or partly murdered, and left in the wood, with the instrument of death by his side. And there he lay for four long months, not forty yards from the high road, yet hid from all but the wondering eyes of the poor idiot boy. *He*, doubtless, had seen the murdered man as he lay fresh in his newly-shed blood,—some think, before life had fled; but, however that may be, there is no doubt that day after day he came and gazed upon the terrible sight, and marked how the birds pecked at its eyes and the rats or dogs fed on its flesh, and how it mouldered away beneath the rains and the dews, until it had become the thing of bones that it was found.

In some respects this undiscovered crime will remind the local reader of a murder—likewise undiscovered—which was committed only nine years ago in the same district, but nearer to Cuckfield. In this case, too, the body of a man unknown was found who had been struck down by a murderous blow, evidently dealt from behind as he was crossing a "gully" in a meadow near Cuckfield Church—the path across this "gully" being a short cut, by which, in going from Hayward's Heath to Brighton, the town of Cuckfield may be avoided. To do this was, no doubt, the object of the murdered man, for it was afterwards ascertained that he had been concerned in some burglarious robberies near London and was flying from the pursuit of the police. The shoes he was wearing were identified as part of the booty of one of these robberies. He was also, it was afterwards discovered, in the neighbourhood of Cuckfield for another purpose. He had had an accomplice in some of his burglaries, and he had threatened this man, who lived at Croydon, with exposure unless he gave him some "hush money." An appointment had been made for an interview in a lonely part of Sussex, and here, at an inn at Balcombe, the murdered man passed some hours on the evening of the night (Saturday, the 27th November, 1869) on which he was to meet his accomplice. Whether he met him or not, who can say? but on the following Monday morning the fugitive burglar,—for such he was,—was found lying dead in a ditch at the back of Cuckfield with a fractured skull, and the instrument with which the blows were inflicted, called a "jemmy," and used by burglars, was afterwards found in an adjacent pond, into which it was doubtless flung immediately after the committal of the crime.

The police were unable to find any clue to the murderer—any, at least, sufficient to charge him with the crime. Both the murdered man (whose name was Greenhead) and the murderer had concealed their movements so well that they were never seen together. The accomplice referred to—a man named Rowland—was subsequently apprehended, and convicted, at the Sussex Assizes, of a robbery at Croydon, where he lived, and was sentenced to a year's imprisonment.

Here, again, in the presence of an undiscovered crime, we may say, in the powerful language which Hood places in the mouth of Eugene Aram,—whose crime was committed under somewhat similar circumstances to the above,— one more murderer

> " Walks the earth
> Beneath the curse of Cain,
> With crimson clouds before his eyes,
> And flames about his brain;
> For blood has left upon his soul
> Its everlasting stain!"

The late Editor of the Sussex Archæological Collections, the

Rev. E. Turner, in one of his latest contributions, expresses his satisfaction,—and surely all humane persons will join with him in doing so,—at the disappearance from our highways and byeways of those gibbets which used to mark the spot where a crime had been committed and where justice had exacted its most fearful penalty. To make it more durable and more terrible, the culprit used sometimes to be hung in what was called "chains"—that is, in a framework constructed of iron hooping, to which the rotting flesh and clothes and the bleaching bones long hung after wind and rain had done their worst upon them. In this way the body of Tapner, the Chichester smuggler, who took a leading part in the cruel murders of Galley, the Revenue Officer, and his witness, Chater, was exposed at the Old Broyle, in the immediate vicinity of Chichester, and another of the same gang, named Carter, was hung near Rake, on the Portsmouth road, in 1749. One of the last exhibitions of this kind, which, not improbably, by accustoming men to the spectacle of horrors, did more to harden than to appal them, took place in Sussex in the instance of two brothers, named Drewitt, convicted in 1799 of robbing the Portsmouth mail on North Heath Common, near Midhurst, and sentenced to be hung in chains. The first part of the sentence was carried out at Horsham, where the men were tried, and then, in accordance with custom, their bodies were brought to the place where the crime was committed and exposed in the way we have described. One of the Drewitt's, the younger brother, died protesting his innocence, and the belief is still prevalent at Midhurst and its neighbourhood, to which they belonged and where they were well known, that he was guiltless of the crime for which he suffered, but that he could not clear himself without implicating his father, and, rather than do this, went a victim to the gallows for the crime of a parent. It is remarkable that the last instance in this County of a barbarous custom should be thus coupled with a noble act of self-devotion on the part of one of the so-called culprits.

Poisoning has never been looked upon as an English crime; and it is remarkable, therefore, that a country town like Lewes should, so early as 1679, have been the scene of a deed of this nature, which would have been more in keeping with the soil and manners of Italy. The story, as told by a Lewes chronicler, has all the elements of a tragic romance.

A close intimacy had long existed between two young men of the town, Robert Brinkhurst, a cutler, and William Moor, "bred a draper" (to adopt the phraseology of our local authority), but heir to a considerable landed property. After some years' friendship, a petty difference sprang up between them, but was soon adjusted, leaving them, apparently, with the old feelings of regard for each other. Shortly afterwards, Moon (who suffered from a tainted breath) received, through the London carrier, a packet signed with the initials of a friend, and containing a powder, which was strongly recommended as a remedy for the complaint he suffered from. The contents of the paper were arsenic, and had been sent by Brinkhurst. The victim did not fall into the snare at once. He was uncertain whether he was to take all the powder in one dose or in parts. He therefore wrote to his friend in London to ascertain this point. Unfortunately, he commissioned Brinkhurst himself to carry the letter to the London carrier, — who then, it would seem, stood in lieu of a Post Office,—and the false friend, destroying the letter, contrived, by the agency of an acquaintance in London, to send a reply to it, purporting to come from the sender of the former parcel, and directing his victim to swallow the powder in one dose. He did so—on the Tuesday— and, after suffering four days' great agony, died on the succeeding Saturday; Brinkhurst waiting on him during that time (as Palmer did on his friend Cooke), and putting on all the show of grief and sympathy. How complete was his hypocrisy, and how real the affection of Moor was for him, was now shown in a way which ought to have overwhelmed him with remorse. By his friend's will, he was not only forgiven a debt of £50 (in all probability, one of the incentives to the murder), but was left a legacy of that amount, together with Moor's watch and other tokens of friendship.

So far, all had gone well for the murderer. The burial took place, and, to quote our authority for these facts, " Brinkhurst returned home, in seeming security, to exult in the consummation and profit of his crime." His triumph, however, was but short-lived. Moor had not destroyed the two forged letters that he received from London, and these, falling into the hands of his friends, raised a suspicion of foul play. The London carrier was questioned, and he now recollected that he had, some time before, brought down a parcel to the deceased, which had been given to him in Southwark by a person unknown; also, that he had somewhere by him a letter addressed to this party in Southwark, which, being refused to be taken in, he—the carrier—brought back again to Lewes, but, not knowing the writer of it, had laid it by. On the very day of Moor's interment, this letter, by a remarkable coincidence, was found by the carrier; and, on being opened, it was found that Brinkhurst was the writer of it, and its purport left little or no doubt that the other communications received by Moor had come from or been suggested by him. He was accordingly apprehended and taken before the Lewes Justices, to whom, we are told, he partly confessed his guilt. Being interrogated as to the nature of the powder he had procured, he pretended not to know its name, but said that, if he saw it again, he should recognise it. The Magistrates, unsuspicious of any design on the prisoner's part, directed an apothecary of the town to bring samples of different poisons that Bringhurst might point out the one he had used. This was done, and the prisoner, to the horror of the lookers-on, snatched up a parcel of yellow arsenic, and swallowed a considerable quantity of it before he could be prevented.

This desperate act stopped all further judicial proceedings. We are not told if any attempts were made to obviate the action of the poison by an emetic or otherwise—only that he "languished from the Tuesday till the Saturday evening"—exactly the same time that his friend had suffered—" tormented alike by bodily pangs and remorse"—and then died. His body was refused Christian burial. It was taken in a dung cart, without a coffin, to the cross roads near Spittle Barn, and there flung into a hole dug north and south, "from some absurd, superstitious notion," says the local historian, "a stake having been first driven, with moral barbarity (!), through the uncovered corpse."

To find a local parallel to this Lewes tragedy of the 17th century, we must pass on to our own town of Brighton in the 19th century, where, on the 23rd of May, 1866, a Dr. Warder arrived from Scotland, and took lodgings for himself and wife in Bedford-square. He had only been married ten months; he was in the prime of life,—45 or 46 years of age,—and yet the lady was his third wife. He had married her five months after the death of his second wife, a Scotch lady—a widow—who had only survived her union with Dr. Warder eight months. Her life had been insured by her husband. This second marriage took place in 1865. The death of the first wife had occurred two years before, in 1863, and followed quickly after a temporary separation; so that with Dr. Warder marriage and death had followed in quick succession.

And now again he had a sick wife. It was partly on that account that she came to Brighton, where she had a brother, like Dr. Warder, in the medical profession, but who had never met his brother-in-law until he came to Brighton. The marriage, indeed, of his sister with Dr. Warder had been a great surprise to him and all the members of her family. But she had been a friend of the second wife, and this, doubtless, facilitated the union; and she possessed a small fortune of some £500. The symptoms of Mrs. Warder's illness set in more strongly after her arrival in Brighton, and were of a nature to baffle all the skill of her brother; of a skilful Brighton physician called in—Dr. Taaffe; and of her own husband. The care and affection bestowed by this latter on the suffering lady were worthy of all praise; he rarely left her bedside, and he performed all the duties of a nurse. Still, the ailment baffled both skill and care; the patient grew weaker and weaker, and was sinking rapidly without any apparent cause.

This did not escape the notice of the Brighton physician; it was abnormal, and at last it aroused a dreadful suspicion in his mind. The form in which he gave effect to this was to request that a nurse should be called in; that another medical man should be associated with himself; and that for some days the husband should not be with his wife. This advice was given to the brother on the 30th of June. On the following day Dr. Taaffe and he were to meet at the house of the latter to arrange their future line of action. Early on the morning of that day—a Sunday —Mrs. Warder died. Her husband had been with her all the Saturday night. How he employed it, who can doubt? It was the last time that he would, in all probability, be allowed to act as nurse to the poor lady. Suspicion, he must have felt, was awake, and what he had to do, if done at all, must be done quickly. On the landlady, in answer to his summons, entering the room on Sunday morning, Dr. Warder, addressing her, exclaimed, "She is dying." Mrs. Warder was, indeed, already unconscious, and, before her brother or Dr. Taaffe could be summoned, she was a corpse. The grief of her husband, after death, was as marked as his attentions to her during life had been unremitting.

But Dr. Taaffe refused to certify to the cause of death. Hence an inquest was necessary, and, as a matter of course, a *post-mortem* examination was ordered by the Coroner, and the enquiry adjourned to await the result of an analysis by Dr. Taylor. The inquest was held on the Wednesday. The burial of Mrs. Warder took place on the Saturday. It was attended by Dr. Warder and Dr. Taaffe,—with what feelings by the former who can realise? Those of the latter were subsequently avowed; he looked upon the husband as the murderer of the wife whose remains he was following to the grave. Suspicion was so far aroused that a watch was set by the police on the movements of Dr. Warder. But, after returning to his lodgings from the funeral, he managed to evade this and went up to London. In the evening of Monday he returned to his lodging—cool and collected, according to his landlady, whom he requested to make out her bill, and on the following morning she found the full amount on the table, with £3 in excess as compensation for loss caused by the illness, inquest, &c. But Dr. Warder himself was gone. He had not passed the night at his lodgings.

The scene of the tragedy is now shifted to the Bedford Hotel, where, at a quarter to twelve on the Monday night, a traveller presented himself, with a black leather bag, and desired to be shown at once to a bedroom. His manner was quite cool and collected. The day was far advanced before the chambermaid thought of calling the late arrival, and when she did so there was no reply. She tried the door. It was unlocked. She entered the room and looked in; and she saw Dr. Warder—for it was he—lying dead on the bed. He was undressed, but the bedclothes were undisturbed. On the drawer by the side of the bed stood a small blue bottle, capable of holding 10 drachms and still containing 4 drachms of prussic acid. Whoever swallowed these 6 drachms could only have had time to put the bottle where it stood; he could not even draw the bedclothes over his face before death seized him.

Of course, an inquest was held on the body, and a *postmortem* examination of the brain shewed it to be healthy and its structure normal; there was nothing to indicate insanity, from which, it was said, some of his family had suffered. A verdict of *felo de se* was returned, and the body was interred in the Parochial Cemetery without any religious ceremony and with no inscription to say who lay beneath. The wife had been interred on the 7th July; the husband was buried on the 12th.

At the adjourned inquest on Mrs Warder, Dr. Taylor attended to report the result of his analysis. There was no vestige of poison in the organs, but they showed no other cause of death, and, from their appearance and the evidence already adduced, Dr. Taylor had no doubt that death had been caused by poison, and the jury returned a verdict that Ellen Vivian Warder died from the effects of aconite, administered wilfully by her late husband, Alfred William Warder.

The letters left by Dr. Warder at his lodgings on the night of his quitting them for the Bedford, addressed to friends, contained a virtual confession of his crime. After giving some directions about his property and his children by the first marriage, he wrote, "There is no escape for me, as you will find when you know all."

There was, indeed, none. Success in former cases (for the second wife died under similar symptoms to those of the last, and of the fate of the first there can be no doubt) had made the poisoner rash, and when he put the finishing stroke to his last crime he rushed on inevitable detection. It seems strange that he should have returned from London after, doubtless, procuring there the means of suicide. But who can explain the workings of a mind enmeshed in such a terrible net? That he fully realised his situation after the holding of the first inquest was demonstrated by the evidence of his landlady as to his frantic action in rushing to the window, from which she thought he would have thrown himself, and by the blow with which he fractured the mirror in the room and cut his face and throat with the broken fragments of glass. But this impulse towards despair and self-destruction was restrained for a time—only to gather force and be carried out in a more terrible, if a more collected, manner.

There is a general resemblance in the circumstances of the two events—at Lewes in the 17th and at Brighton in the 19th century—in the deadly means employed; the chance of escape; and then the sudden flashing out of the truth and the self-inflicted punishment of the culprit. But the relations of the parties in the modern crime were closer and the circumstances surrounding it more terrible.

Passing over the twin tragedies of Celia Holloway and Hannah Hobbs,—the one brought home so completely to the guilty party, the other still shrouded in the mystery which involved it from the very first,—as too revolting in their details to be told again, we come upon another undiscovered crime, connected with, though not committed in, Brighton, which stands out from the ordinary class of "bloody deeds," not only by the social position of the victim, and the utter failure to discover his "takers-off," but by the strange circumstance which preceded the deed, and by the puzzling fact which, after a considerable lapse of time, recalled the memory of it.

We refer to the death of Mr. George Stonhouse Griffith, the owner of the Rock Brewery, in Brighton, on the night of Tuesday, February 6th, 1849.

At the time of his death few men were better known at Brighton than Mr. Griffith. He was indeed a new comer; he had resided in Brighton little more than three years, and he was a stranger when he came; but his manners were open, frank, and pleasant, and his countenance was in harmony with his manners. It was a pleasant and good-looking one. Then his position—as the head of a brewing establishment—(he had previously been connected with the law),—was a good one, and he had taken the popular side in local politics, and distinguished himself as a Commissioner by his spirited opposition to the Clerk of that body, Mr. Lewis Slight, then exercising a predominant influence over that body, but with a growing opposition to his rule in which Mr. Griffith took a leading, if not a very successful, part.

Such was Mr. Griffith's position; a man happy in his domestic circumstances—with a wife and children—at the head of a large and, it is to be presumed, prosperous business,—enjoying good health, good spirits, and the good opinion of his fellow-townsmen, —on the day in February, 1849, on which he set out on that journey from which he never returned alive.

It was customary with the "house" to visit its customers in the north-west of Sussex,—at Horsham, Henfield, &c.,—on the first Tuesday of the month; and at one time Mr. Griffith made the journey himself; but for the twelve months preceding this February of 1849 he had discontinued it; his head clerk, Mr. Martin, taking his place. A circumstance, however, now occurred which induced him once more to make the journey. A warning letter was received early in January by Mr. Martin, couched in the following terms :—

"Sir,—Some parties intend to rob you next time you goes to Horsham, so bee on your gard."

This singular epistle was directed to "Mr. Mertens, Griffis Bruery," and the post-mark showed that it had been put into the box of the Trafalgar-street receiving house of the Brighton Post Office. The handwriting was evidently a disguised one; in the

P

opinion of those expert in such matters it was written with the left hand, and the bad spelling was evidently assumed, it being altogether unlikely that a person who could spell such a word as " parties " correctly, would stumble at " bee " and " gard."

The letter was, of course, shown to Mr. Griffith by his clerk, and its effect was, to induce him again to make the journey himself, taking with him a pair of pocket pistols, which Mr. Martin had borrowed of a friend in case he had gone. An offer made by the Chief Officer of the Brighton Police (Mr. Chase), to whom the letter was also shown, to accompany Mr. Griffith on the return journey by night was declined by him, as was also the company of Mr. Martin. He wished, he told the latter, to give a young friend staying with him a drive. However, he eventually went alone, in a light gig hired for the occasion. He was a fine, athletic man, in the prime of life, between 42 and 43—a formidable antagonist for any single assailant, and, with fire-arms, it might have been thought, a match for many. He seems to have had no fears ; he did not even tell his wife of the anonymous letter. And yet he was a cautious and prudent man, as is testified by the fact that not long before he had insured his life for a large sum.

The out-journey was made in safety. Horsham, West Grinstead, Henfield were called at and accounts collected. At the former place the wife of the landlord, Mrs. Ansell, remarked on the lateness of the hour and the fact that some robberies had been recently committed in that vicinity, whereupon, according to her statement at the subsequent inquest, Mr. Griffith took out of his pocket a red bag containing fire-arms. Never having seen such a weapon before, she asked him if it was a pistol? He replied " Yes," and proceeded to unscrew it, putting in first a round ball, and then, at the trigger part, some powder. As he was replacing the loaded weapon in the bag, the string broke, and he put the pistol in the right-hand pocket of his great coat. He then took out another bag, also containing a pistol, on which a neighbour of Mrs. Ansell who was present asked if that too was loaded? Mr. Griffith replied, " No. I'll warrant the other will

be enough for one man. I shall not give up my money easily."
He did not take the second pistol out of the bag; but Mrs.
Ansell saw the end of the weapon in it.

Mr Griffith was now on his return-journey to Brighton, and
night had set in. But it was not dark; for the moon, though
obscured by a hazy atmosphere, cast a bright light, almost as
strong as day, upon the surrounding country. When he reached
Henfield it was half-past eight. He took tea with the landlady of
the White Hart, who afterwards spoke of him as being in high
spirits, and as playing with her children in his usual kind way.
She paid him a £5 Brighton Union Bank note, the number
of which, with the business habits peculiar to him, he
entered in his memorandum-book. He left Henfield at 10 minutes
to 9, and at 5 minutes past 9 he passed through Terry's Cross-
gate, a mile and a half further on the road to Brighton. He was
then driving steadily at about six miles an hour. The gate-
keeper was expecting him, and exchanged salutations with him as
he passed through without stopping. The next turnpike was
Dale Gate, about three miles further on, and here, too, the gate-
keeper was expecting him between 9 and 10 o'clock. But he
never came. The road between Terry's Cross-gate and Dale
Gate is very lonely, but open. To the right, coming towards
Brighton, the country slopes up to the South Downs in wide open
fields, with "occupation roads," lined by low hedges, running
down from the hills to the highway. Mr. Griffith was now
skirting one of these sloping fields, called the "Deadway's Field."
After leaving Terry's Cross Gate, there is a strong rise in the road,
up which the horse must have walked, and here, one would have
thought, would have been the spot selected for a robbery, for from
neither side is a habitation to be seen. This, however, was passed
in safety, and then, on arriving at the top of the ascent, Newtimber Church comes into sight, and, on the same side, the left,
a farmhouse and a cottage. This point, too, was passed without
obstruction; and now, after a short fall in the road, there is
another rise—not so sharp as the former one, but still sufficient,
with the heavy state of the road and the long journey of the

horse, to bring it to a walking pace. Here the attack must have been made, for at this spot—about 600 yards from Dale Gate—the lifeless body of Mr. Griffith was found, between one and two o'clock in the morning, by a party of gentlemen returning home late from a shooting party at Newtimber, to whom Mr. Griffith was well known. He was lying on his back, with his great coat torn open (a button was off it), and the knees of his trousers and the front part of his dress stained with mud, but no other sign of violence beyond the immediate cause of death. This was a pistol shot in the centre of the chest, high up, and so close to the body when fired that it had scorched Mr. Griffith's shirt and a piece of chamois leather which he wore beneath it, and a part of the wadding had gone into the wound. This must have been instantly fatal; for the bullet, after passing the breast bone, took a side direction and went right through the heart, in which it was found lodged. The conclusion was, that, after receiving it, the unfortunate gentleman fell on his back and was so suffered to remain while he was robbed, his pockets being turned inside out. But in that case he must either have alighted or been dragged from his vehicle, and then shot, for the medical man examined at the inquest, Mr. Harry Mills Blaker, was decided on the point that he was standing when shot, and immediately fell backwards and died. He might have uttered, said Mr. Blaker, one shriek or moan, and such a death-shriek was heard by the keeper's wife at Dale Gate at half-past nine.

But, however instantaneous the death of Mr. Griffith, it was obvious that he was not surprised by his assailants, and did not die without a struggle. It would have been impossible, in such an open country, and on so light a night, to come upon him unawares, forewarned as he had been and prepared as he was for the attack; and then, too, as a proof that he was not so surprised, he had had time to take off his right-hand glove and to draw and discharge, or attempt to discharge, a pistol. The weapon was found on the road two yards and a half from his body. Then, too, his whip was broken, as though by a blow given with it, and the reins had been cut, and a portion of them was found lying on the road, with a clasped knife, by which, no doubt, it had been done; and Mr. Griffith's hat and empty purse, and with them the frame of a pair of spectacles, with some crape attached to it, intended, it may be presumed, to conceal an assailant's face, were also lying in the road near the dead body. When, too, the gig,—which had been turned round towards Henfield,—was examined, it was found that the step had been forced round in a way that could only have been effected by great violence. There were no marks of blood or other signs to denote a struggle in the gig, only the cut reins and the broken whip and the twisted step; nor did the ground, where Mr. Griffith was lying, show any signs of a struggle. But the above facts are conclusive that there must have been a struggle between Mr Griffith and his assailants before the fatal shot was fired.

The booty resulting from the deed could not have been great. It was supposed that Mr. Griffith had upon him about £20 in cash; he had taken a cheque of £13 on the Chichester Bank, and a £5 Brighton Union Bank note. These were missing, and his watch—a gold one—had been wrenched off the gold chain by which it hung round his neck; but a considerable part of the chain itself was found attached to the back part of his neck, as if flung round by the violence of the rupture, and a gold mourning ring was still on his finger.

The excitement caused by the event in Brighton and in the County generally, when made known, cannot easily be described. If such a man, so armed and forewarned, could thus be attacked and murdered on a highway so much frequented as that between Dale Gate and Henfield, who could be safe? A reward of £300 was offered—£100 by the Government, and £200 by private subscription—to anyone who could give evidence that would lead to the conviction of the murderers, and a free pardon to any party who did not actually commit the crime. Both the East Sussex and the Brighton Constabularies put forth their utmost efforts to obtain some clue. But without avail. The Coroner's Inquest, held at the Plough Inn, at Piecombe, brought out the above facts, and ended in a verdict of " Wilful murder against some persons unknown," the jury giving it as their decided opinion that more than one person must have been concerned in the crime. But not the slightest evidence was forthcoming as to the guilty parties. The question was asked by a juror whether the fatal shot might not have been fired by deceased himself, either in a struggle or otherwise? But to this a decided negative was given by Mr. Blaker. It was impossible, he said, that deceased could have inflicted such a wound on himself. The bullet came straight from the orifice of the pistol. This put the hypothesis of a suicide out of Court, and it was never raised by the parties whom it most concerned to do so : the Insurance office.

It has been named that one of Mr. Griffith's pistols was found lying near him on the road. The pan was open and the trigger down, so that it had been pulled. But, upon being examined by the police, it was found that the barrel was clean, and the constable who took charge of it after it was picked up expressed his belief that it had not been discharged, and, therefore, could not have been loaded by Mr. Griffith. A *loaded* pistol was found in the right hand pocket of his great coat—where he had been seen to place one by Mrs. Ansell at Horsham—and at that time, it will be recollected, Mr. Griffith said the other pistol, which was in a bag, was unloaded. The inference, then, is, that when Mr. Griffith saw he was about to be attacked, he drew forth the *unloaded* weapon, and that the *one* shot heard,—for several witnesses spoke distinctly to hearing the report of one shot, and one only, at the time, half-past nine, at or about which Mr. Griffith must have reached the " Deadways field," and that it came from that direction,—must have been that fired by his murderers. That Mr. Griffith should have made such a strange and so fatal a mistake, and that such a powerful man should have been pulled from his vehicle and have suffered a pistol to be discharged so close to him as to burn his clothes, does seem strange, and certainly bears out the conclusion of the jury that more than one person were concerned in the crime. In which case detection should have been easy, especially when the anonymous letter points to the probability, if not certainty, that the criminals were known to the writer of it, and thus brings a third party into the field. Yet neither the writer of that strange letter, nor any other party to the crime, came forward to claim the reward offered, coupled as it was with a promise of forgiveness to any except the actual murderer.

If the motive to the deed had been personal revenge, this could be understood. But the anonymous warning was against robbery, and a robbery *was* perpetrated, though here, again, a remarkable circumstance comes to throw additional mystery over the affair. Seven years after the death of Mr. Griffith, when all hope had died out of any further light being thrown on it, an important part of the booty—the gold watch, with a fragment of the broken chain attached to it—was found in a pond which was being "mudded" at Nutknowl, which lies by the side of the highway between Henfield and the spot where Mr. Griffith's body was found. How did it come there? Did the murderer, fearful of being found in possession of so damning a piece of evidence, fling it away almost as soon as he had got it? Then why did he take it at the peril of his life? Robbers—especially highwaymen —do not act in this way, unless in immediate danger of apprehension, and nobody ran this risk as a murderer of Mr. Griffith. A few people of doubtful character were questioned as to their whereabouts on the night in question; but nobody was ever taken into custody or even lay under suspicion. There was a rumour about two men being seen in the neighbourhood on the day of the murder; but they could not have been Brighton men, or they would have been marked and known; and if strangers, how is the warning letter to be explained? This points to a long-planned robbery, and if so, it must have been planned by men living in the same town as the writer of the letter and the intended victim resided in—that is, Brighton. It must not be forgotten, too, that the warning letter was sent, not to Mr. Griffith, but to Mr. Martin, his clerk—that *he* was the party who, in the ordinary course of events, would have made the journey, and he, therefore, must have been the object of attack, and not Mr. Griffith. This does away with the idea of personal revenge as a motive to the crime.

There is one circumstance in this mysterious crime to which we have not referred, namely, the presumptive evidence of a desire for concealment on the part of one of the murderers, in the shape of the mask formed by the spectacle frame and the crape. Was, then, the assailant known to his intended victim? If so, he could not have been unknown to Mr. Griffith's friends and dependents,— to Mr. Martin especially, whom he must have expected to meet, —and he could scarcely have avoided suspicion. None such ever fell on any individual. How singular, too, that this piece of disguise (which might have led to detection) and the knife with which the reins were cut should have been left in the road, when they might have been, in a comparatively clear night, so easily carried off! for it was some hours before any passer-by came to discover the body. Yet the men who did not do this took the precaution to turn round the horse and gig to prevent an alarm at Dale Gate!

From first to last, then,—from the receipt of the anonymous and warning letter to the finding of the lost watch,—the death of Mr. Griffith is involved in a strange mystery. That an act so foreseen and so guarded against should have been successful, is not the least extraordinary part of it. The chances were a hundred to one against the success of the attack: against the journey being made at all, after the warning given; against its being made alone, or on that day or at that time of night,—without which the crime could not have been committed,—also against the party attacked being unarmed, or rather against the weapon he used being unloaded, and against the one shot fired at him being fatal; and with more than one shot the chances of an alarm being given would have been more than doubled. Even that *one* report was heard by several persons. Then, when the crime had been successfully perpetrated, that the escape from detection, or even suspicion, should have been so complete, is most remarkable. That there should have been a person of some education and intelligence cognizant of a criminal intention, ready to give a warning, and yet, when a great crime *had been* committed, deaf to all the appeals and rewards of justice, does excite our wonder, and lead us to question the truth of the old adage that "Murder will out," or, "though it have no tongue, will speak with most miraculous organ."

Sussex has not furnished many contributions to the romance of County History. Its County families have, for the most part, led a quiet, secluded, respectable life, pursuing their bucolic pleasures, and discharging their Magisterial duties, with a homely kind of ambition that has preserved them from those temptations and dangers, not to say crimes, that attend on a more brilliant mode of life. There have, of course, been exceptions to this rule. The tragical fate of Lord Dacre "of the South," in the reign of Henry the Eighth, was one of these, and has already been recorded in these pages. The adventurous careers of the three Shirley's, whose love of wandering took them into the East and made one of them the favourite of Shah Abbas, are another instance of departure from the home-staying habits of Sussex gentry. But, as a rule, the biography of our Sussex County families furnishes few materials for that romance in which many other Counties are so rich ; and where the novelist or romance-writer has, like Horace Smith, in his "Brambletye House," or Harrison Ainsworth, in his "Rookwood," made Sussex the scene of his story, it is to his invention rather than to historical or biographical fact that he has been indebted for any exciting or tragical events that may have figured in it.

There is, however, one incident in the history of a Sussex family overlooked by novelists and romancists, and, so far as our knowledge extends, unnoticed by our County annalists, which makes good the saying that "fact is strange—stranger than fiction," and, as it casts no slur on any survivors of those who took part in it, may be told without offence.

In July, 1820, a trial came on in the Court of Queen's Bench, before the Lord Chief Justice and a Special Jury, upon the direction of the Lord Chancellor, to try whether the plaintiff, Eliza Ann Harriet Sergison, was the daughter of the late Colonel Francis Sergison, or whether she was a supposititious child imposed upon the family by the contrivance of his wife.

The Colonel Francis Sergison in question was the second son of Francis Jefferson, Esq., a native of Yorkshire, and who had taken the name and arms of the Sergisons of Cuckfield Place, Sussex, on marrying the heiress of that family, and also of the Wardens. His second son Francis entered the army, and must, in those active times, have seen some service, for he rose to the Colonelcy of the 62nd Regiment. But in the year 1806 he was residing in Dublin upon half-pay, having, we are told, dissipated the greater part of his fortune, and being, in fact, so reduced in circumstances that he was thrown into the Dublin Gaol for debt. Here he met with a companion in misfortune—a widow named Cronin—a woman of great personal attractions, but not of the most reputable character, for it was admitted that since the death of her first husband, a journeyman coach-builder, she had borne two illegitimate children, one of whom had been born on the 18th of March, 1806, as her marriage with Colonel Sergison took place, within the walls of the Dublin prison, on the 30th of April following! The Colonel's first wife, too, had only died a few weeks previous to the ceremony, so that little else is needed to bear out the statement made on the trial that Colonel Francis Sergison was a hasty, passionate man, very fond of having his own way!

The newly-wedded couple soon after contrived to gain their liberty, but lived for some time in embarrassed circumstances in Dublin; and it was during this period that the events took place which were the subject of the trial at the Court of Queen's Bench in 1820—13 years afterwards.

During the temporary absence of Col. Sergison—sent out of the way, it would seem, by design, on a visit to one of his wife's illegitimate children—Mrs. Sergison represented that she had been confined, and presented to him, on his return, a female child as his own offspring. It was, to all appearance, accepted by him as such without suspicion, for he had believed his wife to be in the family way, and the child was brought up by him as his heiress. In the following year, 1808, the Colonel and his wife came to live in England, and in 1811, by the death of his elder brother, Mr. Warden Sergison, of Cuckfield Park, without issue, he came into the fine family property at Cuckfield, Sussex. And here he lived, with his wife and his reputed daughter, Eliza Ann Harriet, up to the time of his death, in 1812. Not only was the girl acknowledged as his heiress, but she also inherited a considerable fortune by the death of his mother, the ~~heiress~~ of the Wardens and Sergisons. For some years the widow of the late Colonel must have continued in the enjoyment of this, for the trial to decide the question of birth did not, as we have said, take place until July, 1820, when the child must have been nearly 13 years of age. How long the proceedings lingered in Chancery,—whence they issued by the writ of the Lord Chancellor, Lord Eldon (not the most expeditious of Judges!)—we do not know; but they were instigated at the instance of the Rev. Mr. Pritchard, who had married a younger sister of the Colonel, and who, by his death, became the only surviving representative of the Sergison and Warden families, that is, in case of no issue being left by the Colonel. The legitimacy, therefore, of Eliza Ann Harriet Sergison became a vital question to the family. Doubtless some suspicious rumours had got abroad, which had reached the ears of the Pritchards, and caused them to set enquiries on foot in Ireland. And these at length ripened to a point which justified legal steps, and brought about the trial in England. They must have been conducted with great ability, for Mrs. Sergison, the pseudo-mother of the girl who was made plaintiff in the case, went into Court with the greatest confidence, and her cause, as it really was, was conducted by the Solicitor-General of the day. Mrs. Sergison, described as being a very fine woman, swore positively that the child was hers by her late husband, Colonel Francis Sergison, and appealed to the testimony of several persons who were present at the birth; naming one—Fitzsimmons—as the accoucheur. Several of these persons were called as witnesses, and swore, some to the pregnancy of Mrs. Sergison previous to the birth, and some to the actual birth of the child.

But, at the very time these witnesses and Mrs. Sergison were thus giving their evidence, the most conclusive proof was in the hands of the opposite party of its falsehood, and not a small portion of this proof was furnished by the acts of Mrs. Sergison herself.

Mr. Scarlett (the first Lord Abinger), who conducted the defence, began his speech by telling the Solicitor-General that he (the Solicitor-General) was not aware of the case which he supported and that the lady who had sworn so firmly before the Court had perjured herself in every word she had uttered. He proceeded to prove this by reading letters from Mrs. Sergison to witnesses on the other side, imploring them to go abroad or otherwise keep out of the way, and to communicate with her for that purpose, unknown to her solicitor. He then called these people, including a female—a Mrs. Gibson—whom Mrs. Sergison had called in to aid and assist her in the fraud—also the accoucheur, Fitzsimmons, and the real mother of the child, one Ann Magin, a servant at a Dublin public-house. From their statements it appeared that in January, 1807, whilst Col. Sergison was away, his wife went to Mrs. Gibson, with whom she had previously been acquainted whilst the wife of Cronin, and said she had supposed herself to be with child, and dreaded the Colonel's violence when he should discover her mistake and his disappointment. She had, therefore, in conjunction with her servant, Nelly Cunningham, formed a plan for imposing a supposititious child upon him. This plan she disclosed to Mrs. Gibson, and they proceeded to put it in execution. It had been previously ascertained, by Mrs. Sergison's servant, Nelly Cunningham, that a servant at a public-house, named Ann Magin, had been delivered four days before of an illegitimate child, and this woman was induced to part with the child—a female one, with black eyes and dark hair—for three half-crowns. It was taken by Nelly Cunningham to a house in Angier-street, where Mrs. Sergison and Mrs. Gibson were waiting for it; and there Mr. Fitzsimmons, an accoucheur, was sent for, and, after a conversation with Mrs. Sergison, consented to play his part in the deception. The child was then taken by Mrs. Sergison and Mrs. Gibson in a coach to the lodgings of the former in Parliament-street, and was carried upstairs by Mrs.

Gibson in her muff; something having been given it to make it sleep. In half-an-hour after Mr. Fitzsimmons came. Mrs. Sergison then went to bed, and the child was laid on the bed by her. The trick was never suspected by Colonel Sergison, who looked upon the child as his own, and died in that belief. In all respects it was brought up and treated as the heiress of the Sergison family. Yet, as Mrs. Gibson told Mrs. Sergison in 1819, when the latter went to Dublin with her supposed daughter, in order to induce her (Mrs. Gibson) to go to America, at that very moment the real mother of the child was selling apples at the corner of the street in which they were!

In addition to this *viva voce* evidence, letters were produced from Mrs. Sergison to Nelly Cunningham (dead at the time of the trial) to show that Nelly was acquainted with the secret of the so-called Miss Sergison's birth and extraction, and that she received an annuity as the price of her silence. In fact, there could be no doubt of the fraud, and the jury had no difficulty, under the direction of the Lord Chief Justice, in coming to a verdict for the defendant, the effect of which was to establish the illegitimacy of Eliza Ann Harriet Sergison and to transfer the Sergison and Warden estates to the rightful heirs, the Pritchards, by whom the surname and arms of Sergison were forthwith assumed, and by whose descendants they are now borne.

What became of Mrs. Colonel Francis Sergison and the poor girl who was made the innocent instrument of her fraud, we are not able to say. In all probability, the former had a provision for life, as the widow of Colonel Sergison, and no further proceedings seem to have been taken against her, for perjury or fraud. The child of the Dublin applewoman was, it is to be hoped, either maintained by her or some provision made for it by the Sergison family. The escape of the latter from being made the victims of a cunningly-devised scheme was a narrow one; if successful, it would have been a singular, but perhaps not unique, mode of keeping up the line of descent of two ancient families! As it is, the *sang azule* of the Wardens and Sergisons flows unsullied in the veins of its head, Captain Warden Sergison, of Cuckfield Park, and, seeing how numerous are the branches to the family-tree, there is little likelihood of its being exhausted.

Another romantic incident—and of a more touching character—unstained, too, by any associations of crime, is furnished by the local history of Maresfield, and is told so unaffectedly by the late Rector of that parish, the Rev. E. Turner, that we give it in his language. When touching on the family mansion, at Maresfield, of the Relphes, of " Marshalls," he says:—

"The melancholy circumstances attending the death of a female of this family, resident in Buxted, and of a gentleman named Atkinson, to whom she was affianced, was deemed by Mr. Mitchell, the then rector of Maresfield, of sufficient interest to merit more than a mere formal register of their burial. He has therefore recorded them in a Latin note; and they are certainly, as Mr. Mitchell commences by saying, worthy of being delivered down to posterity. The entries of their burial are:—

"1742. Dec. 14th, buried Mrs. Mary Relfe, of Buxted.
"1742. Dec. 15th, Mr. James Atkinson, of London.

"A mutual attachment, he continues, had for some time existed between them, and the day fixed for their marriage was close at hand, when a special messenger unexpectedly arrived in London, where Mr. Atkinson appears to have held some public appointment, for the purpose of announcing the sad intelligence of the dangerous illness of the lady. He hastened to Buxted, and found the object of his dearest affections at the point of death. Gratified by the sight of her lover, and at this proof of his sincere attachment to her, she revived a little at the sight of him, and lived, contrary to all expectation, two days after his arrival, during which time he continued by her bedside, administering to her wants, and refusing to take food, or to be in any way comforted. She died on the evening of Sunday, on which day, sick in body, but much more sick in mind, he took to his bed, and there lay, overpowered by the intensity of his grief, and praying continually for relief by death, until the following Sunday, when he died, at the very same hour in the evening that she expired;

his death having taken place the day she was buried, and he himself being buried the very day they were to have been married. They are interred, side by side, in the churchyard of this parish, at the east end of the chancel. As the name of Atkinson occurs frequently in the registers about this time, the broken-hearted-swain in this case was probably a native of Maresfield, as well as the lady to whom he was so devotedly attached."

We think it is Dr. Johnson who doubts if such a thing as a broken heart is to be found within the range of pathological science. But, if the above facts be true,—and there is every reason to receive them as such,—the strong sympathy between two human beings which we call love has been the cause of death, and it little matters in what region of the body the cause of dissolution lay. In figurative speech, if not in actual fact, James Atkinson died of a broken heart.

SUSSEX POETS.

IT may be questioned if any County can produce four greater names in English literature than those of John Fletcher, Thomas Otway, William Collins, and Percy Bysshe Shelley. These are the *Dii majores* of Sussex. We have also many poets of the second and third class, not unknown to fame, but better known in their own day than they are now. Amongst these are Hayley, Hurdis, Charlotte Smith, Clio Rickman, George Frederick Richardson, Charles Crocker, and Charles Verral.

To the four great names that head our roll of Sussex Poets it would be impossible for any writer, short of the highest order, to do full justice. To make use of Fletcher's own magnificent language, in which he makes Cæsar mourn over the murdered Pompey,—

> " Nothing can cover *their* high fame but Heaven ;
> No pyramids set off *their* memories,
> But the eternal substance of their greatness,
> To which we leave them."

But, before referring to these great poets, three of whom were dramatists (for Shelley is entitled to take rank with Shakspeare, Marlowe, Webster, Fletcher, and Otway, by virtue of his "Cenci"), we ought not to forget that the precursor of all these sons of fame—the first Englishman who wrote a tragedy worthy to be so called — was a native of Sussex: Thomas Sackville, Lord Buckhurst, afterwards Earl of Dorset. " The earliest tragedy," according to Hazlitt, in his lectures on the Elizabethan Dramatists, "that we have—that of Ferrex and Porrex, or Gordubuc, as it has been generally called," was his production, and was in that blank verse which, as subsequently used by Marlowe and then by Shakspeare, became the most powerful vehicle for passion and pathos since the days of Eschylus and Sophocles. "Gordubuc" was first acted, and with applause, before Elizabeth in 1561, when its author was still a young man. Hazlitt, judging it by comparison with what came later, is severe upon it. "As a work of genius," he says, "it may be set down as nothing, for it contains hardly a memorable line or passage. As a work of art, and the first of its kind attempted in the language, it may be considered as a monument of the taste and skill of the author." He quotes some passages which go far to overthrow his unfavourable judgment. Certainly there is poetic genius in the following lines, in which the heroine laments over the untimely death of her lover, Ferrex :—

> "Ah! noble prince, how oft have I beheld
> Thee mounted on thy fierce and trampling steed,
> Shining in armour bright before the tilt,
> And with thy mistress' sleeve tied on thy helm,
> And charge thy staff to please thy lady's eye,
> That bowed the head-piece of thy friendly foe!
> How oft in arms on horse to bend the mace,
> How oft in arms on foot to break the sword,
> Which never now these eyes may see again!"

Does not this passage recall as well as anticipate those of a great poet of our own days :—

> "So like a shattered column lay the King,—
> Not like that Arthur who, with lance in rest,
> From spur to plume a star of tournament,
> Shot thro' the lists at Camelot, and charged
> Before the eyes of ladies and of Kings."

The thought and feeling are the same in both, and even in the imagery there is resemblance enough to make the parallel a striking one. Both have the true touch of pathos, and the ring of chivalry, in them.

But we must leave Thomas Sackville in his glory as the first writer of English tragedy, to come to a greater than he: John Fletcher, the author of "The Faithful Shepherdess," one of the sweetest and richest Pastoral Poems ever written,—worthy of Arcadia itself in its most palmy days,—and the writer, first in conjunction with his friend, Francis Beaumont, and afterwards by his unaided pen, of a large number of plays, of almost every style, from that of Seneca to that of Plautus. In speaking of "The Faithful Shepherdess," Hazlitt says it comes near to Spenser in a certain tender and voluptuous sense of natural beauty, whilst in the playful and fantastic expression of it he approaches Shakspeare ; and he quotes some passages which bear out the eulogy. Here is one: the description of a spot well fitted for love, described by Chloe to Thenot :—

>———" Here be woods as green
> As any, air likewise as fresh and sweet
> As where smooth Zephyrus plays on the fleet
> Face of the curled stream, with flow'rs as many
> As the young Spring gives, and choice as any ;
> Here be all new delights, cool streams and wells,
> Arbours o'ergrow with woodbine ; caves and dells ;
> Chuse where thou wilt, while I sit by and sing,
> Or gather rushes, to make many a ring
> For thy long fingers ; tell thee tales of love,
> How the pale Phœbe, hunting in a grove,
> First saw the boy Endymion, from whose eyes
> She took eternal fire that never dies ;
> How she conveyed him softly, in a sleep,
> His temples bound with poppy, to the steep
> Head of old Latmos, where she stoops each night,
> Gilding the mountain with her brother's light,
> To kiss her sweetest."

The invocation of Amaryllis to Pan, the God of Shepherds, to save her from the violence of the Sullen Shepherd, for Syrinx' sake—

> " For her dear sake
> That loves the rivers' brinks, and still doth quake
> In cold remembrance of thy quick pursuit "—

this has the magic touch of Shakspeare in it ; and in some

passages it is obvious that Fletcher set a copy which Milton was not loath to follow in his Comus—*Ex. gr.* :—

> "Yet I have heard, (my mother told it me,
> And now I do believe it), if I keep
> My virgin flow'r uncropt, pure, chaste, and fair,
> No goblin, wood-god, fairy, elf, or fiend,
> Satyr, or other power that haunts the groves,
> Shall hurt my body, or by vain illusion
> Draw me to wander after idle fires ;
> Or voices calling me in dead of night
> To make me follow, and so tole me on
> Thro' mire and standing pools to find my ruin ;
> Else, why should this rough thing, who never knew
> Manners, nor smooth humanity, whose heats
> Are rougher than himself, and more misshapen,
> Thus mildly kneel to me ? Sure there's a pow'r
> In that great name of Virgin, that binds fast
> All rude uncivil bloods, all appetites
> That break their confines : then, strong Chastity,
> Be thou my strongest guard, for here I dwell
> In opposition against fate and hell !"

"The lady" in Comus does but repeat this pure sweet strain of our great Sussex poet.

When we consider that the hand that writ this sweetest of pastoral poems was also the author (in conjunction, it is thought, with Shakspeare himself) of "The Two Noble Kinsmen," and that he soars in it to Shaksperian heights—also that he wrote the play of "Philaster, or Love lies a Bleeding," in which, as Hazlitt says, "The passages of extreme romantic beauty and high-wrought passion are out of number "—ought we not to think much of our Sussex poet? Ought not Rye to be very proud of having given birth to him? It did so, it would seem, in 1579. His father, Dr. Fletcher, was then Vicar of Rye, and subsequently held in succession the Sees of Bristol, Worcester, and London—owing them, apparently, as much to his good looks (Queen Elizabeth ever liked a handsome face—in a man) as to his piety or learning. Marrying, however, a second time,—once too often for his Royal and fickle mistress,—he fell into her displeasure, and so pined away and died—most unbishoplike ! It was, probably, this reverse of fortune to his father that caused the son, like so many young men of the day, to take to play-writing. Upon leaving the University, and finding a congenial spirit in Francis Beaumont, also fresh from College, these twin-Poets set up a partnership which aimed at nothing less than rivalry of Shakspeare, and the produce of which was accepted by a later age as superior to his work. This decision has, of course, long been reversed, and the space which separates Shakspeare from all other poets becomes greater and greater as Time rolls on. Yet, so far as Shakspeare *can* be approached, he is approached by Fletcher. Speaking of him and Shakspeare's other great contemporaries, Hazlitt says :—

"They are a mighty phalanx of kindred spirits closing him (Shakspeare) round, moving in the same orbit, and impelled by the same causes in their whirling and eccentric career. They had the same faults and the same excellences ; the same strength and depth and richness, the same truth of character, passion, imagination, thought, and language, thrown, heaped, massed together without careful polishing or exact method, but poured out in unconcerned profusion from the lap of nature and genius in boundless and unrivalled magnificence. The sweetness of Deckar, the grace of Fletcher and his young-eyed wit, Jonson's learned sock, the flowing vein of Middleton, Heywood's ease, the pathos of Webster, and Marlow's deep designs, add a double lustre to the sweetness, thought, gravity, grace, wit, artless nature, copiousness, ease, pathos, and sublime conceptions of Shakspeare's Muse. They are indeed the scale by which we can best ascend to the true knowledge and love of him. Our admiration of them does not lessen our relish for him ; but, on the contrary, increases and confirms it."

Fletcher died unmarried,—in 1625,—it is supposed of the plague then raging in London, and was buried at St. Mary's, now St. Saviour's, Southwark. Little or nothing is known of his habits of life, except that he and Beaumont were gay young men, "about town," "noble-swelling spirits," affecting a more aristocratic, or, as we should say now-a-days, fashionable tone and air than their great contemporaries. With these, however, we know, from Beaumont's poetic description to Jonson of what they did at the Mermaid, they mingled, and the very talk of the two friends is said to have been a "comedy." Sometimes, too, it must have been something higher, for how richly stored must have been the minds of which such gems as these were the out-flow :—

MELANCHOLY.

" Hence, all you vain delights,
As short as are the nights
Wherein you spend your folly;
There's nought in this life sweet,
If man were wise to see't,
But only melancholy.
Oh, sweetest melancholy!
Welcome folded arms and fixed eyes,
A sight that piercing mortifies :
A look that's fasten'd to the ground,
A tongue chain'd up without a sound;
Fountain heads, and pathless groves,
Places which pale passion loves :
Moon-light walks, when all the fowls
Are warmly hous'd, save bats and owls;
A midnight bell, a passing groan,
These are the sounds we feed upon :
Then stretch our bones in a still, gloomy valley;
Nothing so dainty sweet as lonely melancholy."

MAN.

" Like to the falling of a star,
Or as the flights of eagles are,
Or like the fresh Spring's gaudy hue,
Or silver drops of morning dew,
Or like a wind that chafes the flood,
Or bubbles which on water stood :
E'en such is man, whose borrow'd light
Is straight call'd in and paid to-night :—
The wind blows out, the bubble dies;
The Spring intomb'd in Autumn lies;
The dew's dried up, the star is shot,
The flight is past, and man forgot."

There is a honeyed sweetness in this verse which has never

been surpassed. And yet we question if many Sussex ears have feasted on it before. And Rye, has she any memorial of her greatest son? We wot not. Otway has not long had one at his birth-place, and Horsham knows nothing of Shelley. But poets like these need no monuments beyond their own works. They alone are indestructible.

Thomas Otway was born in 1651, in the little village of Trotton (West Sussex), of which his father was curate, and subsequently Rector of the adjacent parish of Woolbeding. The spot is well-fitted by its rural beauty and picturesque scenery for a pastoral poet. But Otway's genius did not lie, like Fletcher's, in this direction; nor was there, in the licentious age of the second Charles, much demand for that kind of poetry. A new taste and a new style of literature had been imported from France, and a license was permitted,—nay, demanded,—of writers for the stage that even the later dramatists of James's days would have scarcely satisfied. The Rochesters, the Davenants, and the Ethereges were now in the ascendant; and even men of true genius, like Dryden and Otway, had to swim with the stream.

At the age of 18 years Otway, like Fletcher, was sent (from Winchester School) to the University of Oxford, which he left in 1670 without a degree, and betook himself, not to his Sussex home, but to London, "to seek his fortune." The reason for this step was pointed out by us in the *Brighton Herald* 20 years ago. An examination of the parish register of Woolbeding[*] at that time led to the discovery, not only of the entry of Otway's birth, but of the death of his father, then Rector of Woolbeding, in February, 1670. The death of the father, in Otway's as in Fletcher's case, threw the son on his own resources, at the early age of 19, and his tastes, probably, as well as his necessities drew him to the stage. In one of his minor poems,

---

[*] Made by the courtesy and with the assistance of the Rev. F. Bourdillon, then the Incumbent of Woolbeding.

"The Poet's Complaint of his Muse," he thus describes his own situation at this time :—

> " I am a wretch of honest race :
> My parents not obscure, nor high in title were :
>   They left me heir to no disgrace :
> My father was (a thing now rare)
>   Loyal and brave : my mother chaste and fair.
> Their pledge of marriage-vows was only I ;
> Alone I liv'd, their much-lov'd fondled boy ;
> They gave me generous education high,
> They strove to raise my mind, and with it grew their joy.
>   The sages that instructed me in Arts,
>   And knowledge, oft would praise my parts,
>   And cheer my parents' longing hearts.
>   When I was called to a dispute,
>   My fellow-pupils oft stood mute :
>   Yet never envy did dis-join
> Their hearts from me, nor pride distemper mine.
>   Thus my first years in happiness I past,
>   Nor any bitter cup did taste ;
>   But oh ! a deadly potion came at last.
>   As I lay loosely on my bed,
>   A thousand pleasant thoughts triumphing in my head,
>   And as my senses on the rich banquet fed,
>   A voice (it seem'd no more, so busy I
>   Was within myself, I saw not who was nigh)
> Pierc'd thro' my ears ; Arise, thy good *Senander's* dead.
> It shook my brain, and from their feast my frightened senses fled.
>
> From thence sad discontent, uneasy fears,
> And anxious doubts of what I had to do,
>   Grew with succeeding years.
> The world was wide, but whither should I go ?
> I, whose blooming hopes all wither'd were,
> Who'd little fortune and a deal of care !
> To *Britain's* great Metropolis I stray'd,
>   Where fortune's general game is play'd ;
> Where honesty and wit are often prais'd,
> But fools and knaves are fortunate and rais'd.
> My forward spirit prompted me to find

>   A converse equal to my mind:
> But, by raw judgment easily misled,
>   (As giddy callow boys
>   Are very fond of toys)
> I miss'd the brave and wise, and in their stead
> On every sort of vanity I fed.
> Gay coxcombs, cowards, knaves, and prating fools,
> Bullies, of o'ergrown bulks and little souls,
> Gamesters, half-wits and spendthrifts, (such as think
> Mischievous midnight frolics bred by drink
>   Are gallantry and wit,
> Because to their lewd understandings fit),
>   Were those wherewith two years at least I spent,
> To all their fulsome follies most incorrigibly bent:
>   'Till at the last, myself more to abuse,
>   I grew in love with a deceitful Muse."

To put this in plain prose, the ex-collegian of 19 joined the Duke of York's company of players, and became an actor. But, like so many other playwrights, his success on the stage was small. It gave him, however, that knowledge of stage business which is so essential to the dramatist. At the age of 25, he produced his first drama, the tragedy of "Alcibiades"—a remarkable work as the first attempt of so young a man, though with many faults. This was quickly followed, if we are to credit Otway's own preface to it, by the tragedy of "Don Carlos, Prince of Spain"—a much higher effort, and containing passages of great beauty; many of them in those triplets which Dryden afterwards adopted and made such good use of in his translation of Virgil. This was succeeded by a translation of Moliere's "Fourberies de Scapin," and by a comedy called "Friendship in Fashion." The character of this latter may be inferred from the fact that when it was revived at Drury Lane in 1749 it was hissed off the stage for its grossness and immorality. Even when originally produced, it could not have had much success. Otway's genius did not lie towards comedy, which became mere buffoonery in his hands, or worse than that.

A break now takes place in Otway's career as a dramatic

author; he accepted a commission as cornet in some troops sent by the English Government into Flanders, and underwent some of the hardships of a soldier's life, without reaping any of its glory or more solid fruit. On returning to England, which he did a beggar, he turned his military experience to account by writing a play, "The Soldier's Fortune," which had a successful run; and any reader of it in the present day will be astonished that it should have done so. It is marked by a coarseness of language and of action which stamps the age that could accept such a piece for a picture of its manners as one of gross licentiousness. How a man of feeling and of genius, as Otway undoubtedly was, could produce such a piece amazes us. His excuse must be, that he was starving, and that he wrote for the age. And this is but a poor one for such trash.

In the play that followed "The Soldier's Fortune" Otway returned to tragedy, and to that vein of pathos in which his strength lay. This was "The Orphan," one of the two plays on which his fame rests for that mastery of pathos and tenderness in which he has never been surpassed, and only equalled by Shakspeare himself. There are some passages in "The Orphan" which rise to the highest point of passion, especially that in which Polydore, after his treachery to his brother and his discovery that Monimia has been secretly married to Castalio, bursts into the following "fine frenzy:"—

"Then thus let's go together,
Full of our guilt, distracted where to roam,
Like the first wretched pair expell'd their Paradise.
Let's find some place where adders nest in Winter,
Loathsome and venemous: where poisons hang
Like gums against the walls; where witches meet
By night and feed upon some pamper'd imp,
Fat with the blood of babes: There we'll inhabit,
And live up to the height of desperation;
Desire shall languish like a withering flower,
And no distinction of the sex be thought of.
Horrors shall fright me from those pleasing harms,
And I'll no more be caught with beauty's charms,
But when I'm dying take me in thy arms."

After an interval unworthily employed in giving a new shape to Shakspeare's "Romeo and Juliet," which was produced under the classical form of "Caius Marius," Otway again asserted his native genius and produced the nearest approach to Shakspeare that the English, or, perhaps, any stage, has seen since the days of Elizabeth and James. This was the tragedy of "Venice Preserved," the chief characters of which have ever been selected by our greatest actors and actresses—our Keans and Kembles, Siddons and O'Neils—as a vehicle for their histrionic powers. This was the highest and ripest fruit of Otway's genius. It was also the last. The life he led in London alternated between excess and starvation,—and it is a tradition of literature that his death was owing to the latter. His means may be guessed at from the fact that he only received £15 for the copyright of "Venice Preserved!" He was in his 34th year, and in the full maturity of his powers: he had genius, experience, the ear of the public, and, if we may believe his dedications to the Duke and Duchess of York, &c., he enjoyed the favour of the Court. But all were thrown away in that reckless and riotous life which was the fashion of the second Charles's days. The closing catastrophe of the Sussex dramatist's career had now come. He was hiding,—so runs the story,—from his creditors at a public house on Tower Hill, in a penniless condition, when, meeting a friend, who gave him a guinea, he hurried to buy a roll of bread, eating which with the voracity of a starving man, he was choked by the first mouthful. So perished, miserably and obscurely, a writer who, according to Johnson, has caused more tears to be shed on the stage for his Belvidera and Monimia than even Shakspeare has for Juliet and Desdemona, and who, in an age when bombast and obscenity divided the stage between them, went to Nature for his materials, and knew how to wring the human heart with sympathy for human suffering. He had great faults, but he had still greater beauties, and these latter were his own, whilst the former were those of the age in which it was his hapless lot to be cast. When it is considered that at the age of 19 years he was thrown upon his own resources for a living, and in such a city as London, in such a reign as that of Charles the Second, it is wonderful that he retained such vigour and freshness of thought—such healthiness of feeling, as enabled him to picture the virtues and sorrows of a wife such as Belvidera. He never apparently re-visited, as Shakspeare so often did, his rural home—the little village of Trotton, with its Church and river and picturesque scenery, nestling under the beautiful hills of Sussex and Hampshire—to drink in the fresh air and draw inspiration from the fair sights of the country. The home-ties snapped by the death of his father were never re-knit. Otway seems to have drifted about, a waif of London life—now in luck, now out of it, but oftener the latter than the former,—until a wretched death closes the struggle. Yet his mother still lived,—and in the old Sussex home of Woolbeding;—she did not die until 1703, and, with a heart capable of such intense feeling as Otway's was, his thoughts must have sometimes travelled to her, and to that beautiful village in which the early part of his life was passed. Perhaps he looked forward to achieving fortune as well as fame before returning "home." For it is obvious that, demoralising as Otway's mode of life may have been, his genius had been ripening. His last production, "Venice Preserved," is far above all his other works. Strike out one or two attempts at comic scenes, and both the incidents and the verse of the remainder have a strength which soars into the highest region of poetry and passion. Love was the natural element of Otway, but whilst in Monimia and other characters there is a dangerous voluptuousness in the pictures drawn of it, in Belvidera it is pure as well as impassioned, and the whole play gave promise that, had Otway lived, he would have reached a still higher point of excellence.

As it was, he sank, at the age of 34, into a nameless grave,—his remains were interred in a vault under the Church of St. Clement Danes,—and it is only within the last 30 years that a tribute to his memory has been erected (by W. Jolliffe, Esq.) in his birth-place, in the shape of a brass-plate let into the wall of the Parish Church at Trotton, and bearing the following inscription :—

> "Hoc monumentum, quantumvis simplex,
> Memoria sacratum sit
> THOMAS OTWAY, Armigeri,
> Poetarum Tragicorum qui in Britannia enotuerunt,
> Facile Princeps.
> · Hoc Pago natus anno 1651.
> Eheu ! egestate acerrima gravatus
> Naturæ concessit 1685.
> Abi, Lector Amice !
> Et vicibus præcellentis ingenii prospectis,
> Quamcunque Deus tibi fortunaverit horam,
> Æternitatem cogita."

The third great name on our Sussex roll of poets is that of William Collins. He also belongs to the western part of the County. He was a native of Chichester, and, like Otway, a Winchester boy, and a graduate of St. Magdalen's, Oxford. But here the parallel ends. The family of Collins, though of the trading class, were in good circumstances ; his father was thrice Mayor of Chichester, and, when he died, his brother-in-law, Lieut.-Colonel Martyn, a distinguished officer in the army, took his nephew, William, under his protection. At his uncle's invitation, after taking his degree as a Bachelor of Arts, Collins went over to Flanders, where Col. Martyn was then serving with his regiment,—it is a curious coincidence that both Otway and Collins should have had a taste of that unpoetical country, Flanders,—but he was pronounced "too indolent" for a military life, and was sent back to England to see if a clerical one would suit him better. For this, too, he was either disinclined, or "there was metal more attractive." Indeed, his tastes from early youth were strongly towards literature ; and having, by the death of his mother, become the owner of a little property and the master of his own actions, he gave the bent to his inclination, and became a man of letters. He had been the school-fellow of the Wartons, Whitehead, Hampton, &c., and he now made the acquaintance of

Dr. Johnson, at that time the head of the London world of wit and learning. The great Doctor, who afterwards became Collins's biographer, speaks highly of him. "His appearance," he says, "was decent and manly; his knowledge considerable; his views extensive; his conversation elegant; and his disposition cheerful." This latter quality contrasts strangely with what we know of the after-life of Collins, for "melancholy had marked him for her own." Even in his school-days he was remarked for being depressed, and once, when questioned by a companion as to the cause, he replied that he had had a dream: he had dreamt that, while walking in the fields, he saw a lofty tree, which he strove to climb, but, when he had nearly reached the top, a great branch gave way and he fell to the ground. On his school-fellow laughing at him for being out of spirits at such a cause, Collins said he looked upon the tree as "the tree of Poetry"; betraying at the same time his poetical aspirations and his constitutional melancholy. The anecdote has some resemblance to the story of Swift—also a prey to mental depression— who, seeing a tree struck by lightning, and its topmost branches leafless, exclaimed, "Ah, I am like that tree. I shall die at the top first."

The dream of the one poet and the prophecy of the other were both fulfilled. Collins climbed high, and reached one of the highest branches of poetry. But here he fell—not, like Otway, by the stroke of Fortune, but by even a harder Fate. Fortune, in the ordinary meaning of the word, was kind to him. When Johnson knew him, he was, indeed, in distress, and, with his usual kindness to literary brethren in trouble, the great Doctor assisted him out of his temporary difficulty by helping him to sell to the booksellers the commencement of a translation of Aristotle's Poetics. This work, however, he never finished, for, soon afterwards, his uncle, Colonel Martyn, died, leaving him a legacy of £2,000, and this sufficed for the wants of the remaining years of his life. Taking lodgings at Richmond, he seems to have indulged in that vein of indolence which was noticed in early life by his uncle. He wrote little, but that little was highly polished, and his "Ode to the Passions" placed him on a level with the finest lyric poets of that, or, indeed, of any other age. It brought him little profit—it was sold for £10!—but it gained him the acquaintance of Thomson, Armstrong, Mallet, and other poets and dramatists of the day, and with some of these it is to be feared that Collins, by free living and late hours, increased that natural debility which lay at the root of his subsequent malady. Perhaps, of all gifts, that of competency—the means of living in idleness—is the most dangerous that a man predisposed to melancholy can receive. If Collins had had his living to earn, he might have preserved his reason for many years. As it was, the cloud which was "no bigger than a man's hand" in youth grew and grew until it clouded the whole of his intellect. Had he had some fixed occupation—had he been compelled to translate the Poetics of Aristotle, of which Johnson speaks, or to write the History of the Revival of Learning, which he planned with Warton, it might have changed his fate, and he might, like Johnson himself, have striven successfully against this morbid melancholy which assailed them both. But his uncle's liberality had relieved him from immediate pressure, and though he afterwards projected many works, prose and poetical, he completed little or nothing,—and the only poem he published was his Dirge for Cymbeline, "To Fair Fidele's grassy tomb," printed in the *Gentleman's Magazine* of 1749. He had now left Richmond, and resided for a time, first in his native place—Chichester—and then in Bath. The clouds were gathering around him. To scatter them, he tried a tour in France, but without success; and, returning to England, was seized, whilst with some friends at Oxford, with the first attack of insanity, and became for a time an inmate of a private asylum. Hence he was removed by his sister to her residence near the Cathedral of Chichester, and in the cloisters of this edifice he was wont, it is said, to wander, giving vent to the distresses of his mind in lamentations and sobs. But, though the branch of the tree he essayed to climb was broken—though no longer able to write, or even to study, all light was not shut out. At this period of Collins's career he was seen once by his old friend, Dr. Johnson. It was after his return from France, and when awaiting his sister at Islington. "There was no apparent insanity (we quote from Mr. M. A. Lower's admirable piece of biography in his "Worthies of Sussex")—but he had given up study and travelled with no other book than a New Testament, such as children carry to school. Johnson took it into his hand, from simple curiosity as to what book a classical scholar (for Collins, besides being a thorough classical scholar, was master of Italian, French, and Spanish) had chosen for his *vade mecum*. 'I have but one book,' said the poor stricken poet; 'but that is the best.'"

It is to this incident that Hayley refers, in those lines (beneath Flaxman's monument to Collins in Chichester Cathedral) which are, perhaps, the finest he ever wrote :—

> " Ye who the merits of the dead revere,
> Who hold misfortune sacred—genius dear—
> Regard this tomb, where Collins' hapless name
> Solicits kindness with a double claim.
> Though Nature gave him, and though Science taught,
> The fire of Fancy and the reach of Thought,
> Severely doomed in penury's extreme
> He passed in maddening pain Life's feverish dream ;
> While rays of genius only served to show
> The thickening horror and exalt his woe.
> Ye walls, that echoed to his frantic moan,
> Guard the due records of this graceful stone !
> Strangers to him, enamoured of his lays,
> This fond memorial to his talents raise ;
> For this the ashes of the Bard require
> Who touched the tenderest notes of Pity's lyre ;
> Who joined pure faith to strong poetic powers ;
> Who, in reviving Reason's lucid hours,
> Sought on one Book his troubled mind to rest,
> And rightly deemed the Book of God the best."

In penning these fine lines, Hayley rose to the level of his theme, and proved, if his age erred in thinking him a poet, that he could at least write poetry. Collins lived until 1759 (he was born in 1721) and then expired in the arms of his sister, and was buried in the churchyard of St. Andrew's, Chichester, immediately behind the house in East-street where he was born. To the world he had long been dead, and though his genius was recognised even then by the higher order of minds, it was not until some years after his death that it received full acknowledgment as of the highest order in one, and that a high, class of poetry—the Ode.

There could scarcely be a stronger contrast inmoral character and course of life than between Otway and Collins. Though the former was the son of a clergyman and educated at Winchester and Oxford, he only refers to the clerical profession (as in "The Orphan") in order to load it with insult and contempt. With regard to religion, he evidently shared in the latitudinarianism of the day. His morals were of the loosest, and some of his plays, as we have seen, were too gross and licentious even for an age which tolerated the works of Afra Behn and Wycherley. Even in "Venice Preserved" there are some scenes which no modern stage would allow. Collins, on the other hand, was temperate and deeply religious, and his writings were pure and moral. "He was," writes one who knew him, "passionately fond of music, good-natured and affable, warm in his friendship, and visionary in his pursuits; and, as long as I knew him, very temperate in his eating and drinking." That his temper was equable, is demonstrated by the following anecdote, told by the same friend:—" It happened, one afternoon, at a tea visit, that several intelligent friends were assembled at his rooms to enjoy each other's conversation, when in comes a member of a certain College, as remarkable at that time for his brutal disposition as for his good scholarship,* who, though he met with a circle of the most peaceable people in the world, was determined to quarrel, and though no man said a word, lifted up his foot and kicked the table and all its contents to the other side of the room. Our poet, though of a warm temper, was so confounded at the unexpected downfall, and so astonished at the unmerited

---

* Hampton, the translator of Polybius.

insult, that he took no notice of the aggressor, but, getting up from his chair, calmly began picking up the pieces of bread and butter and the fragments of his china, repeating, very mildly,

"Invenias etiam disjecta membra Poetæ."

This, by the bye, is not unlike the story told by Boswell of another scholar of the day, who, receiving a glass of wine in his face from a discomfited opponent, coolly remarked, "That is a digression; let us proceed with the argument."

Collins never married—never, indeed, seems to have been deeply in love. In this, and in other respects, in his piety and mental suffering, he bears some resemblance to his fellow-Poet, Cowper, who was one of his fervent admirers.

There is a peculiar pleasure in finding one great Poet recognising the beauties, and sympathising with the misfortunes, of another, and this pleasure is doubled when, as in the case of Collins, such recognition comes from a Poet of the same locality. Collins refers both to Otway and to Fletcher. In his "Ode to Pity" he asks, after invoking the memory of "Pella's bard," Euripides,

> "But wherefore need I wander wide
> To old Ilissus' distant side,—
>   Deserted stream, and mute?
> Wild Arun too has heard thy strains,
> And Echo, 'midst my native plains,
>   Been soothed by Pity's lute.

> "There first the wren thy myrtles shed
> On gentlest Otway's infant head,
>   To him thy cell was shown;
> And while he sang the female heart,
> With youth's soft notes unspoil'd by art,
>   Thy turtles mix'd their own."

And, in the poetical epistle he addressed to Sir Thomas

Hanmer, on his edition of Shakspeare's works, he thus places the Sussex-born dramatist, Fletcher, next in order to the "Swan of Avon":—

> "No second growth the western isle could bear,
> At once exhausted with too rich a year.
> Too nicely Jonson knew the critic's part;
> Nature to him was almost lost in art.
> Of softer mould, the gentle Fletcher came,
> The next in order, as the next in fame;
> With pleased attention 'midst his scenes we find
> Each glowing thought that warms the female mind;
> Each melting sigh, and every tender tear;
> The lover's wishes, and the virgin's fear.
> His every strain the Smiles and Graces own;
> But stronger Shakspeare felt for man alone:
> Drawn by his pen, our ruder passions stand—
> Th' unrivall'd picture of his early hand."

A long dreary night in poetry has to be passed (but feebly lighted up by three Sussex luminaries, Hayley, Charlotte Smith, and James Hurdis), before the close of the 18th century, with its French Revolution, and the breaking forth of new hopes, new ideas, new passions, called forth a new race of poets—first Coleridge, Southey, Wordsworth—all Revolutionists, or, as they called themselves, Pantisocratists, in their "salad days"—then Byron, Keats, Leigh Hunt, and, last and greatest of all, the Sussex boy-poet, Percy Bysshe Shelley. These later poets took up the opinions of the earlier ones of the 19th century at the point they had cast them off for more sober and orthodox views. Hence the bitter feud between them. But literary quarrels are for a generation—poetry is for "all time." Shelley—expelled from Oxford, driven from his home and country—even deprived of his children for his theological opinions, now takes his place beside Coleridge and Wordsworth, and is looked upon as one of the brightest names and purest natures that adorn the literature of England. He did not live to see the change. The clouds were still over him when he went down into that watery element with which, even in life, his nature seemed to mingle, and which he loved more than the tame land.

Never, surely, did the storms of life beat more fiercely than on that girl-like and ethereal being; girl-like in its fragile mould —in its intense sympathies; also in its capacity for suffering. It sounds like a contradiction in Nature when we are told that Shelley was the son of a Sussex " Squire "—a man of broad acres and narrow opinions—one Timothy Shelley—living in the heart of that Bœotia of England, the Weald of Sussex, which was only known to the rest of the kingdom 100 years ago by the fatness of its fowls, the whiteness of its wheat, and the clayey adhesiveness of its soil. Of course, Timothy Shelley was a Tory of the Pitt School—a hater of Bonaparte in particular and of Frenchmen in general; a staunch upholder of " Church and State," as that was understood 100 years ago. How came this man to christen his son Percy Bysshe Shelley—of which it may as truly be said that "it doth poetically sound," as it has been said of Shakspeare that " it doth heroically sound." How came he to *have* such a son? How could such a Pegasus—all " fire and air "—all tenderness and love—more Greek than English—more spiritual than mortal—spring from such fox-hunting, change-hating loins? Expound the mystery, shade of Tristram Shandy! We can only record the fact.

The life of Percy Bysshe* Shelley (he was born on the 4th of August, 1792, at Field Place, near Horsham) was a long conflict,—martyrdom, it will, perhaps, one day be called,—with the Powers of the day, one by one, as he came in contact with them: the power of the Bully at School—of the Tyrant at home —of the Dogmatiser at the University—of the High and Dry spirit of Toryism in Law, Church, and Senate—of the " slashing " and slandering Reviewer in Literature. With the organization of a woman, but with the heart of a hero, and the intellect of a being something higher than man, the Sussex boy turned at bay upon

---

* Bysshe was the name of the poet's grandfather.

these Powers of the day and did battle with them. Discreetly? Temperately? Wisely? No. *He* was but a boy when the struggle began, and *they* were mature Powers, consolidated by ages of victorious battle, and walled round by towers and battlements of rank, wealth, prejudice, caste, dogmas, with all the experience of antiquity and all the prestige of authority. Of course, in his childish hatred of abuses which he felt rather than understood, he blundered—struck wide, and comprehended in his words of hate what in his spirit he loved. And they—the Powers of the day—took advantage of the error and punished him according to the code of the day. He attacked "constituted authorities"—"time-honoured Institutions"—dogmas, social, political, and theological, consecrated by centuries of acceptance; and their champions and defenders did their best, not to convert or convince, but to crush him.

There is but little left of the abuses with which Shelley did battle at the beginning of this century; one by one, they have gone down before more skilful, but not braver or purer adversaries; and the clouds of calumny in which he passed his life, and which settled down so densely on his tomb, are beginning to clear off and to disclose what was pure and strong and beautiful, as well as what was weak and faulty, in his character.

Few lives have, indeed, been made the subject of greater misrepresentation and vilification than that of Shelley, and yet few have been more free from the stains and weaknesses of ordinary natures. His morals were pure—his tastes simple—his habits void of those foibles which often attend youth in the upper circles of life.

"To all sensual pleasures," writes his widow, "Shelley was a stranger. His usual food was bread, sometimes seasoned with a few raisins; his beverage was generally water; if he drank tea or coffee, he would take no sugar with it, because the produce of the cane was then obtained by slave labour; and the unanimous voice of those who knew him acquits him of any participation in the lax habits of life too common among young men."

It was by his opinions that he gave offence, and he was a

mere boy when the announcement of them, at Oxford, induced the authorities there to drive him from its walls, and, as a consequence, to close against him the doors of his father's house. The paper in which Shelley set forth those opinions,—often spoken of as a pamphlet,—consisted of two pages, and was a mere thesis,—a challenge to discuss certain abstract points, after the fashion of those theologians of the Middle Ages who used to pin their propositions to the gates of a Monastery or University. The author of it was 18 years of age, and younger even in experience than in years; for, though he had spent the usual time at school and at College (Eton), to which latter he went at 13, he had never associated much with his fellow-students, and, opposing himself to the practice of fagging, then in full vigour at that place of education, he became an object of suspicion to the Masters and of dislike to those boys who did not understand him, though he won the affection and admiration of another and a higher class. What his feelings were at this period he himself has described in the dedication of his poem, "The Revolt of Islam":—

> "Thoughts of great deeds were mine, dear friend, when first
> The clouds which wrap this world from youth did pass.
> I do remember well the hour which burst
> My spirit's sleep: a fresh May dawn it was,
> When I walk'd forth upon the glittering grass,
> And wept, I knew not why; until there rose
> From the near school-room voices that, alas!
> Were but one echo from a world of woes—
> The harsh and grating strife of tyrants and of foes.

> "And then I clasp'd my hands, and look'd around;
> But none was near to mock my streaming eyes,
> Which pour'd their warm drops on the sunny ground;
> So, without shame, I spake:—'I will be wise,
> And just, and free, and mild, if in me lies
> Such power; for I grow weary to behold
> The selfish and the strong still tyrannize
> Without reproach or check.' I then controll'd
> My tears; my heart grew calm; and I was meek and bold.

> "And from that hour did I, with earnest thought,
> Heap knowledge from forbidden mines of lore ;
> Yet nothing that my tyrants knew or taught
> I cared to learn ; but from that secret store
> Wrought linked armour for my soul, before
> It might walk forth, to war among mankind.
> Thus, power and hope were strengthen'd more and more
> Within me, till there came upon my mind
> A sense of loneliness, a thirst with which I pined."

The expulsion from Oxford, and, as a consequence, from his own home, where he was beloved by mother, sisters, servants—all except his father—led to another misfortune. His sisters, in sending to him such assistance as they could save from their own school allowance, chose for their agent one of their school-fellows, named Harriet Westbrook, whose parents lived in London. She was a beautiful girl, and the occasions which led her to Shelley's lodgings did not diminish her attractions in his eyes. He became a visitor to her father's house ; an attachment naturally sprang up ; and the result was, that, before he was 20 years of age, Shelley was married, and to a girl of 16, whose principal charm seems to have lain in her personal beauty. Previous to this step he had, however, come to an arrangement with his father as to the settlement of the family property, by virtue of which he was to receive an allowance of £200 a year; and on this the young couple lived for some years, until the growing differences of their character, aggravated by the presence in their little household of an elder sister, led to a separation by mutual consent. Previous to this the young poet (for Shelley had now, after writing several minor poetical pieces, and some prose works of fiction, of little merit and which have perished, composed, at the age of 18, his "Queen Mab,") had made the acquaintance of Godwin, the author of "Political Justice" and "Caleb Williams," who was, in fact, to that day what John Stuart Mill was to a later one—and this led, after his separation from his wife and her death by suicide (from causes unconnected with her husband), to his marriage with Godwin's only daughter, Mary

Woolstonecraft. When Shelley first disclosed his feelings to her, Mary Godwin was only 16 years of age, and the scene is thus described in the "Memorials" published by the Shelley family and edited by Lady Shelley (the wife of the poet's son), which are the only trustworthy records of his career, and from which we take our facts :—

"To her—Mary Godwin—as they met one eventful day in St. Pancras Churchyard, by her mother's grave, Bysshe, in burning words, poured forth the tale of his wild past—how he had suffered, how he had been misled, and how, if supported by her love, he hoped in future years to enrol his name with the wise and good who had done battle for their fellow-men, and been true through all adverse storms to the cause of humanity. Unhesitatingly, she placed her hand in his, and linked her fortune with his own ; and most truthfully was the pledge of both redeemed."

Soon after this the death of his grandfather, Sir Bysshe Shelley, and the succession of his father, Sir Timothy, to the Baronetage, placed the young poet in easier circumstances, by his allowance being increased to £1,000 a year. At this period, in order to qualify himself for those offices of kindness and charity to the poor for which he destined himself, and some of which he had already discharged when living in Wales, he "walked" one of the London Hospitals, though suffering intensely from the delicacy of his own health. This, in fact, drove him from London, and, after a temporary sojourn on the borders of Windsor Forest, where "Alastor" and other poems were composed, induced him to go abroad. Returning to England in 1816-7, he formed the acquaintance of Keats, doomed, like himself, to so brilliant and yet to so melancholy a career, and a friendship with Horace Smith, so long an esteemed resident in Brighton, which only ended with his life. It was at this period of Shelley's life that another of those blows fell upon him which seemed intended to crush out his fragile life, but against which his indomitable spirit rose with the strength of a martyr. During the life of his first wife their two children—a boy and a girl—lived with her. On her death, their father claimed them. The claim was opposed by the mother's father, on the ground of Shelley's religious and moral opinions, and, on the case being taken to Chancery, the Lord Chancellor (Eldon) pronounced against the father being custodian of his children, and they were committed to the charge of an utter stranger. Against this decision, which, it is needless to say, in the present day would be scouted, Shelley protested with all the vehemence of his nature, wounded in the tenderest part, but he was impotent against the Law, as it was then administered, and, in order to put the children of his second wife beyond its arm, he left his native country, and never returned to it. He went to Italy, and there, in a climate which suited his delicate constitution and amidst scenery which excited his imagination, he composed those great poems and dramas, "Prometheus Unbound," "The Cenci," "Adonais" (the elegy to Keats), "the Witch of Atlas," "the Sensitive Plant," "the Ode to the Skylark," &c., &c., on which his poetic fame rests. "Queen Mab," the crude and premature, though marvellous, fruit of his youth, he never intended to publish. He himself condemns it, in stronger language than, perhaps, many of his critics would apply to it, as "a poem written by me at the age of 18—I dare say in a sufficiently intemperate spirit—but even then it was not intended for publication, and a few copies only were struck off to be distributed amongst my personal friends. I doubt not that it is perfectly worthless in point of literary composition, and that in all that concerns moral and political speculation, as well as in the subtle discriminations of metaphysical and religious doctrine, it is still more crude and immature."

Most certainly, Shelley lived to modify many of the extreme opinions which find expression in "Queen Mab;" and his later writings—prose and poetical—indeed, his whole life—clear him from that odious charge of atheism which his enemies sought, with a malice worthy of the irreligion they attributed to him, to fix on him. If anything were wanting to rebut such a calumny, it would be supplied in the unfinished "Essay on Christianity" found amongst Shelley's papers after his death, and attached by his daughter-in-law, Lady Shelley, to the "Shelley Memorials" published by her. It breathes the very spirit of Christianity, and vindicates its principles, though drawing a line between the great Master who promulgated them, and those who followed Him and proposed to interpret and embody them.

Passing from the vexed subject of Shelley's religious opinions, never very fixed, and which most certainly were greatly modified in his later years, let us turn to the closing scenes of the poet's life in Italy. After many trials and sufferings—some from those unavoidable attendants on humanity—ill-health, death of children, and depression of spirits, to which Shelley was peculiarly subject—and some from the persecution and detraction by which he was pursued to the last, Shelley seemed to be floating, after a storm-tost career, into smoother waters. His "Prometheus Unbound" and "Cenci" compelled the world to acknowledge him as a great, though not a popular, poet; in Leigh Hunt, Horace Smith (the custodian of his monetary interests in England), Trelawny, Williams, and many others, he had found a knot of true friends, who stood between him and the outer world; and in Lord Byron, whom he met in Italy, he had found a congenial spirit in poetry, though in the pure and lofty spirit of Shelley there was a barrier between them which both felt, and which could not be over-passed by either, so as to lead to friendship. In all these circumstances there seemed to be a brighter and calmer future opening upon the young Sussex poet— not yet 30 years of age. In his own mind there was brooding the performance of something greater than anything he had yet done —though how gigantic is that work, if measured by his years, compared to the works of most other men!—when the fatal event took place which closed his labours, and quenched one of the brightest, and, if sometimes erring, yet, surely, one of the purest spirits that ever lit up the later ages of this world.

The tale has been often told, and will be told and re-told thousands of times yet; for it is full of a terrible charm.

Shelley, with his young wife and only surviving child by her, christened Percy Florence, had, in conjunction with his intimate friend, Williams,—also accompanied by his wife and children,—taken a villa in a wild and romantic site, called Lerici, on the shores of the Bay of Spezzia. Here he was visited by Trelawny, who acted as Captain of Lord Byron's yacht, "The Bolivar," and here he was expecting a visit from Leigh Hunt and his wife. These latter were, in fact, already arrived at Byron's Palazza at Pisa, and hither, to meet them, Shelley and Williams, with a young English sailor, named Vivian, set out in their little yacht, which they had had built for them at Genoa, and in which they had been making excursions in the Italian seas. They reached Leghorn in safety, and spent several days with their friends at Pisa; but Shelley receiving a gloomy letter from his wife, who seems to have had the cloud of an impending calamity hanging over her, hastened his departure from Leghorn; Williams and he and the sailor-boy Vivian embarking again in their little yacht on the 8th July, (1822) for their home at Lerici.

The weather was very sultry, and clouds were gathering in the south-west when they set sail from Leghorn; but a profound stillness overspread the Bay. By and bye a sea-fog came on which concealed Shelley's boat from the watching eyes of his friends, Trelawny and Roberts. At half-past six (they had started at 3 p.m.) it was almost dark, and the wind began to rise, in short, panting gusts; and big drops of rain struck the water. "There was a commotion in the air," says Mr. Trelawny, who records these particulars, "made up of many threatening sounds, coming upon us from the sea." The vessels in the harbour were all in hurried movement, and the tempest soon came crashing and glaring, in the fury of thunder, wind, rain, and lightning, over the port and the open waters. The storm only lasted about twenty minutes, and during its progress Captain Roberts watched Shelley's vessel with his glass from the top of the Leghorn lighthouse. The yacht had made Via Reggio when the storm began. "When the cloud passed onward," writes Mrs. Shelley, "Roberts looked again, and saw every other vessel sailing on the ocean except the little schooner, which had vanished." Mr. Trelawny thought for some time that his friends would return to port; but he waited for them in vain.

They were never to return alive. After an agonising suspense of some days for wives and friends, the terrible truth was made certain by the casting ashore of the bodies, first of Shelley and then of Mr. Williams. The latter was nearly undressed, having evidently made an attempt to swim. Shelley had probably gone down at once, for he was unable to swim, and had always declared (according to Mr. Trelawny) that, in case of wreck, he would vanish instantly, and not imperil others in the endeavour to save him. His right hand was clasped in his breast, and he appears to have been reading Keats's last volume of poems at the time of the catastrophe; as the book, doubled back, was found thrust away, seemingly in haste, into a side pocket. In another pocket was a volume of Sophocles. The copy of Keats had been lent to Shelley by Leigh Hunt, who told him to keep it till he could give it to him again with his own hands. As the lender would receive it from no one else, it was burnt with the body.

A great deal of unnecessary scandal was caused by the burning of the bodies on the sea-shore. It was, in fact, a police necessity. According to the Italian laws of that day, every thing cast by the sea on the shore had to be burned, to prevent the possible introduction of the plague. It was only through the influence of the English Consul at Florence that Mr. Trelawny was permitted to superintend the cremation and to convey the ashes of the deceased to their two widows. He discharged this painful duty with a devotion to which Mrs. Shelley does full justice. He himself collected the ashes in his scorched hands,—(Leigh Hunt and Byron looking on from the latter's carriage),—and afterwards deposited them, where they now lie, in the Protestant burial-place at Rome, by the side of Shelley's own son, William, and of his brother-poet, Keats. To the two words "COR CORDIUM" and a Latin inscription of the cause of death, &c., are added the lines from Shakspeare's *Tempest* (one of Shelley's favourite plays)—

> " Nothing of him that doth fade
> But doth suffer a sea change
> Into something rich and strange."

Subsequent enquiries left no doubt that the boat had been run down, though there is no reason to believe that it was done designedly. On its being raised up from where it lay, 15 fathoms deep, all was in her—books, telescope, ballast—lying on each side of the boat, without any appearance of shifting or confusion : the topsails furled, topmast lowered ; the false stern broken to pieces, and a great hole knocked in the stern timbers. When she was brought to Leghorn, every one went to see her, and the same exclamation was uttered by all : " She was run down."

In the " Shelley Memorials," to which reference has already been made, some extracts are given from Mrs. Shelley's " Private Journal" which were written in the October succeeding the death of her husband. They are most touching, but also of an exalted character, and point to the spiritual belief of both husband and wife. "You will be with me," she exclaims to his spirit, "in all my studies, dearest love. Your voice will no longer applaud me, but in spirit you will visit and encourage me: I know you will. What were I, if I did not believe that you still exist ? It is not with you as with another. I believe that we all live hereafter ; but you, my only one, were a spirit caged, an elemental being, enshrined in a frail image, now shattered. Do they not all with one voice assert the same ? Trelawny, Hunt, and many others. And so at last you quitted this painful prison, and you are free, my Shelley ; while I, your poor chosen one, am left to live as I may."

In a subsequent passage she thus bursts forth, in the agony of separation :—" Mine own Shelley ! the sun knows of none to be likened to you—brave, wise, gentle, noble-hearted, full of learning, tolerance, and love. Love ! what a word for me to write ! Yet, my miserable heart permit, me yet to love—to see him in beauty, to feel him in beauty, to be interpenetrated by the sense of his excellence ; and thus to love, singly, eternally, ardently, and not fruitlessly ; for I am still his—still the chosen one of the blessed spirit—still vowed to him for ever and ever ! "

No being ever bore stronger testimony to the worth of another than did Shelley's wife to him ; and the testimony was sealed by a widowhood of 29 years, consecrated to him and his child, during which she was left by his father to bear the full weight of the burthen; for she indignantly spurned the only condition on which Sir Timothy would continue to the mother and son the allowance made to the husband and father, namely, that she should give up the custody of her only child ! She also declined to take part in the work to which she was invited by some of her friends,—the apostleship of the Rights of Women, for which she felt she had no mission; but she devoted her time and talent to literature, and so, like the worthy daughter of Godwin and wife of Shelley, maintained herself and son until the death of Sir Timothy, in 1842, put Shelley's son, Sir Percy Florence Shelley, in that position as to fortune and title which he still fills.* Mrs Shelley died in 1851, in the 54th year of her age.

We have referred to the delicate, and almost feminine organisation of Shelley. Here is a picture of him by Captain Kennedy, a friend of the Shelley family, who saw him during a stolen visit which he paid to his mother, at her request and his sisters'—it was his last visit to Field Place—in 1813, whilst his father was away :—

"I fancy I see him now, as he sat by the window, and hear his voice, the tones of which impressed me with his sincerity and simplicity. His resemblance to his sister Elizabeth was as striking as if they had been twins. His eyes were most expressive, his complexion beautifully fair, his features exquisitely fine; his hair was dark, and no peculiar attention to its arrangement was manifest. In person he was slender and gentleman-like, but inclined to stoop; his gait was decidedly not military. The general appearance indicated great delicacy of constitution. One would at once pronounce of him that he was something different from other men. There was an earnestness in his manner, and such perfect gentleness of breeding, and freedom from everything artificial, as charmed everyone. I never met a man who so immediately won upon me."

" He was," says Captain Kennedy, in closing his description of him, "an amiable, gentle being." Such, indeed, was the tes-

---

* Sir Percy Florence Shelley filled the office of High Sheriff of Sussex in 1865.

timony of all who knew him intimately, and it is a remarkable illustration of the hardness of the age in which he lived—an age of iron in many respects—that such a spirit—so gentle, so loving, so filled with sympathy for his fellow-men and for every breathing creature—for, as Captain Kennedy tells us, "he had a horror of taking life and looked upon it as a crime,"—that such a spirit should have been so cruelly buffeted by the world and almost driven from it to the communion of Nature, in which, indeed, when not assisting in some act of charity or resisting some act of oppression or injustice, it was his greatest delight to live. In one of his letters to his wife, after a more than usually vile attack by some journal upon her as well as him, he thus writes to her :—

"My greatest comfort would be utterly to desert all human society. I would retire with you and our children to a solitary island in the sea ; would build a boat, and shut upon my retreat the flood-gates of the world. I would read no reviews, and find talk with no authors. If I dared trust my imagination, it would tell me that there are one or two chosen companions, besides yourself, whom I should desire. But to this I would not listen. Where two or three are gathered together, the devil is among them ; and good, far more than evil, impulses— love, far more than hatred—has been to me, except as you have been its object, the source of all sorts of mischief. So, on this plan, I would be *alone*, and would devote, either to oblivion or to future generations, the overflowings of a mind which, timely withdrawn from the contagion, should be kept fit for no baser object. But this it does not appear that we shall do."

What such a mind as Shelley's might have produced had his life been prolonged, it is, of course, impossible to say. But, by the admission of all judges of poetical genius, if measured by what he did in the ten short years of his life of authorship, between 20 and 30, he was the greatest poet that England has produced since Milton, whom, in some respects—in the purity of his life, in the extreme to which he carried his opinions, in his mastery and love of Greek literature, and also in the feminine beauty of his face,—he resembled. He is the greatest of the four great Sussex poets, and, though no trace of any reference to his native County is to be found in his works, we may be sure that the beautiful woods round Horsham, in which he loved to wander, and often lost himself as a boy, had their effect upon him, and that even Horsham, though oblivious, as it was and is, of him in the pursuit of its bucolic pleasures and profits, had yet a place in that " Cor Cordium."

In looking back over the careers of Fletcher, Otway, Collins, and Shelley, the reflection is provoked how little they were connected with the places, or even the County, in which they were born ! Collins, indeed, returned to die in Chichester, and alone, of our four great poets, rests in his native soil. Even he passed the greater part of his life away from it; and as for Fletcher, Otway, and Shelley, they all left Sussex in early youth, never to return to it, and all lie amongst strangers. Nor do their works contain the slightest evidence that their thoughts ever reverted to their native soil. They gave themselves up, heart and soul, to the wider sphere to which they were attracted, and merged their provincialism in the larger atmosphere of literature.

Not so the lesser Poets of Sussex. They linger about the old familiar ground, as though they drew from it part of their strength and depended upon it for their after fame. Perhaps they lacked the strength of wing to fly far from the parent-nest. Be that as it may, it is a fact that Hurdis, Hayley, Charlotte Smith, and Charles Crocker all linger in Sussex, and take delight in singing of the beauties of Nature and of Art to be found in it —beauties for which their greater brethren had no eye or ear.

The sphere and the themes of James Hurdis were purely local. He was born (in 1763) at Bishopstone; Bishopstone was the living to which he was appointed after a previous curacy at Burwash; at Bishopstone he passed the greater part of his life; at Bishopstone he is buried; and the subject of his chief poem, " Favourite Village," is Bishopstone. Only in one thing does his quiet placid life resemble the turbid ones of his fellow poets. He died young—at 37 years. But he lived long enough to be appointed Professor of Poetry at Oxford, and perhaps this fact will suffice to prove that, though an accomplished, amiable man, he was not, in the true sense of the word, a poet. Certainly, the axiom of Shelley, in his "Julian and Maddalo," as echoed by him from Byron, that

> "Most wretched men are cradled into poetry by wrong :
> They learn in suffering what they teach in song,"

did not apply to Hurdis. He had no such cradling, and no such lesson is conveyed in his poems. He was content with singing the external attributes of men and Nature; he never dived into the depths of the human heart or sought to fathom the higher mysteries of Nature. Mr. M. A. Lower quotes, in his "Sussex Worthies," a passage from the "Village Curate" as one of "startling beauty," "amidst much that is prose-like and unattractive." Here it is :—

> " It wins my admiration
> To view the structure of that little work,
> A bird's nest. Mark it well, within, without ;
> No tool had he that wrought, no knife to cut,
> No nail to fix, no bodkin to insert,
> No glue to join : his little beak was all ;
> And yet how neatly finished ! What nice hand,
> With every implement and means of Art,
> And twenty years' apprenticeship to boot,
> Could make me such another ? Fondly then
> We boast of excellence, whose noblest skill
> Instinctive genius foils."

With every deference to the talented author of "The Worthies of Sussex," we fail to see the "startling beauty" of this. To us it is the perfection of common place—the antipodes of Poetry !

There was one poetical incident in the life of Hurdis. He met Cowper at Eartham, the country-seat of Hayley, near Chichester. There, in 1792, says Mr Lower, "the three poets met," of whom *one* certainly was a poet. "But as for the other two"——

But this meeting was at the close of the 18th century—that

sterile period in English poetry—and Coleridge, Southey, and Wordsworth, like young eagles, were as yet purging their eyes in the light of that poet-awakening event, the French Revolution. At no other period could such platitudes as are contained in the foregoing lines have been sent forth as poetry.

Hayley was almost as local in his poetic sphere and themes as Hurdis. He was born at Chichester (in 1745); his two principal places of residence were at Eartham and Felpham, spots within half-a-dozen miles of that City; and round them and London his life revolved. It took in a wider range than that of Hurdis, and also embraced a longer period of time; Hayley lived until 1820, and thus witnessed the rise of that young, varied, and vigorous race of poets—the fruit of a new age and new thoughts —in which such pretensions as he had to poetic fame were to be utterly extinguished. It was a melancholy career—opening as it did with so much promise, and closing in such a "starless night;" for "The Triumphs of Temper," Hayley's principal poem, produced about 1780, was received with a shout of applause, and the fact itself serves to mark the lowest point in the long and glorious line of English poets. It is a fitting commentary on it that the post of Poet Laureate (vacant by the death of Richard Wharton —only one degree above the standard of Hayley as a poet) was offered to the Sussex versifier, and refused! If it be true that Hayley declined the honour and the benefit attached to the post (at that time £20 a-year and a pipe of malmsey), because he wished Cowper to enjoy them, it is honourable to him. It was, indeed, to Hayley's credit that he recognised the genius of Cowper, and paid homage to it as that of the greater poet. Himself a man of the world, moving in excellent society, enjoying an independent fortune, and all the delights of such a country as that round Eartham, and such a coast as that of Felpham,—acknowledged as the poet of the day, and the friend of such artists as Romney and Flaxman—it is to the credit of Hayley that, in the midst of these gifts of fortune, he bowed to the superior genius of the author of "The Task," and throwing aside all idea of rivalry, sought for his acquaintance, visited him in his seclusion, drew him

S

from it to become an honoured guest at Eartham, retained his friendship to the close of the unhappy poet's life, and became his biographer. This shows that Hayley had none of that spirit of jealousy which has so often been the bane of literary men and the disgrace of literature. He was, indeed, an amiable and accomplished man; intended by Nature to be rather a patron and a friend of poets than a poet himself; and it was his misfortune, not his fault, to be born in an age so barren of poetic genius, and so unable to distinguish between good and bad, that it mistook him for a poet. He did all he could to undeceive it; going so far as to write an "Essay on Old Maids" and "Ballads on Animals," the very acmé of bathos. And at last he succeeded! No man ever more completely outlived his reputation than Hayley. From having been at the top of the tree of poetry (to adopt Collins's figure) he fell, branch by branch, to the bottom, until there is scarcely a bough so low as to give him a resting-place. If allowed one, it is to mark zero on the poetical thermometer!

And yet he could write poetry,—the epitaph to Collins proves it,—and his prose was elegant, and his plays (he wrote three comedies in rhyme and two tragedies), were acted with success. His knowledge of Art was considerable, and his conversation and manners were pleasing. In fact, he was an accomplished gentleman, such as are to be met with by thousands in the present day, and was only remarkable in his own age because, during the close of the 18th century, the cultivation of literature and of the polite Arts did not enter into the education of the English gentleman as it does now. They were limited almost entirely to a narrow professional clique in London: the smaller descendants of Johnson, Goldsmith, Reynolds, and Gibbon. It needed such a thunderclap as the French Revolution, and the new ideas it excited, to dissipate this artificial atmosphere—to let in the fresh air of Nature—the passions of humanity—and begin a new school of poetry. Hayley lived to witness this change and to be forgotten in his retirement —first at Eartham and then at Felpham, where it was a singular fact, which has something of the irony of Fate in it, that Blake, the Poet and the Painter—the child of Nature and Imagination—the very antipodes of Hayley in art, in literature, in thinking, and in living—this forerunner of a new and greater era came to live side by side with the representative of a by-gone age and effete literature. It was like Nature coming to live on the threshold of Fashion. What they thought of one another we do not know; but they exchanged civilities; Blake even illustrated some of Hayley's poems, and when Blake got into some trouble by chastising the insolence of a disbanded soldier, who invaded his little garden at Felpham, and had to answer a charge of disloyalty before the Chichester Magistrates, Hayley stood his friend, and Blake was *not* sent to gaol as a *sans culotte*.

Hayley died at Felpham (where his house and Blake's humble cottage still stand in their integrity), and was buried at Eartham. The offices that he had so often performed for others were now performed for him; his epitaph (in Felpham Church) was written by his friend, Mrs. Opie, and his autobiography was published in two quarto volumes by a Reverend friend. His name lives, and always will live, in the history of English literature, because it fills up a niche of time, like that of a *roi fainéant* in French history; but his works are entirely forgotten.

Charlotte Smith (*née* Turner) is the only poetess of note Sussex can boast of.* And *she* was not Sussex born. She first saw the light in London (in 1749). But her family were Sussexian; the family seat was Bignor Park, near Arundel; and her grandfather filled the office of High Sheriff of Sussex in 1714. The chief part of her life, too, was passed in Sussex. She went to school at Chichester; her holidays were spent at Bignor; and when she married it was at Storrington and at Woolbeding that she chiefly lived and wrote. She was a contemporary and a friend of Hayley, and, like him, she was unhappy in her matrimonial life, separating from her husband, as Hayley had separated from both his wives. It seems, indeed, to be left to the present day to prove that poets

---

* We refer to poetesses of the past. Our own days have been richer in this respect. Mrs. William Sawyer (*née* Andrews) is only one instance of Sussex ladies, still living, who have wooed the Muses with success.

and poetesses can enjoy conjugal felicity! The experience of preceding ages was almost uniformly in the other direction, and our Sussex poets, when they married,—and Fletcher, Otway, and Collins never married,—were no exception to the rule.

In the case of Charlotte Smith, however, it was the husband who was to blame. He spent his fortune in extravagance and thoughtless speculations, and when he had to take up his abode in the Queen's Bench his wife accompanied him thither, and it was to her exertions that he chiefly owed his liberation. It was to support herself and her children that she turned to literature. She was a voluminous writer, producing no less than 38 volumes, chiefly in works of fiction (the most popular of which was "The Old Manor House"), but also in other ways—in works for the young and in Essays and Elegiac Sonnets. It was in this latter line that she won her place in literature—a place which she retains, and is likely to do so, for no collection of English Sonnets could be perfect without some specimens of the Muse of Charlotte Smith. They are, perhaps, a little over-strained in their melancholy; they border on the sentimental as distinguished from the passionate. But still they are full of tender music, and the love of Nature comes to soften and divide the sorrows that struggle for utterance.

It was in Sussex that Charlotte Smith chiefly found the subjects of her verse, and the Sonnet addressed by her to the Moon, and another written in Middleton church-yard (long since swept away by the encroaching sea) may be taken as samples of the smoothness, the sweetness, as well as of the sentimentality of her verse :—

TO THE MOON.

Queen of the silver bow ! by thy pale beam
  Alone and pensive I delight to stray,
And watch thy shadow trembling in the stream,
  Or mark the floating clouds that cross thy way.
And, while I gaze, thy mild and placid light
  Sheds a soft calm upon my troubled breast,
And oft I think, fair Planet of the Night,
  That in thy orb the wretched may have rest ;

The sufferers of the earth perhaps may go,
  Released by death, to thy benignant sphere,
And the sad children of despair and woe
  Forget in thee their cup of sorrow here.
Oh! that I soon may reach thy world serene,
Poor wearied pilgrim in this toiling scene!

Written in the Churchyard at Middleton in Sussex.

Press'd by the Moon, mute arbitress of tides,
  While the loud equinox its power combines,
  The sea no more its swelling surge confines,
But o'er the shrinking land sublimely rides.
The wild blast, rising from the Western cave,
  Drives the huge billows from their heaving bed;
  Tears from their grassy tombs the village dead,
And breaks the silent sabbath of the grave!
With shells and sea-weed mingled, on the shore,
  Lo! their bones whiten in the frequent wave;
  But vain to them the winds and waters rave;
They hear the warring elements no more:
While I am doom'd—by life's long storm opprest,
To gaze with envy on their gloomy rest.

Other Sonnets of Charlotte Smith are addressed to the South Downs and the river Arun, in which latter she couples Hayley as a fellow-poet with Otway and Collins! It was in these local effusions that her strength lay; out of Sussex and the Sonnet her Muse droops.

We may almost apply the same words to Charles Crocker, who, in our own days, sustained the reputation of Chichester as a birth-place of poets. He was born there in 1797, of humble parents; received his education at the Grey-coat School; and was apprenticed before he was 12 years of age to a shoemaker. It was whilst he was earning his living at this handicraft that he made the discovery—first of his taste for poetry, and then of his own power to compose verse—at first, "in his head," and, after a time, on paper. Some of his effusions coming to the knowledge of his fellow-townsmen, they were printed and published, and established the title of Charles Crocker to the fame,—if not of a poet, at all events, of one who could write poetry. One piece, at least, will live in our English Parnassus, viz., the Sonnet to the Oak, which Southey, when including Crocker amongst the poets of the day, declared to be one of the finest ever written. Few Englishmen, we think, will be disposed to dispute the *dictum* of the then Laureate :—

TO THE OAK.

When, sacred plant, the Druid sage of old,
  With reverential awe, beheld in thee
  The abode or emblem of Divinity,
Methinks some vague prophetic vision rolled
Before his wondering eyes, and dimly told
  Thy future fame—thy glorious destiny.
  Haply, e'en then, deep musing, he might see,
Within thy trunk revered, that Spirit bold
  Which sprang from thence in aftertimes, and stood,
  Rejoicing in his might, in Ocean's flood,
The guardian genius of Britannia's Isle ;
  At whose dread voice admiring nations bow,
  In duteous homage—tyrants are laid low—
And fierce Oppression's victims learn to smile.

As might be expected, the themes which inspired Crocker were purely local : Kingley Vale, The Lavant, Kingshame—all within a walk of his native city. Chichester was his world. We almost doubt if he ever slept out of it. If ever poetic power was unaccompanied by ambition, it was in the case of Crocker. He was contentedness itself. In his placid look and calm expression it shone out unmistakeably, and it found expression in his unpretending address and unadorned language. It was, to his unambitious spirit, a great step in advance when he left the shoemaker's board for the bookseller's counter, being selected for this more congenial post by his friend and patron, the late Mr. William Hayley Mason, a godson of Hayley, and the owner and occupier of the house in which Collins was born (now Mr. Wilmshurst's) in East-street, so that he was brought, as it were, into a literary atmosphere and kindred associations. Here he remained, quiet and contented, and little troubled by visitations of the Muse, until a bit of ecclesiastical patronage fell to the poet (may we say "from the rich man's table?") in the very unpoetical shape of the office of sexton to Chichester Cathedral, afterwards supplemented by that of Bishop's verger. In this office he reached, to use Massinger's language, "the *ne plus ultra* of his proudest hopes." He now passed the greater portion of his time in the Cathedral, which he loved with a love that only those who have been born under the shadow of a Cathedral can understand. His latest literary work was a descriptive Hand-book of it, written in as prosaic and matter-of-fact a style as though by the veriest Penny-a-liner. In fact, Crocker's prose style was singularly bald and trite. His fancy seemed to desert him when he ceased to rhyme. He was, indeed, in everything, except his love of Poetry, as marked a contrast to Collins as one poet could be to another: happy, contented, seeking his joys in domestic life, and finding delight in that building amidst which Collins wandered and raved in agony of spirit.

One great misfortune Crocker was doomed to, arising out of his love and pride for the chief ornament of his native City, and that was in the fall of the Spire and Tower of his much-loved Cathedral. This occurred on February 21st, 1861, and Crocker's death followed in the same year; hastened, his fellow townsmen believed, by the shock it gave him. He was followed to the grave by Dean Hook, and by many of the clergy, Magistrates, and principal citizens of his native place; and never did the grave close over a man with any pretensions to poetic genius —and most certainly Charles Crocker had such,—his Sonnet to the British Oak attests it,—whose life disproved more completely the notion that the gift of poetry is fraught with danger to him or her on whom it is bestowed.

In Crocker we are brought down to our own times. We knew him well, and, like all who knew him, loved and respected him. He represents a class of men by no means uncommon in this country, who, born in humble life and with very unpoetical surroundings, possess a natural taste for literature and pursue it with an ardour that amazes men of higher culture and to whom there are other roads of distinction open. The secret of this devotion lies, perhaps, in the fact that Letters *are* a Republic, and that the veriest drudge or outcast of society—a slave like Epictetus, a tradesman like Defoe, a tinker like Bunyan,—can win the highest literary honours and inscribe his name amongst the Immortals. The lists are open to all—the weapons are easily caught up—it is a melée in which king, noble, squire, yeoman, peasant, all fight with little or no advantage of rank or position; and if the prizes come "tardy off," they are, in the end, most equitably distributed by that ultimate Court of Appeal, the voice of Fame. The names of many Sussex competitors in this "gentle passage of Arms," which, like that of Ashby-de-la-Zouche, has its list of killed and wounded, might be added to the instances we have given, male and female. The columns of the *Brighton Herald* have for the last 70 years borne weekly testimony to the large amount of poetical talent that floats about the world, and, like other "airy nothings," seeks to give itself "a local habitation and a name." We have already tried to do a little justice to three lesser Sussex poets in Clio Rickman, a native of Lewes; Charles Verral, of Seaford; and George Frederick Richardson, of Brighton.

With this latter we might associate two other Brightonians, both of whom gave promise of distinction, but passed away and "writ their names in water." The ties of friendship, in the one case, and of near relationship in the other, must be our excuse if we are guilty of partiality in singling out the names of Charles Stanhope Busby and William Henry Fleet as having given token in early life of more than average literary, and especially poetical, ability. The first was the author of the papers which, under the title of "RANDOM THOUGHTS," appeared weekly in the *Brighton Herald* from January 12, 1833, to December 27th, 1834, and which included not only Essays, Criticisms, and Sketches of Character, in which extensive reading, good taste, and considerable powers of fancy and invention are displayed, but some poems rising above the average. Such, we think, the reader will admit, was the following one, entitled

DREAM.

Airy vision!—thou'rt to me
The spirit of tranquillity—
Whispering to the sleeping-breast
Tales of all it loves the best;
Lulling sorrow's pensive note
With a soothing antidote;
Bringing hither friends we love,—
Friends that o'er the wide world rove,
Like some lovely falling star,
Leaving all its mates afar.
Oh! I woo thee, gentle dream,
As a wanderer woos the beam
Of moonlight o'er the troubled stream,
When all around his trembling bark
Is doubtful, desolate, and dark.
Would that the spirit could awake,
And not thy bright illusion break,
But dream through life so sad as this
In one fair harmony of bliss!
Dear Spirit! in thy wide domain,
Misery drops her fetter-chain—
Envy's tumult-voice is still—
Raging passions cease to thrill—
Hope is there with laughing eye,
Beaming in her extasy;
Every feeling, every sense,
Is mingled with benevolence.
How should hatred e'er invade
The silence of thy spirit-shade?
There, within thy twilight realm,
No jarring shouts of strife o'erwhelm;
But thought and action blend and shine
Like Nature at the day's decline.
I know not if thou always art
As soothing to the troubled heart!
Some say that terror's fitful gleams
Hover o'er the land of dreams;

That fearful phantoms wildly frown—
That sorrow there usurps a crown !—
That all the woes of life appear
Doubly deep within thy sphere !
Dear Spirit !—can it, can it be ?
Thou never hast seemed thus to me !
If ever, in day's beam of gold,
Fickle friendship's heart was cold,
Within the hour of thy reign
All was warm and bright again !
If wandering love forgot her vow,
Who led her back as soon as thou ?
But if indeed thou canst assume
Terror's image, terror's gloom—
E'en then, when rous'd by anger's will,
Enchantress, I would woo thee still !
What are thine airy woes or strife
To the realities of life ?
The fickle sons of guile forsaking
The wanderer when his heart is breaking—
The eye of love, when chill'd by pride,
Turning its azure glance aside—
The pomp, the pride, the seeming free,
Pleasure—all false, all vanity !
' Mid things that so delusive shine,
Where, Spirit, can be joys like thine ?
And who that ever felt thy kiss
Would grudge the penalty of bliss ?
I know not if it be my fate
To meet thy terror, or thy hate—
As yet thou hast but been to me
A refuge from reality !—
And surely they who sorrow share,
Can well surmount thine airy care—
For tho' slumber yield no more
Her balmy visions, as before,
Her pictur'd ills are far less deep
Than daylight's woes. O maid of sleep !
I love thee now ! Thou art to me
The spirit of tranquillity !

Mr. C. S. Busby was the son of the talented architect of that name who designed Brunswick Square, Brunswick Terrace, and other of the best parts, architecturally, of Brighton. The son was brought up to the law, and left Brighton to follow that profession,—successfully, we are glad to say,—in another part of England. If still alive, and if they meet his view, he will doubtless smile as he reads the above verses, and thinks that he too,—if Blackstone and Chitty had not come between him and the Muses,—might have been a Poet!

William Henry Fleet was the eldest son of the then proprietor of the same Brighton journal in which the compositions of Mr. Busby appeared, but in the columns of which his name appears only once attached to his productions. His poems were thrown undistinguished into the stream which sweeps the contents of a newspaper into the Pool of Oblivion. Yet there were some pieces that deserved a better fate. From a large number of fugitive poems which appeared in the *Brighton Herald*, the *Merthyr and Cardiff Chronicle*, and the *Montreal Courier* (of which two latter William Henry Fleet was the Editor for some years before entering upon a legal career in Canada, which was closed by a too early death), we take, almost at hazard, two samples of his work : the one of a serious, the other of a humorous character, for he excelled in both :—

THE WANDERER'S RETURN.

Years had flown—his hair was grey,
   Who sought again the much-lov'd spot,
Where youth's first hours had passed away
   'Mid friends who ne'er might be forgot.
The path he trod—he knew it well,
   The ancient oak its shade still shed ;
But those he sought no one could tell,
   But, wondering, answered—" They are dead."

He sought the cot of one he'd left
   A laughing, merry-hearted thing ;
Who near his youthful heart had crept,
   As tendril round a flower of Spring ;
Where is she now? the laughing voice,
   The happy, tripping, blithesome tread,

No longer bid his heart rejoice,
  But echo whispers —" She is dead !"

His sisters, say, ah, where are they,—
  Companions of his youthful hours?
He sought them where they used to play,
  But sad and cheerless were the bowers.
The trees they'd planted side by side,
  Now proudly waved above his head ;
He asked, " Where are they ? " They replied,
  " Thy sisters, Wanderer—they are dead ! "

He turned away—his brother dear,
  The bud his mother doated on ;
How is it that he is not here,
  To welcome back the wandering one ?
He called him by his well-known name,
  But echo answered in his stead—
Again the chilling response came,
  " Thy brother, Wanderer—he is dead ! "

His sire was full of manhood's pride
  When he had left, a boy, his home ;
His mother's cheek had time defied,
  He fondly thought, for years to come.
He sought them both, but there, alas,
  Within the churchyard's narrow bed,
A tombstone told him as he passed,
  " Thy parents, Wanderer—they are dead ! "

He sought again the ancient hall,
  Where desolation held her sway,
And heard the owls' dull croaking call
  And bats against the casement play.
His footsteps on the marble floor
  Aroused th' intruders, and they fled ;
Shrieking, " Thy friends, they are no more ;
  Maid, brother, sisters—all are dead ! "

The following lines were a mere *jeu d'esprit;* but they showed an ability, which is rare, to deal airily with a bubble :—

THE CHINESE LOVERS.

I'll tell you a tale of a young Chinese
Who wore her petticoats up to her knees,

And put her feet, so pretty and small,
Into a walnut-shell, heels and all,—
There never had been such a prize to win
Before in the town of old Pekin !

There lived a youth in the very same town,
Whose tail to the heels of his shoes came down,
And he met the maid as she walked one day,
With a servant to fan the flies away ;
And, stopping a moment near to sneeze,
Walked off with the heart of the young Chinese !

That very same night, as in bed she lay,
There came a note from her Pa to say
As how as what a person had been
To ask her hand for a Mandarin,—
A very great merchant who dealt in teas,
And who was coming next day for the young Chinese.

Then many a tear the maiden shed,
As she put on her clothes and jumped out of bed ;
The moon shone cold on the river's stream
As the maid plunged in — one feeble scream
Is borne along on the passing breeze—
'Tis the dying moan of the young Chinese !

And ever since that time, they say,
Those who by the spot do stray
See the form of a skeleton maid
Dancing along 'neath a willow's shade ;
And they know it to be the young Chinese,
For it wears its petticoats up to its knees !

By a singular coincidence, two other Sussex names, with claims to be called poets, passed over in early manhood to the other side of the Atlantic, after issuing volumes in which decided proofs of their talent were given, viz., Edmund Parsons, a member of a well-known and highly respected Brighton family ; and Richard Realf, the son of an Uckfield peasant, and whose remarkable career will doubtless some day be writ down. He was once " Secretary of State " to " Old John Brown," the Champion of Freedom in the South, and whose spirit still "marches on." He was taken prisoner at the abortive rising against Slavery at Harper's Ferry, and nearly shot by the Southerners, but escaped, to fight through the War of Freedom, and to rise to the rank of Colonel in the Northern Army—also to write such stirring verses as have won for him a high name in the States, which he still enjoys.

These three young men—of whom Colonel Realf alone survives—carried their poetical talents with them to the New World; and thus it is that England flings her intellectual "superflux to the poor." Of those Sussexians who still "confess the soft impeachment" and sacrifice to the Muses we will say nothing, but leave some future scribe, when they and ourselves and all who belong to the breathing Present shall come under the venerable denomination of "Ancestors," to glean such "Glimpses" of them and their poetical productions as may have floated down the stream of time.

SOCIAL CHANGES IN SUSSEX.

SERVANTS AND THEIR WAGES.

THERE are few things in existence at the present day in which the revolution has been so great, even within living memory, or which has been brought home so completely to us, as the relations of servants to masters. We mean more especially domestic servants—the servants of in-door life, whose office it is to wait on the person or minister to the daily wants of their masters or mistresses: such as the cook, the housemaid, the footman, &c. To listen to the lamentations of a modern *mater-familias*, we might infer that the age of domestic service in England had come to an end, or was about to do so. There is no such thing as a decent cook or well-conducted housemaid to be got for love or money, or, if got, they cannot be kept. " Love," indeed, as a means of retaining domestic servants, has passed away altogether. That once-powerful tie between master and man, maid and mistress, personal attachment, has ceased to be felt at all. Money is the sole consideration, and in a market where the demand seems to be continually increasing and the supply to be falling off, this money-value rises so fast that it threatens to limit the luxury of domestic servants to the higher classes altogether—that is, to those who can alone afford to give very high salaries.

Perhaps, after all, this disappearance of domestic servants in our households would only be a return to the normal state of things, as regards the larger part of society. It can only have been since the rise of the middle classes in England into wealth and the introduction of a luxurious style of living that domestic service, as we know it, came into existence at all. Three or four hundred years ago—perhaps less than that—the wives and daughters of our farmers and traders did their own domestic work, with the help, perhaps, of a poorer neighbour, if in the country, or of an apprentice in towns. As to hiring men and women at large fixed salaries, for domestic services, as cooks, housemaids, butlers, footmen, coachmen, &c., &c., that must have been unknown to the middle classes of England in the days of the Plantagenets. It was confined altogether to the establishments of the great nobles. In these, indeed, domestic service was of a severer, more stately, and more ponderous character than anything that is known in the present day, even in the abodes of Royalty. The "Book of Orders and Rules," drawn up by Anthony, Lord Montague, who lived at Cowdray, Midhurst, in the reign of Elizabeth, for the government of his household, gives us a lively idea of this. Hundreds of servants of all kinds and degrees, from the "Principal Officers" and "Gentlemen Ushers" who waited on the person of the great man, down to "the groomes of the Great Chamber" and "the Scullery men," helped to fill the house and empty the purse of the great Noble in the Tudors' day, and to give occupation to the sons and daughters (for, of course, My Lady the Countess had her gentlewomen, chambermaids, "lavenderers," &c.) of the inferior classes.

The enormous expenses, not to say inconveniences, attendant upon such a style of living doomed it to extinction, in an age when the price of labour was rising, and when the vast estates of the old families were being broken up by civil war, the attacks of the Crown, and other causes. Amidst these troubles to the higher ranks, the middle classes grew up in the days of the Tudors and the Stewarts; and the Great Revolution of the 17th century put its seal on their victory. They were now the masters of the political situation, and we may be sure that there was an accompanying development in the social situation. The merchant's wife and the scrivener's wife,—nay, the draper's wife, the clerk's wife, and the yeoman's wife,—"looked up" in the world, and called in that help and aid for their increasing family wants and comforts which their more homely mothers had not needed, or managed to do without. Their "good men" wanted their dinners to be more varied and better cooked than they were wont to be, and the fittings-up of the hall and refectory and withdrawing-room required to be looked after with more care and by more skilful hands. So cooks and housemaids, and, as things went on, footmen and coachmen became part and parcel of the more well-to-do middle-class establishments, whilst, at last, scarcely a household above the mechanic or labourer's rank could do without a " general servant."

And for a time all went on well. The supply was equal to the demand. The drain of war had ceased to be felt by the labouring classes ; food was cheap, or, in a time of scarcity, there were the Poor-law and out-door relief to fall back upon ; no Malthusian doctrines were yet promulgated to check the force of the divine command to " increase and multiply," and so there was a class of labourers increasing in number, and decreasing in means, on which domestic service could draw almost without limit for its supply. It was the golden age of Masters and Mistresses, to which the present generation looks back with regretful eyes. These were the days of long and faithful servitude, when the relations of man and master, maid and mistress, extending as they did over long periods of time, were of that kind that Shakspeare speaks of, "when service sweats for duty, not for meed"—when there was something like a personal friendship between the served and the server, and when the discovery had not been made that " service was not inheritance," for the servant scarcely thought of closing the service except by death or marriage.

Of these days—which, perhaps, the *laudator temporis acti* is apt to over-colour—does the late Rev. Edward Turner speak in his paper on "The Mode of Life of a Sussex Gentleman" in the last century, when he says, " My grandfather's principal manservant lived nearly half a century with him ; and it was his boast to the day of his death, that he had waited at dinner upon twelve squires at once without being anyways da'nted. And in later days I have often visited at a house in the western division of the County where the cook of the family was nearly 90, and had never lived as a servant in any other house. My estimable friend was her second master, she having lived with his uncle previously ; and after he had passed his seventieth year she generally spoke of him as her *young* master."

T

Referring, too, to the servants of the Stapleys, of Hickstead, he observes that "the men-servants were not like the pampered menials of the present day, but men who, though they could wait upon their masters and their mistresses, their families and their friends, at their usual meals, could also, when not so employed, turn their hands to anything that might be required of them, either indoors or out, and who became so attached to the families in which they lived that the thought of 'bettering themselves' rarely entered their heads."

As we have said, those were the golden days of masters and mistresses, when they had "the pick" of the girls and boys of the labouring class, and there was neither the recruiting-sergeant, nor the manufacturer, nor the milliner, nor National or State Elementary Schools to interfere with them. It was, in many cases, a choice between service out, or hard work, and sometimes starvation, at home.

We propose to take a peep at these early days of domestic service in Sussex. The earliest record that we find of it in the Archæological collections of Sussex is in the journal of the Rev. Giles Moore, Rector of Horsted Keynes, who settled there in the days of the Commonwealth and lived to see the Restoration of Charles II. He had a wife and a daughter, and he was, it is evident, a man of some property independently of the revenue he derived from his living, and seems to have lived in a comfortable, if not liberal, style. One of his earliest entries (in 1656) is as follows:—" I entertained for my yearly servant John Dawes at Old Lady-day, promising to make his wages as good as they were under Mr. Pell [his predecessor in the Rectory]. I payed him his *half-yeares wages on the 2nd of Oct., £2 10s.* Rose Colman came to me on the 7th Sept. *I bargained to give her £3 per annum.*"

We need hardly say that money was worth more in 1656 than it is now; but even double or treble £5 a-year for a manservant, or £3 a-year for a female, and what house-wife would not rejoice?

Sometimes, too, lower wages than the above were taken. Thus, in 1666-7 (writes Mr. Moore), "Anne Sayers, of Lindfield, came to live with me as mayd servant, with whom I bargained not, *for under 40s. a-year she said she would not serve.* I gave her 6d."

What an unreasonable personage Anne Sayers, of Lindfield, must have been! We wonder if there are any "of that ilk" still in the parish! Not to come for a mayd servant under £2 a-year! Domestic wages must have been rising to justify such ideas!

A little further on we read as follows : "Mary Ward packed up and went her way, having lived with me 1 quarter and a weeke, for which I payd her 12s. 18th Feb., being Shrove Tuesday, Anne Grove, from Mr. Wyatt's [a neighbouring farmstead, we presume] came to live with mee, for whom I bargained at the rate of 45s. per an." So Mary Ward got an advance of 5s. a year on Anne Sayers!

It seems curious to us that Mr. Moore, and not Mrs. Moore, "bargained with" female as well as male servants. But so it was. And the Rev. Gentleman does not seem to have been particularly lucky in his choice. *Ex. gr..:*—" Thos. Dumbrell came to mee as servant to dwell with mee, with whom I agreed to give after the rate of £5 a yeare. On the 22nd Dec. I payed him up to that time £1 8s. : that same night I found him sleeping with my mayd Mary, and I packed them off."

So that Masters and Mistresses had their domestic troubles even in the days of the Commonwealth! It speaks to the kindheartedness of the Rev. Giles Moore that, immediately after the above, he records, "I marryed Thos. Dumbrell and Mary his wyfe, gratis ; and I gave him on his wedding 8 stone of beefe (16s. 8d.), a hind qr. of mutton (3s. 4d.), and a lambe, (7s. 6d.), besides butter, wheatt, and fewell." So that Thos. Dumbrell and "my mayd Mary" had made their peace. There were, doubtless, "extenuating circumstances."

As the Rector of Horsted Keynes married one of his men, so did he bury another. " I payd John Dawes his halfe yeare's wages, £2 10s. On the 7th of March he dyed, and I buryed him on the 10th in the ground on the south side next to the yew tree."

The above, we presume, were in-door servants. Out-door labour was better paid. *Ecce signum:* "I payd John Warde for 4 days work about the garden in setting it to rights, 6s. 8d., and for 5 dayes worke in clearing out 5 trees growing about the Glebe, 9s." This rate of payment, taking into account the higher value of money at the time, was as high as that of the present day, and much higher than that to which it fell in the succeeding century.

There is one kind of labour which the Rector of Horsted Keynes had to pay from which we are free in the present day—at least, in the form in which he was mulct. *Ex. gr.:*—"I payed John Ward in ready money at the Parsonage, 10s., *hee having gone out in my arms for 4 days.* For the harm he received in my service at the muster I gave him 5s."

The latter part of the foregoing entry explains the earlier. John Ward was *not* carried out for an airing by the Rev. Giles Moore, as the phraseology might imply, but took his place in the yearly muster of the Militia. Thus even the clergyman, in those days, was obliged to attend drill, or find a substitute. This entry occurs periodically in the Journal. Nor were humbler people exempt, as we see by the following:—"8th May, 1677, John Divall came to live with me. I bargained with him for £5 wages per an., besydes my kindnesses, I being to give him 6 weekes warning and hee mee also as much. I must remember out of my man John's wages to deduct 12s., *payed to his brother for supplying his absence while he souldiered."*

Here we will take leave of the Rev. Giles Moore and his servant-bargainings and troubles, and pass on to Mr. Timothy Burrell—Councillor Burrell, as his neighbours called him—of Ockenden, Cuckfield. His Journal touches closely in point of time on that of the Rector of Horsted Keynes, the first entry in it bearing date April, 1686,—the reign of James the Second. Wages had not risen in the meanwhile, for, writes Mr. Burrell in 1689, "Thos. Godsmark came to me as footman, at the wages of 30s. per annum, with coat, breeches, and hat;" and, in the following year, "John Piccomb came as footman, at 30s. per an., and a livery. Anne Baker came as cook, at 55s."

Thomas Godsmark, therefore, did not stay very long at

Ockenden. His successor seems to have done better, for, in 1691, we find this further reference to him :—" I payd Jack Piccomb in full of his quarter's wages 7s. 6d. To mend his coat and breeches, 1s., and to buy stockings, 1s. 6d." Just previously, " Two hats for my fellows liveries, 10s."

As he speaks of his "fellows" in the plural, perhaps Mr. Burrell had two footmen. He was, we must bear in mind, a gentleman of family and property as well as a barrister-at-law. And yet he did not disdain to pay his servants in kind ; *ex. gr.* :— " I paid John Coachman (John the coachman) part of his wages in money and 14lbs. of wool, 10s." A modern gentleman, or, for the matter of that, a modern coachman, would think it rather strange to pay or be paid in wool !

Mr. Timothy Burrell had a wife,—indeed, he had three, for he was thrice married,—and yet he, like Mr. Giles Moore, seems to have done the "bargainings" with his servants, male and female. Nor did he, any more than the Rector of Horsted Keynes, escape the troubles consequent thereon. Here, under date March 26th, 1693, is an illustration :—" I paid Frances Smith all her wages due to this day, £2, and discharged her, *she being a notorious thief.*"

These, and other corresponding entries, may console modern housekeepers for their little domestic troubles, which, as we see, may occur in the " best regulated families," under Cromwell and William of Orange, as well as under the Stewarts or Guelphs. Nor, it is evident, by Mr. Timothy Burrell's entries, had those golden days of servants yet been reached of which Mr. Turner speaks so enthusiastically, when boys and girls grew into old men and women in the service of their masters and mistresses. For we have only to pass on to April, 1694, to come to a new footman to Mr. Burrell :—" Marian Hall (it is a singular Christian name for a man), footman, came at the wages of 30s. per an. and a livery once in two years. I laid out for him, in part of his wages, linen sleeves, shoes, hat, and frock, 17s. 8d."

The Ockenden coachman, however, kept his place better :— " 1700, May. Paid John the coachman, in full of his year's wages, £4 3s. I payd him 2s. 6d. for Thos. Gates for a goos, but he kept it for ale, and to widow Goldsmith, for mending his stockings, 1s. 6d."

Wages, it is evident, had not risen much at Cuckfield. 30s. a-year and his livery for a footman and £4 3s. for a coachman are not very high rates of payment. What would the present generation of footmen and coachmen say to them?

Yet we have a proof, in the following entry, that the men who took, or rejected, these wages might "go further and fare worse:"—" 14th Sept. Goldsmith departed my service, by consent, this day. On the 29th October he repented, and returned, half-starved."

And here we arrive at one of those facts which would have made the late Mr. Turner's heart rejoice, and at which modern masters will shake their heads in melancholy guise:—"1704. Will. Gates came to me as footman at 50s. per annum; he is to have a hat, coat, and breeches once in two years. If I turn him away the first year, I am to give him 5s. more and take his livery. He died in 1713."

That is, after a service, and doubtless a faithful one, of nine years. If we mistake not, it is the master or mistress who, now-a-days, holds out the bait of higher wages to servants if they remain in their places. In Timothy Burrell's time it was the servant who sought to guard against the chances of dismissal.

Yet masters still had their troubles, and in 1706, as in 1877, it is the drinking that is the *fons et origo malorum.* Ex. gr.:— "Aug. For a periwigg for John, 14s. So he has had in all £6 2s. 5d. in full of his year's wages, and 2s. 5d. over; and I gave him notice that I would not allow him any longer for the livery being worn two years, *since 'twas to be all spent in drunkenness.*"

The next entry gives us a glimpse of female servants' wages:—"Paid Nanny West her wages in full, due 25th, £2 and more 1s. 10d. Paid Sarah Wade two years' wages, £5."

Thus £2 and £2 10s. were still the salaries of female servants in a gentleman's family 170 years ago.

Later on, in 1710, he pays W. Gates £3 10s. as his year's wages; to Mary Chaloner (how low had the Chaloners, once the first people in the County, sunk !) £5 for two years' wages; and to Mary, the cook (in 1715), for her year's wages, £2 15s."

This is the last entry of Mr. Timothy Burrell as to payments to servants, and it shows that during his life the wages of domestics had not risen much; for in 1686,—above 30 years previously,—he paid his cook £2 10s. a-year. A rise of 5s. in 31 years ! As much in as many days would be expected now-a-days !

The Stapley Diaries, extending from 1682 to 1743, come next in order of succession to those of the Rev. Giles Moore and Timothy Burrell, Esq., as documents throwing light on the wages of domestic servants in Sussex in past days. The social position of the Hickstead Stapleys was something between that of Squire and yeoman. They farmed their own land, and did a good deal in what may be called the retail business of farming, such as selling of wood and of meat as well as of stock. The first of the diarists, however, Anthony Stapley, was, like Timothy Burrell, a Councillor or barrister-at-law, and he was also a Justice of the Peace.

The Hickstead Stapleys (they were settled in other parts of Sussex) kept a good establishment, and their house or kitchen staff consisted of three maid servants and three men servants. Let us see how they paid them. "The wages of domestic servants," Mr. Turner remarks, *à propos* of the Hickstead establishment, "both male and female, were then marvellously low"; and the figures that he proceeds to quote from Anthony Stapley's account-book leave no doubt upon this point. The earliest of these entries refer to a period anterior to the Rev. Giles Moore's —that is, to the earlier part of the reign of Charles the First, before the troubles of the Civil War. Thus, in 1636, " To William Dennett, for half-year's wages, £1 10s. To my own man, Robert, for one year, £3 10s. To William Matthew, for ditto, £3 2s. 6d. To Elizabeth, for half-year's wages, £1. To Rachel, for ditto, £1. To Mary, for ditto, 8s. To the Nurse, for a quarter's wages, £1."

These entries, it is clear, embrace all classes of in-door's servants; and they are all equally low. £3 a-year for men-servants, £2 a-year to women, and 16s. a-year to girls,—these were the wages of domestic servants in a country gentleman's house in the time of Charles the First. It was a prosperous time for the country, though, politically, a very troublous one, as the Stapleys, who took sides both with King and Parliament, well knew. Food was abundant, and, of course, cheap. Wheat (in 1662) £7 10s. a load; cows and steers, £3 to £4 each; oxen, £5 or £6 each; 30 ewes selling for £20 0s. 6.; lambs, 7s. 6d. each; and 30 ewe lambs for £5 5s.! So that it was not expensive to feed servants.

In the next 20 years—to 1656—there was a slight rise in wages. "My man," writes Mr. Anthony Stapley, "came with me to dwell, and is to have £4 5s. per annum wages. Martha Earle came to me April 10th, and Elizabeth Lancaster May 5th. The former is to have £2, and the latter £2 10s. per annum." And again, in 1657, "My man George came June 1st, and I am to give him £3 15s. a-yeare, and he is to brew besides his other work. George Virgoe came to me as helper in the garden, and is to have £4 per annum and to live in the house."

Anthony Stapley, Justice of the Peace, was gathered to his fathers and was succeeded by his son, also an Anthony, who continued the diary. But for the next 50 or 60 years there is little or no change in the rate of domestic wages at Hickstead. Passing on to 1730, we learn that "Mary White began her year May, 1731. Hannah Morley came, and is to have £2 if she stay to Lady Day next. Paid Edward Harland and George Virgoe half-a-year's wages each, £3 5s. James Hazlegrove came to live with me at £6 5s. per annum."

From these entries it may be inferred that, whilst women's wages had remained stationary, or had even fallen, men's had risen a little. But then we must bear in mind the lower value of money. Perhaps £6 5s. in 1730 would not command much more of the necessaries of life than £3 in 1630. But even the former sum sounds very small compared with a man-servant's yearly wages in 1877.

There is no reference in the Stapley Diaries to such domestic troubles as disturbed the peace of mind of the Rev. Giles Moore and Mr. Timothy Burrell. Servants came and went, of course; but no moral delinquencies are recorded. One motive for their leaving was, that they might not gain a settlement in the Parish by a twelvemonths' service; and so they left their service just before the year was completed and returned in a few days' time. *Ex. gr.:*—" 1743, March 25th, Richard Mitchell left my service, and I paid him £3 10s. *He came to me again on the 29th.*" This was the consequence of one of those provisions of the Old Poor Laws which have been swept away in the present century with so many other fetters on the labour-market. It was a matter of policy not to allow a man to get a settlement,—that is, a right to be relieved out of the Poor-rates in a parish, and so he was discharged previous to the completion of a twelve months' service, and then taken back again.

To all appearances, things went smoothly at Hickstead Place in respect to indoor service. There was no want of good servants, and these seem to have known when they had good masters and mistresses. The latter part of the Stapley Diaries reaches to the times of which Mr. Turner had experience—the golden age of Masters and Mistresses, and the fabulous one of servants, or, shall we say, the age of fabulous servants?

Pari passu with the later Stapley Diaries runs the Diary of Richard Marchant, of Little Park, Hurst, beginning in 1714 and ending in 1728. But Mr. Marchant's references to servants and wages are few and far between. One point of interest, however, is touched upon, under date March 28th, 1716 :—" Bargained with Edward Morley at 35s. until Michaelmas, and if his *vailes* be not 5s., I have promised to make them so."

This matter of "vailes," as *douceurs* to servants were called, was one of no small importance in the last century, both to those who received and to those who paid them. These latter were the visitors and guests of the Master. They were expected to " tip " handsomely to the servants, and at length the practice grew into a system of extortion which made hospitality a grievous tax to the recipient of it and a disgrace to the host. The "vailes" which Edward Morley expected to receive at Little Park were, it is obvious, not very formidable; but at the houses of the great, and especially in London, nothing less than gold was taken by the "pampered menials," and sums of £5 and £10 were expected at some noble houses ! Pope often refused invitations because the price of the dinner, in the shape of "vailes" to servants, was too high a price for the honour or the enjoyment. To whom the world (and especially the dining-out world) is indebted for putting down this system of vailes, we do not know. Doubtless the abuse of it brought its own cure, as the same extortionate system, transplanted from private houses to hotels, has led in our days to a remedy in the shape of a fixed charge for attendance. How grievously must the thought of "vailes" have interfered in the 18th century with that "good digestion" which ought to "wait on appetite"!

After all, Edward Morley did not come to Little Park. On Easter Monday Richard Marchant wrote, "Edward Morley's mother was here, and made some scruples about her son's service. So away they both went together."

Perhaps the "vailes" of Little Park were not tempting enough !

Except that on Christmas Day " the workmen [that is, the farm labourers] dined in the house as usual," there is no further reference to servants in the Marchant Diary. Servants, it is evident, were more easily procured in those days than now, and not so difficult to be kept. Very regular hours were observed in most families, especially in the country. Dinner at 1 or 2; tea at 5 or 6; a little card-playing or smoking and drinking, and then to bed at 9 or 10—to be up again "with the lark." The servants were not worn out by late hours, or spoilt by over-dainty, ignorant mistresses; they were kept to their house-work, and, when that was done, were put to needle-work, or, in earlier days, to the spinning-wheel, the drone of which was the music of the old farmhouse. Then, as we have already pointed out, there was little competition for female labour. There were not two mistresses running after one maid, or columns of advertisements in newspapers tempting young women from their places by higher wages. In thousands of households even the "servant of all work" was not yet known,—the wife did the housework with the help of her daughters or a poor relative or dependent, and the domestic labour-market was rather over than under supplied. It was a good thing then for a young woman from the country to get into a good family even as a servant.

In illustration of this period, when there was little to separate the middle classes of society from that class immediately beneath them, which was the nursery of domestic servants—that is, the agricultural labourers—we may turn to the journal of Thomas Turner, general dealer, of East Hothly. It takes in the middle of the 18th century, from 1754 to 1765; and it is evident that at this time not only did all classes below the highest aristocracy mix and mingle much more easily than they do now, but that the trading classes—in country-places, at least—and the serving class approached very closely to each other—so closely, indeed, as to touch and mingle. Such was the case in the household of Thomas Turner himself. He was a man of education and a prosperous tradesman, associating on equal terms with the Parson and the Doctor of the Parish, and yet he and his maid and shop-boys all took their meals together and went to church together, and he tells us of all this as of an ordinary matter-of-course thing. *Videlicet*: "I and the maid staid the Communion :"—a kind of association which we do not think is common in the present day! There was, it is obvious, no great social gap between Mr. and Mrs. Thomas Turner and their housemaid or shop-boys. They all dined together in the kitchen, and, doubtless, passed the evening in the same apartment. The trading classes had not yet taken,— at least, not in country places,—that bound upwards which has carried them to the very top of the tree, and the labouring classes had not begun that downward march which did not cease until the great mass of them had become paupers. Thomas Turner himself, though with good blood in his veins and a coat of arms in the family, does not seem to have been conscious of any great disparity between him and the serving class. When he lost his first wife, and was looking about for another help-mate, he advisedly selected Molly Hicks, servant to Luke Spence, Esq., of South Malling, and he so describes her in his Diary. "She comes," he further tells us, "of respectable parents, and may, perhaps, one time or other, have some fortune."

In fact, a little further on, he tells us that "her fortune seems to be rather a flowing stream." "As to her education, I own," he adds, "it is not liberal; but she has good sense, and a desire to improve her mind, and has always behaved to me with the strictest honour and good manners." Molly Hicks was, in fact, as the editor of Thos. Turner's Diary (Mr. Blencowe) informs us, the daughter of a substantial yeoman at Chiddingly; and it was frequently from this class that servants were drawn in the last century, and no shame thought of it. Their position was that of one of the family—not mere menials—and, as we see, they often became the wives of men in the middle ranks, and made good wives too. This only lasted for a time. The middle class rose rapidly; the labouring class as rapidly sank; the drawing and dining room received the one; the kitchen was left solely to the other: and a very wide gap grew up, or rather down, between them, which there seems to be no modern Curtius capable of filling up.

It was about this time—the rising period of the tradesman, the declining one of the agricultural labourer—that the general servant, "or maid of all work," came into existence. Like most other classes, she was created by circumstances—adverse to her own peculiar class, that of the farm labourer; flourished for a time—during the struggle upward of the middle classes—and then disappeared—with their initiation into wealth and luxury, and the increasing demand for servants of all kinds. For we ask such of our readers as can look back a few years, has not the "servant-of-all-work" passed out of existence as one behind the times? Only such as have arrived at a certain age can recall that patient, hard-working, uncomplaining—what shall we call her—slave?—no, she was too active and willing for that—but certainly a domestic serf, a drudge—a hewer of wood and a drawer of water—who used, in the times of our grandmothers, to last a mistress a whole life-time, and whose whole being seemed to be summed up in one word—housework. Patient, hardy, cheerful, loving too—with a very high feeling of respect for their "masters" and "missises," and with a strong feeling of affection for their children—was this race of "servants-of all-work." Of course, their cooking abilities were limited—confined chiefly to roast and boiled—suet puddings and apple turnovers. But it was careful and cleanly cooking, and they "cleared as they went." They were up early—always on their feet—got their dinner when they could, but managed to "tidy up" by tea-time, and then did a bit of work for themselves or their mistresses, and could even sometimes find time for a romp with the children before they put them to bed. Cannot you, reader, remember such a household creature as this—a very part of the house and family—scarcely ever quitting it from year's end to year's end—only to go to Church on Sunday evenings or do a "little shopping" once or twice in the year—and not leaving "for good" except to marry, and then in a shower of tears? Cannot you remember some such faithful, simple, active-handed creature as this, who knew nothing and did everything? They are gone—"clean gone." They did their work, or rather the work of their mistresses, in their generation, and went and left no successors. It was quite right, perhaps, that they should pass away, for they marked a very low point in the fortunes of the working classes, and many of them came from starving homes, and some even from the Workhouses in which their parents had died. They could, as a rule, neither read nor write, and do nothing but the simplest household work. But they did it with a will, and carried into the homely families which they entered a strength of affection as well as of body which may in vain be looked for now-a-days in a better-instructed class. Cooks we have now, and housemaids, and parlour-maids, and scullery-maids, and we don't know how many classes of domestic-servants, who make or mar each other's work. But the general servant, or "maid-of-all-work" is extinct, and some lachrymose housekeepers go so far as to say that in a few years there will be no servants at all in England—only "ladyhelps"! But we hold to the adage that "what has been will be," and looking back and seeing that service is of very long standing in the country, and that it has never been without its troubles—each age, perhaps, thinking its troubles the greatest,—we incline to believe that, until the advent of the Millennium, there will be servants in the land, and masters and mistresses to complain of them!

SUSSEX ROADS.

DR. BURTON, of Cambridge (from whose journal we have already quoted) had some experience of Sussex roads in the middle of last century; and his evidence is not of a favourable character. He entered the County from the Surrey side, by way of Stone Street, a relic of the ancient Romans and their road-making (whence the name of the village), which called up all his classic enthusiasm. "As to the Romans," he exclaims, "I praise them for many of their high-souled and magnificent ideas, but not least for their public establishments and works; *and on this very day most especially do I praise them, while travelling on this stone causeway;* for, from the moment I left it, I fell immediately upon all that was most bad—*upon a land desolate and muddy,*—whether inhabited by men or beasts a stranger could not easily distinguish,—and upon roads which were—to explain concisely what is most abominable—*Sussexian.*"

He had previously described Sussex as "a muddy, fertile, and pastoral country, smooth and flat, indeed, when seen from afar, but not easy to ride or drive through; so that, having thereby earned a bad name, it has passed into a by-word, and any difficulty hard to get through or struggle against, may, by a simile, be called "the Sussex bit of the road."

This is hard, indeed, upon Sussex; but "worse remains behind." Going into details (which in this case, we take it, meant rucks and quagmires and "fondering roads)," the learned Doctor declares that "No one would imagine them to be intended for the people and the public, but rather the by-ways of individuals, or more truly the tracks of cattle-drivers; for everywhere the usual footmarks of oxen appeared, and we, too, who were on horseback, going on zigzag almost like oxen at plough, advanced as if we were turning back, while we followed out all the twists of the roads. Not even now, though in summer time, is the wintry state of the roads got rid of; for the wet, retained even till now in this mud, is sometimes splashed upwards all of a sudden to the annoyance of travellers. Our horses could not keep on their legs on account of these slippery and rough parts of the roads, but sliding and tumbling on their way, and almost on their haunches, with all their haste got on but slowly."

At the time this was written Horsham was the metropolis of the Weald, and is described as "ancient and populous;" the Assizes being held there, and salesmen from London resorting thither "to buy with ready money so many thousand of the chicken race."

Travelling thence through the forest of St. Leonard's, "we fell again," says the Doctor, "upon the especially impassable Sussex roads." "The surface of the earth deceived and impeded us in our advance, for, although apparently dry, and looking firm, yet it entrapped us, so we went on, into tumbles and much muddiness, so that the day was already fading away, when we arrived at the long-desired dwelling" (the Rectory house, Shermanbury).

We cannot omit Dr. Burton's description of the natives of Sussex at this period (1751), for it is obvious that he looked upon their manners as smacking of their soil. "The men there, as not being accustomed to quit their homes for the sake of traffic, or any other purpose, generally live by themselves, and, being born on the soil, continue unrefined. Nor does it seem at all strange, if mixed up with so much mud, some sordidness should also stain in some degree the frame of their minds. Their manners, therefore, are not the most gentlemanlike or agreeable, but neither are they quite barbarous. In their persons not corpulent, but rather spare and thin-shanked; in their diet generally frugal; and in their cookery, being neither dainty nor expensive, they care most for pork, which, indeed, they prepare skilfully, by steeping in brine."

To the Sussex ladies he was a little more lenient; but upon that head we have already quoted him. And now we come to the *fons et origo* of that often-repeated witticism which assigns to the stiffness of Sussex clay the length of Sussex legs :—" Come now, my friends," exclaims Dr. Burton, " I will set before you a sort of problem in Aristotle's fashion :—Why is it that the oxen, the swine, the women, and all other animals, are so long-legged in Sussex? May it be from the difficulty of pulling the feet out of so much mud by the strength of the ankle, that the muscles get stretched, as it were, and the bones lengthened ? "

The association of the fair sex with men and swine, "and all other animals," somewhat detracts from the merit of the learned traveller's preceding eulogy on Sussex women. But we must allow something for the manners and language of the times, and for a learned and unreclaimed bachelor! And then he does not spare himself; for, after compassionating the *status* of his step-father, the Rector of Shermanbury, "a man in slender circumstances, *stuck and buried in that irresistible Sussex mud*, in a poor spot," he exclaims, " How disgusted I immediately felt with myself when looking on him! how, in comparison of him, I despised myself, sleek and fat, with a well-fed body, *like a pig* from the reverend herd."

Verily, the clerical estimate of the Doctor was not a very high one!

So much for the Sussex roads in 1750.

At a still earlier date, in 1731, an Itinerary of the roads in England and Wales was edited by John Owen, gent., of the Inner Temple, and in the Sussex map, which he gives, there are only three high roads laid down from London to the sea-coast, and of two of these Shoreham was the terminus! The other one passed along the coast to Brighthelmstone and Newhaven, and from thence through Lewes to London. It was traversed by one stage-coach, which started at a very early hour on the Monday morning, and arrived late in London on Tuesday evening; returning in the same way on Friday and Saturday.

The work thus edited by Mr. Owen, "Britannia depicta," was undertaken in the preceding century by a Mr. Ogilby by the express command and at the expense of Charles II.; and, of the 73 roads there described, only five are assigned to Sussex; 1, from

London to Arundel; 2, from London to Newhaven,—with a continuation to Shoreham; 3, from London to Rye; 4, from London to Chichester; 5, from Oxford to Chichester.   Ogilby anticipates the complaints of Dr. Burton as to the character of the Sussex roads, and more than once advises the traveller to break off the road either to the right hand or to the left, to *avoid the mud.* These are samples of his warnings to travellers :—" Backward turnings to be avoided : at the end of Maudlin, the left to Petworth ; in Amberley, the left," &c.   He also takes note of "the gallows" being a frequent direction post to the traveller ! as they were doubtless intended to be a warning to ill-doers *not* to persist in the path leading to *them.*

De Foe, who published his Tour through Great Britain in 1724, says he has seen a tree drawn on a " tug " by 22 oxen, and even then it was sometimes two or three *years* before it got to Chatham ! Not far from Lewes he had seen a sight " I never saw in any part of England before, namely, going to a Church at a country village I saw an ancient lady,—and a lady of very good quality, I assure you,—drawn to Church in her coach by six oxen ; nor was it done in frolick or humour, but from sheer necessity, the way being so stiff and deep that no horses could go in it."

Judith, the widow of Sir Richard Shirley, of Preston, was a wise and provident woman; and also, no doubt, a loving one. She desired, when she died, to be laid by the side of her first husband, at Preston ; but she knew what Sussex roads were, and that the possibility of her being so buried—the home of her second husband being in Kent—depended upon the season of the year at which that event took place.   So, in her will, dated the 10th of January, 1728, she directed that her body should be buried at Preston, *if she should die at such a time of the year as that the roads thereto were passable; else, where her Executors should think fit.* Dying in June, her wishes were complied with.

The earliest legislative action with respect to Sussex roads appears to have taken place in the reign of Henry VIII. (quoted by Mr. Dodson in a paper to the Sussex Archæological Society), but its object was simply for the diversion of roads, not their improvement. The extension of the iron-works in the Sussex Weald made some steps towards this latter object necessary by reason of the heavy traffic to and from the mills, and an Act was accordingly passed with this view in the 27th year of Elizabeth's reign, entitled "An Act for the preservation of Tymber in the Wildes of the Counties of Sussex, Surrey, and Kent, and for the amendment of High Waies decaied by carriage to and fro Yron Mylles there." The "occupiers of.all manner of yron workes whatsoever as Owners or Farmours of the same which shall at any time hereafter cariee, or caused to be caried, any coales, mine, or yron to or for anie their yron workes," &c., are, for every six loads of coal or one tun of iron, to lay down one cart-load of "sinder, gravel, stone, sande, or chalke" for the repairing and amending of the said highways.

This payment in kind not succeeding in its purpose, in the 39th year of the same reign a money-payment was substituted of 3s. for every three cart-loads of coal or mineral and every ton of iron conveyed a mile along any roads within the County. This statute was not repealed until the Act of 1 George 3, c. 42, which consolidated and amended the then existing Highway Acts, and by which time the iron-works of Sussex were nearly extinct.

It was, however, the introduction of turnpike-gates, by which tolls could be levied under private Acts of Parliament, that those roads so much needed in Sussex were supplied. These were chiefly passed between 1756 and 1780, and in a list of them given by Mr. G. Slade Butler in Topographica Sussexiana (Vol. 15 of S.A.C.) we find an Act for repairing and widening the road from Lewes to Brighthelmstone, and another from Brighthelmstone to the County Oak on Lovell Heath.

Whilst, to people *out* of Sussex, the roads of that County were a reproach and an abomination,—"Souseks full of dyrt and myre" was the description of it in a rhyme of the 8th Harry's time,—by people *in* it they were regarded as a safeguard and protection both from the rogues and cut-throats of the metropolis and the attacks of an invading enemy. There were, however, two sides to this question. If bad roads were obstacles to criminals and invaders, they also stood in the way of the opponents of these gentry, who, if they once got a footing in the country, were more difficult to be got rid of. Highwaymen and smugglers, less than 100 years ago, set the local authorities at defiance and it was necessary to call out the militia to apprehend one of the former, and to besiege towns and to fill them with troops in order to check the latter. Speedy lines of inter-communication are now looked upon, and with good reason, as one of the best safeguards of a country, both from internal and external foes, and it is the ill-doer who has most cause to curse the well-kept highway which ensures a rapid pursuit and the electric telegraph which cuts off escape. These may at times facilitate crime or aggression; but, if put to their right use, they are instruments in the hands of order and safety, and the better the roads of a country, the easier it is to protect and defend it. In this respect, both as to highways and to railways, Sussex now stands as well as any other County of England; its country roads are also, as a rule, a credit to it, especially in the Western Division, and where formerly there was nothing but a horse track, or a "fondering" road, good hard, though narrow, roadways now connect village with village, homestead with homestead, facilitating traffic, economising labour, and giving denizens of towns easy access to the pleasant places of the country. So Sussex is no longer open to the reproach of being "full of dyrt and myre;" or, at all events, its dirt is to be found in the right place, in its fields, not in its roads, and the proverb of Dr. Burton, in the way of "the Sussex bit of the road," signifying an especially disagreeable bit, may be erased, as having lost its meaning.

MUSIC IN SUSSEX.

A Hundred years hence, whoever looks back upon our age as we are looking back upon the century that preceded us, will have no reason to note the absence of evidence of the love and practice of music amongst the people of Sussex, not only in towns but in the smallest country villages. In this respect the 19th century will contrast most remarkably and most favourably with the 18th and the 17th; indeed, with all the centuries, for aught we know, that preceded it. For if there be one thing more conspicuous than another by its absence in the archæological records of Sussex, it is all reference to Music. As a Science it certainly had no existence out of the Cathedral at Chichester, in which, as in all Cathedrals, the practice and the traditions of an ecclesiastical school of music, dating from the Tudors, were kept up with more or less ability, according as the Cathedral dignitaries were more or less inclined to music, or their organist was more or less a musician.

But, setting aside this ecclesiastical class of music, as an exceptional and esoteric growth, scarcely touching the people, music had no existence in Sussex, as a Science, and scarcely as an Art, 100 years ago. There were, of course, both in towns and villages, musical instruments, and people who played upon them, and here and there, of course, there was a man of genuine musical taste and knowledge, who, in happier days for music, might have acquired fame as a musician. But they were *raræ aves*, and their musical taste and talent obtained little fame for them, and not much profit. Still, there was a certain demand for music, and, in this as in other cases, the demand brought a supply. There were then, as now, festive occasions on which music was required, if only for dancing, or processions, or "waits" at Christmas. In almost every village, at the commencement of this century, what was called "a case of viols" was to be found, consisting of the treble viol (or violin), the tenor (or alto), and the bass viol; the latter a title by which the violoncello is still known in country places. And there were certain persons who could play on these instruments after a certain fashion, singly or in concert. The "fiddle" has always served for the votaries of Terpsichore, and a fiddler was seldom wanting in country places. It may be questioned, indeed, whether greater difficulty would not be found in getting one,—that is, a local fiddler, "to the manner born,"—now than there was 50 or 100 years ago. And for this reason: the pianoforte has superseded the fiddle, and there are few houses now above the cottage class in which a pianoforte is not to be found, and also some one (of the feminine gender, as a rule) able to sit down and play a quadrille or a waltz. The pianoforte is to the woman of the present generation what the violin was to the man of the last. In our grandfathers' days, there was really no instrument for a woman to play upon. A Queen, like Elizabeth, might play on the virginal, and, after the virginal, the spinet might be found in a few "great houses," and, at a later date, the harpsichord became more common. But these were the rare luxuries of the rich and great. The middle classes, and even the classes above them, the gentry and clergy, knew little or nothing of them, and, though Fielding might make Sophia Western play her father to sleep upon one, and Scott depict Flora Macdonald as fascinating Waverley with her harp-playing, yet to play on any instrument 150 years ago was a rare accomplishment for an English woman of the middle classes, because musical instruments for women were almost unknown. The only music heard in the cottage, the farm-house, and even the manor-house, was that of the spinning-wheel.

So, in the diaries of the Gales, and the Stapleys, and the Marchants, we find no mention of music; it did not enter as it now does into domestic life, or form a common source of public entertainment. Even in Churches it was of a very rude kind. Organs are of modern date in Sussex country churches, and there was either no instrumental music at all,—only a pitch-pipe to give the key-note to the choir or congregation,—or it was a rude kind of orchestra, made up of the beforementioned treble, tenor, and bass-viol, with, perhaps, a hautbois or flute. This served our forefathers well up to the end of the last century, and, indeed, to a much more recent period in many places. We ourselves have listened to the dulcet tones of a village band in a West Sussex Church within the last thirty years. We believe they are all now extinct. One of the last to hold its ground was in Sidlesham, near Chichester, where the village band and choir (with their " Anthem," as it was called) flourished up to about thirty years ago ; and when the then Vicar, the late Rev. E. Goddard, proposed the introduction of simple psalmody, the whole of the performers, with their instruments and books, rose and indignantly left the Church !

The only reference we have found to the vocal performances of our Sussex forefathers in the Archæological records of the last century, is in the Journal of Dr. Burton (1750), who, *à propos* of the church-psalmody at Shermanbury, writes :—" The more shrill-toned they (the Sussex people) may be, the more valued they are, and in Church they sing psalms, by preference, not set to the old and simple tune, but as if in a tragic chorus, changing about with strophe and antistrophe, and stanzas, with good measure ; but yet there is something offensive to my ear when they *bellow to excess, and bleat out some goatish noise with all their might*" (!)

One might suppose the learned Doctor was talking of a set of savages in some newly-discovered land, and not of his fellow-subjects in an almost adjoining County. But, in fact, to the polished clergyman of Oxford these Sussex boors *were* savages.

A few words of explanation are needed as to the "chorus" ("anthems" they called it) sung by the choir of Shermanbury instead of "the old and simple tunes." The old and simple tunes, introduced chiefly from Germany in the days of the Reformation, and of which "the Old Hundredth" (that was its numerical place in the Psalm-book) is almost the sole remnant, were superseded in the Stuarts' days by a more florid and pretentious kind of hymn, "with," as Dr. Burton says, "strophe and antistrophe and stanzas," and these were often "bleated out," to use his language, with more vigour than taste or discretion. They have, in their turn, been superseded by a simpler and higher class of hymn in our own days.

In few things, indeed, affecting social life and manners, has there been such a change in England, and for the better, as in instrumental music. Vocal music, in some form, must always have held its ground, and we know that in Elizabeth's and the 1st James's days it was widely cultivated, and hence the rich inheritance of madrigals, glees, rounds, catches, and other part-songs that we boast of, and which used to be sung, and still occasionally are sung, without accompaniment. But in instrumental music there was almost a blank up to the invention of the piano. Even Handel's scores were only written for violin, alto, bass, and hautbois, with an occasional flute accompaniment,—that was, the English flute,—and now and then a bit for the French horn. The more recent introduction of the German flute gave an impetus to the study of music by men, and, 50 years ago, there was scarcely a house of the middle classes without a German flute. But it was the improvement of the harpsichord into the pianoforte that, by giving an instrument suited for women, caused music to be introduced into the homes of the English people, and has done more to soften, refine, and polish their manners than, perhaps, anything else. If it has not made us a musical people, like the Germans, the Bohemians, the Hungarians, and other Sclavonic races,—and only Nature could have done that,—it has made us fond of music, which is next door to it. The rest may come in good time! Poets, and great poets too, we have had in Sussex, but there has been no Sussex composer yet,* nor is there that we are aware of such a thing as a genuine Sussex air.

---

* This reproach might have been removed from Sussex forty years ago but for the premature death of a young musician (Alfred Bennett, the eldest son of the then Organist of Chichester Cathedral), who promised fair to keep up the succession of great composers of Church music. At 24 he was chosen (in public competition) Organist of New College, Oxford, and had composed Services and Anthems which are still played in our Cathedrals, besides other compositions. But his career was cut short by a fatal coach accident whilst proceeding from Oxford to the Worcester Musical Festival. So the advent of a great Sussex composer was deferred,—may we predict,—till our own days?

There can be little doubt that, at one period of our history, music in Sussex, as known and practised by the people, had all but died away; and it is still a belief with some that Sussex people lack both ear and voice for music. Certainly the singing at sheep-shearing feasts and other rural meetings gives little token of either; it is a dreary monotonous sing-song of two or three notes, repeated through interminable verses of equally dreary rhyme. Some specimens of these rude rhymes are given in the paper on " The Sussex Sheep-shearer," and Mr. M. A. Lower, in his " Old Speech and Manners in Sussex," after stating that there are still in existence " two or three rhythmical compositions once familiar to Sussex men," quotes, as one of these, a Sussex whistling song, "which," he says, "was formerly popular and is not yet entirely forgotten." Here it is :—

A SUSSEX WHISTLING SONG.

There was an old Farmer in Sussex did dwell,
      [*Chorus of Whistlers.*

There was an old Farmer in Sussex did dwell,
And he had a bad wife, as many knew well.
      [*Chorus of Whistlers.*

Then Satan came to the old man at the plough—
" One of your family I must have now."

" It is not your eldest son that I do crave,
But 'tis your old wife; and she I will have."

" O! welcome, good Satan, with all my heart;
I hope you and she will never more part!"

Now Satan he got the old wife on his back,
And he lugged her along like a pedlar's pack.

He trudged away till he came to his gate,
Says he —" Here take an old Sussex man's mate."

O! then she did kick all the young imps about;
Says one to the other, " Let's try turn her out!"

She spied seven devils, all dancing in chains;
She up with her pattens and knocked out their brains.

> She knocked old Satan against the wall:
> "Let's try turn her out, or she'll murder us all."
>
> Now he's bundled her up on his back amain,
> And to her old husband he's took her again.
>
> "I've been a tormentor the whole of my life;
> But I ne'er was tormented till I took your wife!"

Certainly, when the musical knowledge of the people was reduced to whistling, it could not descend much lower; but still it sufficed to prove that the taste for music was not quite extinct, and, in course of time, that musical knowledge which has grown so rapidly within the last half-century in the middle classes of England will doubtless extend to the lower,—especially through the instruction of the children at school—and England—nay, even Sussex— may wake up some fine morning and find that it is musical!

www.ingramcontent.com/pod-product-compliance
Lightning Source LLC
Chambersburg PA
CBHW021956220426
43663CB00007B/844